Keeping Score: Interviews with Today's Top Film, Television, and Game Music Composers

Tom Hoover

Course Technology PTR
A part of Cengage Learning

COURSE TECHNOLOGY
CENGAGE Learning

Australia • Brazil • Japan • Korea • Mexico • Singapore • Spain • United Kingdom • United States

COURSE TECHNOLOGY
CENGAGE Learning™

Keeping Score: Interviews with Today's Top Film, Television, and Game Music Composers
Tom Hoover

Publisher and General Manager, Course Technology PTR: Stacy L. Hiquet

Associate Director of Marketing: Sarah Panella

Manager of Editorial Services: Heather Talbot

Marketing Manager: Mark Hughes

Executive Editor: Mark Garvey

Project Editor: Sandy Doell

Editorial Services Coordinator: Jen Blaney

Copy Editor: Melba Hopper

Interior Layout Tech: Macmillan Publishing Solutions

Cover Designer: Luke Fletcher

Indexer: Sharon Hilgenberg

Proofreader: Dan Foster, Scribe Tribe

For product information and technology assistance, contact us at
Cengage Learning Customer & Sales Support, 1-800-354-9706

For permission to use material from this text or product, submit all requests online at **www.cengage.com/permissions**
Further permissions questions can be emailed to
permissionrequest@cengage.com

All trademarks are the property of their respective owners.

All images © Tom Hoover unless otherwise noted.

Library of Congress Control Number: 2009933317

ISBN-13: 978-1-4354-5477-4

ISBN-10: 1-4354-5477-4

Course Technology, a part of Cengage Learning
20 Channel Center Street
Boston, MA 02210
USA

Cengage Learning is a leading provider of customized learning solutions with office locations around the globe, including Singapore, the United Kingdom, Australia, Mexico, Brazil, and Japan. Locate your local office at:
international.cengage.com/region

Cengage Learning products are represented in Canada by Nelson Education, Ltd.

For your lifelong learning solutions, visit **courseptr.com**

Visit our corporate website at **cengage.com**

Printed in the United States of America
1 2 3 4 5 6 7 11 10 09

Dedicated to the creative spirit in each of us.

Acknowledgments

I would like to first thank Mark Garvey, from Cengage Learning, who first brought the idea of this interview compilation to my attention. Mark has been extremely helpful, responsive, and professional in his dealings with me, and it's been a pleasure to work with him.

I'd like to especially thank my editor Sandy Doell for the steady assistance and valuable guidance she provided throughout the entire process. This book would not be what it is today without her help and that of copy editor Melba Hopper, so I am quite grateful—and fortunate—to have worked with such a stellar team.

The Composers. Without their music, there would be nothing to keep score of! My gratitude and appreciation for their work are immense, and I hope that I have produced a book that earns their respect in some small way.

The role of the Publicists and Management in this endeavor was crucial, and I would like to thank each of them for their hard work and dedication in seeing this through. To you, Caitlin Owens (ID-PR), Greg O'Connor-Read (Top Dollar PR, music4games.net), Michael Boosler and Ron Moss (Chapman Management), Karoline Brandt (CW3 Public Relations), Alison Wright (Air-Edel), Neil Kohan (GreenSpan Artist Management), Jo Carpenter, Bryce Jacobs, Ree Kadivar, and Amanda Pettit—my heartfelt thanks. Special thanks also to Beth Krakower of Cinemedia Promotions and Christopher Coleman of Tracksounds.com for their great work in the industry.

I'd also like to pass along my gratitude to my terrific friends who have assisted me in their own way, whether they know it or not: Rich Grover, Jeff DeSimone, John Bejko, Ted Buehler, Steve Sikoryak, Terrance Littlejohn, Christopher Crum, and Robert Drummond.

My family: Your support is always near and dear to me. Thanks for being there.

And lastly, to my beautiful wife, Dana, and my magnificent, inspiring son, Cody—yours is the music I enjoy listening to most each day!

About the Author

Tom Hoover is the founder and producer of ScoreNotes.com, a web site that offers audio interviews with some of today's biggest names in film music and entertainment.

With over 10 years of experience in the business, and having conducted well over 100 interviews in all, Tom has an ongoing interest in finding unique and creative ways to present soundtrack and film coverage to audiences.

His future goals include the development of a multimedia concept related to ScoreNotes as well as pursuing screenwriting interests.

Tom currently lives in Mount Laurel, New Jersey, with his wife, Dana, and son, Cody.

Web Site: SCORENOTES.com

Email: TomH@ScoreNotes.com

Contents

Overture

The movie, *Jaws*. The main character, a vicious shark coursing through the deep blue ocean taking victims along the way. Who among us can't hum the ominous musical accompaniment to this? Would *Jaws* be what it is today without its recognizable score? What about the theme to *Star Wars*? *The Good, the Bad and the Ugly*?

Now for a moment, try to imagine a world of movies without film scores. It's a concept that's hard to even consider. Movies and music go hand in hand; neither can exist alone. Is the "shower scene" in *Psycho* made eerier with the musical score that plays hauntingly in the background? Absolutely! For some, simply hearing the music from movies such as *The Exorcist* is enough to evoke goose bumps and shivers. Music is powerful. Music is moving. As Carlos Santana put it, "While some may use tiny brushes and watercolors, musicians work in a field of mystical resonance, sound, and vibration." Ludwig van Beethoven calls music "a higher revelation than all wisdom and philosophy; the electric soil in which the spirit lives, thinks and invents."

Being a film composer is a marriage of the highly complex and the abundantly creative, a merging that takes a unique set of skills to bring to fruition. In my opinion, composers are often the unsung heroes of movie productions. They have the unenviable task of drawing just the right amount of attention to a scene but not stepping over the imaginary line toward dominating its space. They must represent emotions in an honest, natural manner, but still deliver enough drama to make it theatrical. The composer must also take into account the sound design of a project. Specifically, when there are action scenes in a film, they are often dominated by impactful sound effects, and the composers must find the precise layer in which the music can coexist with these competing elements.

Incredibly, through a vast number of scenarios such as these and other potential pitfalls in a film's lifecycle, the composers of today more often than not deliver what they are asked for and more. I am often amazed that we get the quality of scores that we do given the narrow gaps of time and extreme pressures the composers generally work under. You can also add to that the inner politics of a film's production along with expectations driven on them as a result of temp scores. With such constraints, one might think it's a surprise when a really innovative soundtrack emerges on the other side. That we get so many is a testament to the immeasurable talent of so many composers, both young and experienced, working today. Indeed, such worthy efforts required some notoriety.

Roughly three years ago, I set out to create a small Web site, www.ScoreNotes.com, to demonstrate my respect and appreciation for the film music craft. As I got underway with it, I noticed that there was a void in which many composers were not often heard from on the press circuit tours of a particular film, and in general, were rarely spotlighted for their work. I set out to change that in some small way and created a *Composer Interview* segment on the Web site, presented in audio. It was my contention that followers of film music would enjoy hearing the "voices behind the music," and as it turns out, I was right. With over 70 interviews to my credit and a high number of segment downloads each month, the *Composer Interviews* segment turned out to be the real deal. With this book, I have been able to update many of the interviews I've done as well as present all new segments for you to enjoy.

As you read about what the composers have to say, you'll find that their words present a new manner in which the typical movie fans can access "behind-the-scenes" information about their favorite films. You'll also notice that these composers are as creative with their words as they are with their music. I find each conversation to be unique in its own way.

I have a philosophy that genuinely interesting dialogue can be had in an interview format without asking any uncomfortable or controversial questions. With that, you'll take a journey that is positive yet informative and hopefully one that presents some insight that perhaps you didn't have before.

Without further ado, it's time to raise the curtains and cue up the first track—your *Keeping Score* experience is about to begin...

Interviews with Today's Top Film Composers

Let's face it, we have all, at one time or another, seen or read press interviews that are associated with new film releases as part of their publicity machine. And my, does this publicity machine do its thing, so to speak! However, it's rare that I hear any commentary from these sound bites regarding the music of the movies. Instead, we hear a lot about the characters, actors, actresses, and often some information about the director, but where is the composer in all of this?

Look no further.

In Part I of *Keeping Score*, we're going to catch up with the composers behind some of today's biggest films. The criteria I used for this segment was based on my personal opinion of each composer's overall work and the commercial impact of their films. We're talking movies like *300*, *Harry Potter*, *Iron Man*, *Watchmen*, and more! Each interview, at a minimum, offers project-specific commentary, while others are career-oriented, broader-ranging pieces. In either case, these are conversations that will appeal to film music devotees and casual movie audiences alike. Let's get to it.

Keeping Score with Brian Tyler

Photo by Florian Schneder.

Brian Tyler.

Brian Tyler represents the best in today's modern film composer. He's developed a cutting-edge sound without relying on electronic influences to define it—a characteristic that holds great appeal to me. He also has a knack for delivering high-energy scores that are driven by strong, thematic foundations—an unmistakable style that I feel is his trademark.

I first started listening to Brian when his score for *Children of Dune* debuted in 2003. It's been a great ride ever since. He has a natural talent for writing film music—a skill further accentuated by the hard work he's put into his craft. At one point, he worked on 53 consecutive films without taking a hiatus. That's passion!

Even if you're a casual filmgoer, I'm sure you've heard his work at some point. He's scored commercial hits like *Eagle Eye* and *The Fast and the Furious* sequels, yet he's also delivered sweeping, romantic efforts for smaller independent movies like *Partition*.

The following interview was recorded during the time frame of *Dragonball: Evolution* and *Fast and Furious* in early 2009 and features excerpts from some of our previous chats. In the discussion, Brian breaks down his scoring strategies for his recent films, while also touching on some other topics of interest, including the manner in which his music is used in today's popular movie trailers, and his thoughts on a rather exciting science fiction film he is involved with...

Brian Tyler (2009)

ScoreNotes: Let's begin by touching on your foundation a bit. I find that the great thing about your work is that your style is immediately recognizable. Is that something you have to maintain a focus on, or does your original musical voice develop naturally in this manner as you're writing?

Brian Tyler: For better or worse, I think there is a sound that I have that I almost can't get away from. When people hire me, there's going to be a sense of what the vibe is depending on the genre. I've never worked for another composer, so I was never greatly influenced by how they did things, and I didn't learn their craft. I didn't go to film school, and I wasn't in a film composition program, so I really just learned it on my own...guessing along the way [laughs]. That's where my sound comes from—I really didn't have an influence except for the fact that I love soundtracks and I love listening to scores. You know, you've gotta just do what you do and find your own voice. As much as I admire the contemporary composers that came before us, I don't want to be them. And I really am adverse to any type of listening to temp scores because I don't want that to unduly influence me. It's a matter of pride to do your own thing.

ScoreNotes: I'd like to get into your work on the film *Dragonball: Evolution*. How much did you enjoy writing the music for this martial arts/fantasy-inspired world?

Brian Tyler: I've been a *Dragonball* fan for some time and knew they were making a live-action version of it for Fox, so I actually let Fox know that I would like to do it. And this was before they even shot the film, which was great. I was on board early, and I just kind of wanted to dive into the world of *Dragonball*.

The story is a lot longer, both backwards and forwards in time, than in the movie. There is a ton of history on the scale of thousands of years that exists for all the people who know *Dragonball* apart from the movie. So I wanted to give it the feel that this exists outside of just this little sliver of time that the movie covers and capture the fact that it continues on for a long time after that. Whether there is another *Dragonball* movie in the future or not, I wanted to make sure that it felt like this was going places and that there was a lot of history to it. So I loved doing it.

ScoreNotes: As a fan of the series, did you draw any inspiration from the existing source material, or did you let the picture alone speak to you?

Brian Tyler: Well, I really started writing the scenes before I saw pictures, so I suppose it was drawn from the source material. And watching the anime, everything from *DBZ, DBGT,* and the original *Dragonball*, it has a certain quality to it. But also there is a lot of variety to it, especially with the music that existed beforehand, so there was no way to redo or do new versions of all the music. It really had to be its own thing, but it was definitely inspired from just knowing the series.

ScoreNotes: It sounds like it was a fun bit of research on your part getting ready for this.

Brian Tyler: Oh yeah, it was great. You know I have all the DVDs and everything like that, so I dove back in and watched everything I had again.

ScoreNotes: Now, it is kind of interesting that you put a feeler out that you were interested in this movie. How often does that happen with you?

Brian Tyler: You know, it's only every once in a while that I can actually kind of put that out there, but sometimes it's just by coincidence. Early in my career, I just happened to work on things that I was really familiar with, like when I scored *Children of Dune*. I mean, I was a big fan and had read the *Dune* books. *Dune Messiah* and *Children of Dune* were being combined into one, and then I was just lucky enough to do it. *Star Trek* is another one; *Rambo* is another. All the *Aliens* and *Predator* movies, *The Fast and Furious*…huge fan ahead of time. You know, coming into some of these series already as a fan is a lot of fun. I also read *Timeline* before I scored the film, and I really loved the book, but I really wanted Jerry Goldsmith to score that movie. So that was one of those kind of weird events where I ended up scoring the movie for a book that I really loved. I also was, and still am, a huge Jerry Goldsmith fan.

ScoreNotes: If you can step aside from being the composer of *Dragonball* and strictly answer this as a follower of the series…did the movie work for you?

Brian Tyler: Oh yes! It's very different actually in terms of tone, only because I think that something happens in the translation from animation to live action, where certain things can be done and certain things just can't be captured. There is just no way that certain aspects to anime can make it to screen. Not only is it [the *Dragonball* series] animated, but it's a very long kind of running series that you're going to invariably pare down.

A lot of my favorite characters weren't in the film, but there was just no way they could be; you can't include everyone. But a lot of my favorite characters were in the movie as well—Roshi, Piccolo, Goku, Gohan, and all those characters. So it was really cool to see it come to life and be something I could write a score for that spanned an epic amount of time outside of just the movie. I almost felt a sense of responsibility, like "I'm not just scoring the movie, but I'm writing *Dragonball* themes," and I know the fans really take ownership of it. It's a big responsibility for me to actually be writing themes for something that existed for so long and has so many legions of fans regardless of the movie; so, you know, to me it was an important task to cover.

ScoreNotes: I do admire and appreciate your sensibility for looking out for the fans of the series as part of your approach to the work.

Brian Tyler: As a fan myself, it's something that comes naturally…just cruising along doing my thing…but when I score, it's like what I wish someone else would do if I weren't; that's the kind of approach I take.

ScoreNotes: Now moving on to your next movie, *Fast and the Furious*—can you tell us about the new style of music behind this fourth installment?

Brian Tyler: I think the music is getting increasingly more dramatic as the series goes on because the characters are getting older. Especially this one has steered further and further away from being the kind of movie that has girls in bikinis and just fast cars. Now, it's a story about love and love lost, vengeance and the underground and drug trafficking, and all sorts of stuff that have a lot more weight to them. So I think that's why there's been a shift from the first movie, which was primarily songs with some score, all the way to this one, which is almost all score and just a small amount of songs.

You can see that, from the way Justin Lin directed it and the way the story was previously, this was supposed to be kind of your grown-up version of *The Fast and Furious*. Granted it's still a blast, it's still fun, and it has spectacular car chases in it and everything, but the tone has changed. Also, there's the fact that this is a vengeance film, and there is a murder in it that is pretty significant and devastating to the story.

You actually don't just have action music, you have quite a prominent melancholy theme that is used throughout the movie that could very well be from a very serious film. That's "Letty's Theme," which is also in the suite and in different tracks on the soundtrack, for instance. But it occurs quite a lot in the film. And so there is an orchestral component, a Spanish guitar component, and you do have your action, groove, and electronic rock thing underneath a lot of the tracks. But it's a much more grown-up kind of score than I think you would at first expect from a *Fast and Furious* movie.

ScoreNotes: Sounds really promising. And I'm always curious—when you're dealing with an action movie like this, do you work closely with the sound designer to mix in your score in a way that it doesn't get lost in all the sound effects?

Brian Tyler: The sound supervisor on this is Peter Brown, and I've worked with him a million times. We're good friends, and he's part of a team that Justin Lin, the director, works with. We're able to discuss everything and make sure that we're not stepping on each other. We're real careful about that, and we collaborate to make it something that is nice and smooth so that when you watch the scene, you still get the emotion of the music, but you still get the slam of the car impacts and things like that. And for certain scenes, you wish the music was a little bit more. Sometimes you win and sometimes you lose, but I think the process is pretty open when working with this team.

ScoreNotes: It's a give and take, I suppose.

Brian Tyler: It is.

ScoreNotes: Looking back at your score for the fourth *Rambo* installment (2008), can you reflect on your experience of working with a director and actor like Sylvester Stallone?

Brian Tyler: Working with Stallone is pretty amazing because he works on two levels: he's a director, but he's an actor. Especially since *Rambo* is an icon in film history, it is kind of a trip sitting and working with the character you're scoring. Since he *is Rambo*, it's like *Rambo* is sitting on my couch. It's a mind blower. Sometimes I'll look at him, and I don't know what to call him when we're working on a movie like that. The great thing is I didn't have far to go to ask THE guy, *"What is Rambo thinking here?"* There is no higher authority than the dude himself. He's very articulate, he knows music, and he's a great writer. He can be very underrated as a creative force because his characters are kind of these brute types of dudes, but he's really bright, and I loved working with him.

ScoreNotes: Next up, I'd like to ask you where you're at with *Battle: Los Angeles*.

Brian Tyler: *Battle: Los Angeles* is in the stages of being made. I'm kind of on the ground level with the director, Jonathan Liebesman, who is doing something that I haven't seen before. It's like the coolest science fiction invasion film to ever come about. I mean, it really is definitely a film that will redefine science fiction. It is really, really exciting. Just wait until you see this stuff! It is pretty incredible. So I'm on very early and coming up with musical ideas early, and I'm just pretty blown away with what he's doing, and so I'm feeding off that. I can't wait till that one gets to be seen.

It's kind of his [Jonathan's] breaking out into doing what he wants, because really he is a dramatic director, and he's done horror pictures, but that's not really his thing. Even as a viewer, that's not really where he resides as much as with a film like this one, which just has tremendous impact. He's doing this almost like a *Saving Private Ryan* or *Black-Hawk Down*. It is not what you would think. It is not kind of a slick, shiny CGI alien picture at all. It's gritty battle. I remember some of the things I've seen that he's working on; it kind of reminds me of the impact of that first opening scene in *Saving Private Ryan*, that kind of thing. So I'm really excited about it, for sure.

ScoreNotes: From the sound of it, I'm ready to sign up!

Brian Tyler: Yeah!

ScoreNotes: Recently, one trailer of the new *Star Trek* (2009) film featured your music.

Brian Tyler: Right.

ScoreNotes: I'd like to ask you what your opinion of it is. Do you like how it was used?

Brian Tyler: Oh yeah, I loved that. I'm a huge *Star Trek* fan. I think what J.J. Abrams is doing is pretty awesome. It looked amazing. I remember when that all kind of went down. J.J. worked on a screenplay of *Eagle Eye*, which also involved Alex Kurtzman and Bob Orci, and of course they wrote the new *Star Trek* movie, and that's actually when the trailer was being done. I remember they were temping the movie with my *Children of Dune* scores, and that's how the trailer music came about. They did an expanded recording of the piece from *Children of Dune* that was originally used. They extended it and even had recording sessions to expand the length of the piece. So that was kind of cool. You know, it was something that I could have to do with the *Star Trek* world. I'd love to score the film of course, but I'm sure Michael [Giacchino] is doing a great job; he works with J.J. Abrams all the time. I'm really looking forward to that movie.

ScoreNotes: Often it boils down to the people who know one another in the business.

Brian Tyler: Sure.

ScoreNotes: But if they're going to the point where they're adding on to your existing material, perhaps next time, they can just simply plug you in there.

Brian Tyler: [Laughing] Hey, I wouldn't mind!

ScoreNotes: Well, thankfully, it looks like there will be sequels down the road with this *Trek* movie.

Brian Tyler: I think it's going to reinvigorate the franchise. Yeah.

ScoreNotes: Actually, I see your trailer music popping up in all these different movies, and it's something that has been happening for quite some time now. I don't think any other composer's work is being picked up in the unique manner that yours is. Is that flattering for you?

Brian Tyler: Yeah, it's great. Of course, invariably, when you're used in trailers for *The Departed* and movies like a lot of the Ron Howard pictures, *Cinderella Man,* and all those kind of things…you go *Wow!* I'd love to do that!

ScoreNotes: Yeah, *Indiana Jones* got in on the act, too!

Brian Tyler: Of course, that was part of the Spielberg connection that got me on the map for doing *Eagle Eye* because he was producing [it].

ScoreNotes: Oh, nice.

Brian Tyler: It's always great to hear your music in these trailers. It's just one of those things. You don't even know that your music is being used for the trailer often until it is chosen. I just saw *State of Play*, the trailer, and sure enough the track "Prague" from *Bangkok Dangerous*, my score, comes up and it's playing. And I was like, "Oh wow, I didn't know that that was in there." I find out often in the theater.

ScoreNotes: Wow, that's something else!

Brian Tyler: It is kind of crazy. This company that keeps track of trailer music actually has *Summon the Worms* [*Children of Dune*] as the most-used piece of music from a film in trailers in the last six years.

ScoreNotes: Moving on a bit to look at your upcoming slate—are you going to squeeze in a summer break this year?

Brian Tyler: I'm going to try. It's been a while.

ScoreNotes: Because I can envision you working through season after season just turning out these great scores.

Brian Tyler: Yeah, it's kind of strange. I was just wondering the other day truly how many movies I had done in series. Not counting shorts or anything I have done in the past, but I added up that I had done 53 movies, and I kept thinking, "How did I manage to do that?" I can't even imagine that it was that many; I've been going kind of nonstop. Which is good, I suppose.

ScoreNotes: It's good, but take a moment to enjoy things, too.

Brian Tyler: I know! Well, I'm going to catch some Lakers. I've got plans for tickets.

ScoreNotes: Well, there you go!

Brian Tyler: Maybe catch some Formula One this year. . .catch a couple of races, maybe overseas. So we'll see, but I'm going to mix in some fun for sure.

ScoreNotes: Sounds good Brian. It's always a pleasure to catch up with you.

Brian Tyler: All right Tom, you too.

2 *Keeping Score* with John Ottman

John Ottman.

Used by permission.

I t was great getting a chance to speak with composer **John Ottman** about his career. He's been working as a film score composer since the mid-'90s when he first collaborated with Bryan Singer on *The Usual Suspects*. Since then, John has been on a sustained roll, both as a composer and an editor (he's even done some directing, too!) on some of Hollywood's top films.

The following interview hits key touch points on his career path as we discuss his music from *The Usual Suspects*, *X-Men 2*, *Superman Returns*, *Valkyrie*, and more. No doubt, John's career to date is full of interesting and challenging projects, but I feel the best is still yet to come from this multi-talented composer...

John Ottman (2009)

ScoreNotes: What has the John Ottman Hollywood journey been like thus far?

John Ottman: I'm pretty fatalistic and try to be realistic about the world of freelance. I always prepare myself that every next gig might be my last one for a while. And then, lo and behold, another comes up right on the tail end of the previous, and it never seems to cease. That, thankfully, has been pretty much the way it's been. This way, I prepare myself for the worst, try to enjoy my life; and then if anything good happens, I'm pleasantly surprised. In fact, I've been so "surprised" all the time that I don't ever get much of a life to enjoy!

ScoreNotes: At the time of *The Usual Suspects,* did you have a hunch that you and Bryan Singer would be destined for great success together in this business?

John Ottman: Not really [laughs]. *The Usual Suspects* to me was like a glorified student film, as far as I was concerned. It was just Bryan and me making another movie, and if people liked it, great. But it always felt as if we were making the movie to please ourselves, which means it was never made by committee. I never really had seen that many movies of this sort going into it. I was a sci-fi freak who watched a lot of *Star Trek*, so I didn't know who the actors were in the movie, which was sort of good because I treated them as the characters I saw them as. I didn't have any preconceived notions about who these characters were until I was helping to create them in the editing room—which was an old Steinbeck reel-to-reel console, a tape splicer, and heaps of film strewn about my living room. Those were the days! So for me, it was just to make a film that pleased us, and if at the end of the day other people liked it, it was icing on the cake.

We ended up having a screening of the movie that went pretty well, but I basically thought that the movie would come and go, and I would end up going back to my day job. As it turns out, *The Usual Suspects* changed our lives…unexpectedly.

ScoreNotes: In what ways has your writing technique evolved from the early days of that film?

John Ottman: I think as you grow more comfortable in your own skin and have more faith in yourself, your style inevitably evolves. When I do more projects and start to have confidence in myself and throw out some of the fear, then I go to the keyboard and start playing with the keys and have something come out from myself rather than refer to any other music, which I used to do early on. I actually think a lot of new composers do this because their butts are on the line, and they want to impress everyone. There's a lot of temp love that goes on. New guys might take the safe way and emulate a lot of the style from the temp score. That's why in a lot of the early scores by prominent composers, you can hear them ripping off other composers. They were either made to because they didn't have a name at the time or they were in fear of not making everyone happy.

It's also a crutch. My mind is far more free now, and ideas come to me so much easier if I just let all that go and just sit here and fiddle on the keyboard without referring to anything. The fringe benefit of that, which is a godsend, is that you end up having your own signature style. Goldsmith, Williams, Barry—you always know for certain that it's their score you're listening to. It's great to have people pick you out because you have a sound that differentiates you from other composers, and that's only going to happen if you let go of your insecurities and just write.

ScoreNotes: When Bryan took on the first *X-Men* film, you were unavailable since you had a directing feature of your own. Have you had any further interest in returning to the director's chair since then?

John Ottman: Yes, I've always had an interest. All my friends around me are always harping on me to go direct more. I do have offers all the time to develop projects, but it's a lifestyle issue since I basically bought a lot of stuff [laughs] and depend on a certain income that I depend on from my composing. So to leave my day job to go invest a year and a half on something that's not going to pay as well for a second-time director is a scary prospect. It's really fear keeping me from directing. But I loved doing it, had a great time, and it felt very natural to me. But who knows, I'm always looking at stuff. It's funny—I ask myself "How many people have all these offers all the time?" I'm like the one person who has all these offers and isn't doing anything about it. It was 20 years ago when I was coming out of film school and would have been in disbelief that I would be receiving so many directing opportunities. And now that they're coming, I'm like, eh, maybe! So it's funny how life works.

ScoreNotes: How much were you looking forward to scoring the *X-Men* sequel?

John Ottman: I couldn't wait. That was a huge thing for me. I just knew in the back of my head that I had a knack for doing that sort of superhero and lyrical type of score. I grew up with that kind of music, and that's the kind of film scores I lived and breathed when I was growing up. I knew I had it in me, so it was really devastating when our schedules collided. It was a big bummer for both of us.

ScoreNotes: Fundamentally speaking, and this can apply to any franchise, should the musical themes in a series carry over, or at least be referenced, from one installment to the next?

John Ottman: I'm a huge believer in that. In fact, having musical continuity in a film franchise is a soapbox issue for me. It just drives me crazy. It would be as if you were watching a James Bond film and the theme were changing from film to film. That franchise doesn't do that, and every series should be that way. I guess this type of thing happens because another composer comes on a franchise, and my assumption is that perhaps they have an ego and want to do their own theme and not use the theme from a previous film, and so this discontinuity is created. When I get on a film with a previous standing theme, like for instance *Superman*, I want to keep the world alive and add my own original style to it. It's almost sacrilege to me to go away from the theme.

That's what made it hard for me not to be involved in *X-Men 3*, because I had to abandon something I was basically planting the seeds for. In *X-Men 2*, I had written themes that were intentionally designed to evolve into the next movie. And then to have that ripped out from under me when Bryan yanked us to go work on *Superman*, I was really distraught about that. Of course, the double whammy is I was thrown into a franchise that already had an existing theme [laughs]!

ScoreNotes: Staying in the "Marvel Universe," can you tell us how the theme for the *Silver Surfer* originated? To this day, it's one of my favorite modern hero themes.

John Ottman: That's kind of a funny story. I had written the *Silver Surfer* theme when I had read the script with this character having this pathos, inner turmoil, and pain, which all superheroes do, really. It actually came to me during a plane trip, and I just thought, "This is it, this is the Silver Surfer theme."

I presented it to a music exec at Fox, and he didn't respond to it, as he wanted something that sounded like *300* because he was anticipating that the powers that be at the studio might want something electronic that sounded similar to that because it was the flavor of the moment. *300* had made all this money, and you know how Hollywood is—they have to jump on the bandwagon of whatever was a hit and do the same thing. But I was thinking to myself, *Fantastic Four 2* is a completely different type of movie than *300* and is a continuing franchise with an existing type of score—one that I was hired on to write an orchestral, romantic superhero score.

So we went down this road of doing all these crazy electronic themes that were really forcing a square peg into a round hole and didn't make any sense. So I did this big, crazy electronic acid rock demo [laughs] of the *Silver Surfer* theme. To my delight, the powers that be were horrified! It was then that I had a rare moment of complete respect for film executives. They said they wanted the John Ottman sound like for Wolverine in *X2*. I was so relieved! I went back to my original theme and presented it to them, and they loved it.

ScoreNotes: Can you also touch on the overall tone you were looking to convey in the *Fantastic Four* films?

John Ottman: *Fantastic Four 4* is definitely superhero light. That was fun for me because when things are so serious, like in *X-Men 2* and so forth, you have to be very careful about riding that psychological line between darkness and light. But when something is just completely comic book, you can really have fun as a composer. Even the sinister and dark characters have a sense of fun to them. Plus, you can go over the top and not worry about being too subtle, and that's always a lot of fun for me as well. Yet, having said this, you always gotta take the story and characters seriously as a composer, because you're telling your own story musically, or should be.

ScoreNotes: When you moved on to work on *Superman Returns,* did you feel any additional pressure in following John Williams in the series?

John Ottman: Let's just say I was practically getting death threats on the Internet from die-hard fans telling me to use the original theme. I had always intended to use the original theme, but people would e-mail me to beg me to keep the theme alive. They would also ask why I was doing the score and not John Williams. I don't know how so many people found my e-mail address!

It got to a point where I finally stopped worrying about what everyone else wanted me to do and just did what I thought was right. It was crippling my creative process, and I was completely hung up on trying to anticipate what everyone else would want. So, I said to myself that I would just walk into it like I would any other film and score it with my own sensibilities. Otherwise, it was going to sound like I was imitating someone else, and that's the worst kind of score when it's not coming from within the composer. And I can hum any moment of Superman because it's part of my psyche, so it was very easy to intertwine it with my own stuff. So what came out of it was a very personal score that sounded like me but also gave the nod to Williams, and that was the only way I could get through it and score it effectively.

At the same time, as threatening as the fans were, I could completely relate to them because not only was I a huge fan of the Richard Donner version (and didn't want to disturb that world), I also likened them to how I was prior to the first *Star Trek* movie. I would go to *Star Trek* conventions and grill the actors with questions about what the transporter room looked like, what the Enterprise looked like, etc. I was completely concerned about my entire world being destroyed by the making of a movie that could have potentially ruined *Star Trek* for me. So, I completely understood where the Superman fans were coming from…but at the same time, you have to embrace the new a little bit, too. And in retrospect, I believe that one of the problems with *Superman Returns* is that we were all so concerned, almost in a religious way, with preserving the Donner version that the film was inhibited from evolving. It was almost like a love letter to the Donner world, which is fine and good, but I think the next generation needed something newer to see.

ScoreNotes: A more recent project of yours was the Tom Cruise thriller, *Valkyrie*. Given the delays on the movie, how much of a time commitment did that become for you both in the editing phase and with the score?

John Ottman: Way too long! [laughs] It was originally supposed to be a low-budget, six month, in and out gig, like a TV schedule. I remember lamenting to Bryan on the phone when he called about it, and I said, "Wait a minute, we just finished *Superman* a few months ago; you're supposed to leave me alone for a couple of years so I can go and write film scores and make some money." He said, "Don't worry; it'll just be this little thing. You'll be in and out, and you can go back to writing scores."

So of course, the project ended up being a year and a half and one of the most difficult projects I've ever worked on, both professionally and personally. It wreaked havoc on my relationship. It was a very hard year and a half on me.

But that isn't to imply anything about the people involved. They were great. Tom Cruise is one of the most awesome people and a gifted filmmaker as well. He is rarely concerned about his performance; it's all about the story and about pleasing the audience in terms of the movie itself. He was a positive part of the hell we went through. It was a hard movie to put together. Here you have a story where you know the outcome, you know they aren't going to succeed, you know Hitler is going to live (if you're over 12), and the main event of the bomb going off takes place halfway through the movie. So how do you keep everyone enthralled and interested in the story to the end? On top of that, you have a bunch of old men talking about convoluted plots in small confined smoking rooms, so how do you make that a fascinating thriller? That was the challenge. I knew when I read the script this was going to be my personal nightmare because it was all going to come back to the editing and the music to pull this thing off. And that's pretty much how it went down. Endless tweaking!

And what didn't make it any easier (and I know I shouldn't care about gossip) was what people were saying on the Internet. We had this movie that was shaping up to be a strong film from day one, and we never had any problems with the film. I really learned a lot about the news media and "journalism" through this whole "destroy *Valkyrie*" campaign that started ensuing on the Internet. It was just unbelievable to know the reality and then read the fiction that was being believed by everyone. And yet you couldn't really say anything because to go out and try to counteract the rumors would lower yourself to them and would almost look like propaganda the moment you tried to dissuade any rumors. We sort of had to learn to bite our tongues for all that time, which was very frustrating.

ScoreNotes: The film turned out to be both entertaining and informative, a rather rare combination for a Hollywood movie!

John Ottman: Yeah, despite the hardships of the film, the first day I received the dailies I was really starting to enjoy it. I thought it was fascinating, the actors were fantastic, and we've got a great story. It would have been fine if there weren't people who were trying to make the film crash and burn before it even started. That was pretty much what made it difficult to get through. And in the end, it actually affected the film as well. The studio didn't want to release any DVDs for the Academy members early on because they were afraid they would leak onto the Internet and all these people would get their hands on the films and do God knows what with them on sites like YouTube and so forth. So given the machine that was out there to destroy *Valkyrie,* it was too much of a risk to get it out there. Because the film was out in December, by the time the film had been shown in theaters, there was no time to get the DVDs out to the Academy members because the voting deadline is in January. So actually it did affect *Valkyrie* in terms of, I think, cheating some people out of nominations.

ScoreNotes: It really is a shame to hear that. On the bright side, the movie did turn out extremely well, and it is something to be proud of.

John Ottman: Thank you. We're all proud of the work and passion we put into it.

ScoreNotes: Was that the first time in your career you were able to write a choral piece with such dramatic impact at stake?

John Ottman: I've obviously done choral stuff before, but not with lyrics. I didn't know how to leave the audience because at the end of the movie is the execution with this very emotional orchestral music. And then to start the end credits with the same kind of material would have been too depressing with no juxtaposition of something new when people are leaving the theater. We desperately wanted the audience to feel the sense of sacrifice, heroism, and hope—that there were these people who, against all odds, almost changed history.

I had written this orchestral piece for the end credits, and it just wasn't working for me. So I decided on writing a choral piece. But what the hell was I going to have them say?

So a friend of a friend found a poem from the German poet, Gerta. I looked at the lyrics, and it just gave me chills. It was sort of a loose allegory to what had happened to the men in the movie. So I took this poem and adapted the lyrics to the melody, which was not easy because I did it with a friend of mine and neither of us spoke German and we had no idea what we were doing [laughing]. So we actually adapted the lyrics to the melody, and unknown to us, we didn't do it so well. It sounded great to us as English-speaking Americans, but when we played it for a couple of German people, they were scratching their heads. We had to consult language scholars along with music scholars and put our heads together, and literally a couple days before the recording session, we were changing whole notes to half notes and quarter notes to eighth notes just to try to alter the theme to fit the lyrics in properly.

ScoreNotes: Wow, quite a task it sounds like!

John Ottman: It ended up sounding beautiful, and when the choir sang it without scratching their heads, I thanked God [laughs]. I wanted to submit it to the Academy for the song category, but the lyrics had to be original.

ScoreNotes: I'd like to ask about your take on some of my favorite, perhaps lesser known, works of yours. First, where would you rank the music of *Eight Legged Freaks* on your personal rating scale? I found it to be terrifically entertaining on multiple levels!

John Ottman: Wow, that's been so long I can barely remember it now! I do recall it was a fun time. Again, it was one of those movies where you can let your hair down and not worry about riding the line too closely. It's often the films off the beaten path that are my favorites and most rewarding musically—like *Kiss Kiss Bang Bang*, and even little gems like *Pumpkin*.

ScoreNotes: Would you say that a score like *Incognito* is also recommended listening for your fans?

John Ottman: That's at the top of my list for sure. It's well known that it's one of my favorite scores. It's very classical in nature, so someone new to my work who is looking for a superhero kind of score might get the wrong idea. But to me, I often feel like I'm just not going to do anything better than that. It was a rare opportunity for a composer —a film designed with four- and five-minute sequences without any sound design or dialogue, just basically a road map for a composer to compose onto. So the music could be very expository and didn't have to hide; it was basically like being commissioned to write a symphony. So yes, I would say that it was one of the highest points in my career...until I learned that the film didn't come out, which was extremely depressing.

ScoreNotes: Earlier in the discussion, you shared the sense of uncertainty you have about maintaining a steady workload in this business. Do you think you will always carry a sense of fear or angst about where the next project is coming from?

John Ottman: The angst never stops and the fear never stops, with me at least. It's just the way I am. But it makes the highs higher and the lows not seem so bad [laughs]. As much as I'd like to go direct and have all these other things in my life, I'm always excited about writing film music. I just had a realization the other day while working on *Astro Boy,* which is a joy by the way, that film music is something that will always be fresh to me, and I will always be happy doing it. It's like giving birth to something. And that's a really lucky thing to be able to say because not everyone can continually find joy in their work. Obviously, this career, like with any other in the business, is peppered with a lot of pain and anxiety as well, and horrible personalities, ridiculous deadlines, and sleep deprivation, but I realize I wouldn't have it any other way.

3 *Keeping Score* with David Newman

David Newman.

David Newman has a rich history when it comes to film music. His father, Alfred, was the legendary composer behind many of the cinematic blockbusters from yesteryear, while his brother, Thomas, is one of the most sought after composers currently working today. His cousin Randy has etched quite a name for himself in the industry as well. Truly, the positive impact that the entire Newman family has had on film music would require a book of its own to tell the tale.

A successful and prolific composer in his own right, David has composed music for over 90 films* in his career. For this interview, I had a chance to speak with David soon after *The Spirit* was released in theaters. David spoke candidly about the film's

*Statistic captured from IMDB.com.

21

fate and also shared his strategy behind the artistic, noir-inspired score he created for it. We also spoke about some of the other noteworthy projects he previously worked on, including cult favorites like *Galaxy Quest* and *Serenity*.

One of the real gems of this discussion, however, is David's recollection of growing up in the Newman family and how he first became interested in the craft. It's a great read that even the casual movie fan will enjoy…

David Newman (2009)

ScoreNotes: From a composer's perspective, can you please tell us how interesting it was for you to work on a film as creatively imagined as *The Spirit?*

David Newman: Well, I've done a lot of films in my life, but very rarely do I do a film where I'm working almost exclusively with the actual filmmakers, with the director and the producer, who is really more of a creative type person. I'm really sorry that it didn't do as well as we all thought it would do [at the box office]. I think it's a little ahead of its time in terms of its tone and its sort of tongue and cheek "noir-ish" kind of quality, but it was an absolute pleasure for me to work on *The Spirit*.

ScoreNotes: Do you think the lack of box office success might have to do with viewers maybe too closely associating the film's style with that of *Sin City?*

David Newman: I think there might be some of that; *The Spirit* is a very unusual film. It's so against expectations and perhaps people are almost flabbergasted by some of the scenes. I always liked the film, but there is a lot of detail and interesting stuff in it, and so I can't really say why it didn't do as well at the box office. There is much more intelligence in it than is normal in a film, a lot more of western culture, literary kinds of things, believe it or not. The timing may have been the worst thing. Generally in movies, no one really knows what's going to happen, and the further you go away from what's expected in a genre, the more risky it is. I think he [Director Frank Miller] went pretty far away from the genre. Frank did what he does, but there is an odd tone to the movie that maybe people weren't ready for yet. But I always thought, and I thought to the end, that it's a really terrific movie. Aside from that, doing the music for it was a complete, utter pleasure because of the way in which the film was set up, that it was just working with filmmakers. I worked a lot with the sound people; it was a completely collaborative, pleasurable experience for me.

ScoreNotes: Do you think more movies should have productions like that of *The Spirit?*

David Newman: Well, I wish! As a composer and as a part of the filmmaking process, I wish they were all made like that. But they're not. I've done lots of very commercial studio films and a fair amount of art films, and generally you learn to deal with what it is. I'm used to all kinds of crazy things, all kinds of rewriting and having to go all over the map. But when you work with people who make decisions fairly quickly and are committed to their decisions, obviously you don't worry so much about improvising your way around to please everyone. But it's not to say that I don't enjoy the other part of the Hollywood industry which is trying to figure out what people mean by what they say and what the film needs. And when you go out and test the movie, what does the audience think, and where in there do you follow the audience? Do you lead the audience and all those kinds of things? But that's just part of the job, which is actually really kind of interesting. *The Spirit* was a different type of movie. It was more like doing an art thing where it's really all about the art and not so much about the commerce. Maybe to the detriment, I don't know.

ScoreNotes: Do you feel a film such as this might find resurgence once it hits the DVD shelves?

David Newman: You never know about these things, so you just move on and see what happens.

ScoreNotes: I felt, for this movie, your score was quite artistic and unique. What were some of the musical ideas or styles you explored in developing the score?

David Newman: Well, there were a lot of obvious references. There's the harmonica, which is an obvious reference to spaghetti westerns because there is an aspect of that to the movie. The whole movie is a big duel between The Spirit and the Octopus, and it almost has an old western standoff style to it. And so I used the harmonica as sort of the soul of *The Spirit*. Obviously, there are a lot of other characters. There's a lot of reference to noir film scoring in a sort of tongue and cheek way. A lot of the movie is tongue and cheek, which I don't think people got exactly. There was a noir element with the women characters, especially with Sand Saref. Additionally, there was a kind of quirky element with Silken Floss, so they all had sort of different kinds of aspects to them with the music. And then I did as I said: I worked with the sound people a lot. I tried to stay out of the way, scoring it where I wasn't going for these big action sequences where I'm going at full tilt while the effects and visuals are going full tilt and then everybody deciding at the mix who's going to win. It was much more like, "I'll get out of the way here, and then you get out of the way there." But again, that's a kind of an unusual approach as well, because most of these films are just slammed with sound. There's just sound going at all times. We didn't approach it like that. We tried to give it air and breath in places where we could recede into the background or move into the foreground, depending on what we wanted to do, and we really worked it out.

ScoreNotes: That's an interesting point about a "sound versus music" standoff, as it were, because you're correct about how that dynamic usually plays out. Especially so with summer blockbusters or event movies; they try to jam it all in at one moment, and you can't really identify what it is you're watching or hearing.

David Newman: Right, I think that's the normal thing that's done now. Everyone tries to push everything to the front. If you think of the movie as a room, a sound stage, or a concert hall where you're sitting in the audience and then there can be depth in the screen, something can seem to come from the back to the front. I think mainly in these kinds of comic book movies, or these sorts of sci-fi or action movies, everything is slammed to the front. It's the only way to win in a way, so we experimented with a completely different approach to the sound in the movie.

ScoreNotes: Now, how does a project like *The Spirit* stack up with another high-quality film like *Serenity* that you worked on a few years ago?

David Newman: *Serenity* is really similar in the way that I was working with an artist, Josh Whedon, who was in charge of the movie except that movie was for a big studio, so there was a little more pressure on Josh. He was quite a bit more experienced than Frank was, so it was a little more about kicking things back and forth to find the soul of that movie. But again, in that movie, too, we did a bit of the sound design kind of thing. It was similar in the way that it was all about the art of it and not so much about the commerce. That was a terrific experience, too. Coincidentally, that had sort of a western feel to it as well. *Serenity* also had some other issues involved because there was such a rabid fan base and the music was such a big part of *Firefly*, so Josh and I had to kind of deal with that and talk about what we were going to do about that. I think some people liked what we did and some people didn't like it, depending on how fanatical they were about *Firefly*. I did some of that sort of down-home stuff in it, but there were a lot of other elements in it because Josh really wanted it to be a big movie. He felt that a movie is a different experience than an episodic television series.

ScoreNotes: Absolutely…it's on a different platform, and the music has to follow suit.

David Newman: Yeah, but you live and learn this stuff. The reason the movie got made in the first place is because of the fan base. When you're in it, you do what you think is the best thing to do. *Serenity* was a fantastic experience for me as well.

ScoreNotes: I have to say, you seem to have a knack for picking dynamic and interesting projects.

David Newman: I'm glad you say that because most people don't say that! I've done so many movies, part of my aesthetic in doing this is that I like to do lots of different things. But I'm also a working craftsman as well, so I can help movies. I feel like my job is to help; I don't know if the word *sell* is right because that sounds too corporate...but my job is to collaborate with the movie, which is this immutable thing that demands collaboration from the artist's side but not from itself. It's not going to collaborate with you, and so I've had a lot of what I thought were interesting projects. I've done a lot of big studio comedies. I've actually done quite a few art films and various bizarre things. I've had a lot of other things in my career. I've done a lot of conducting. I used to run the Sundance Composers Program for five years, and we've got a lot of music recopied and performed. I was a violinist in my twenties. I worked on all of Jerry Goldsmith's and John Williams' movies that were recorded in Los Angeles in the late '70s to middle '80s. I've done a lot of things, so I'm glad you say that!

ScoreNotes: I think the neat thing about film music is that fans can identify with a favorite composer and really pick out, from the breadth of a career, the particular soundtracks that kind of shaped that composer's voice. I think that's one of the neat aspects of being a follower of soundtracks. For me, one such movie from your career is *Galaxy Quest.* When you completed the score for that film was there ever talk afterwards of maybe doing a sequel?

David Newman: We're all actually still really close, Dean Parisot and all the people that made that movie, including the editor, Don Zimmerman, and my music editor, Jeff Carson. We hang out from time to time and still go out drinking and eating, or whatever. I've never heard anybody talk about doing a sequel. I just did recently a film that Tim Allen directed called *Crazy on the Outside* that we just finished. I was talking to Tim about the movie, too. And he had such a great time, but no one ever mentioned to him about doing a sequel either. That was such a bizarre experience because that was DreamWorks, and no one knew what that movie was. There was another movie like *The Spirit* where nobody got what the tone was. When it came out, it didn't do all that well. It wasn't like *The Spirit,* but it certainly wasn't a huge hit. But some people really got that movie. I think I remember talk about [how] the studio wanted to make the movie for kids, 10- to 15-year-olds, and we were always baffled because obviously it's a *Star Trek* television series type of movie.

ScoreNotes: Right.

David Newman: And so, what would that age group know about that? I mean, I know they would know what *Star Trek* was, but we were always scratching our heads about what that meant. And we didn't end up doing that obviously. It's a parody. I was on that movie from really early on from when they were shooting, so I kind of watched the whole thing develop. I wrote the little theme that was for the TV show really early on, and then I really didn't do anything until the film was done, and we sort of finished it, but I was kind of in the mix there as they went and screened it and talked about it and all the machinations that happen with a studio movie. No, I never heard anyone talk about a sequel.

ScoreNotes: Well, if you're ever in that circle again, I think it's a good time to bring it up because I have a feeling *Galaxy Quest 2* would do very well at the box office.

David Newman: I think it would do better than the first one. I think it's a really good idea.

ScoreNotes: In looking at your career, and specifically with you being in the musically inspired family that you are, can you just touch on what it was like to grow up in the environment that you did?

David Newman: Sure, my father was much older when I was born. My father was 54 when I was born, and he died when he was 70. I was born in 1954, he died in 1970, and I had just turned 15 when he died. We were really trained classically, my brother Tom and me, and my younger sister. I played violin from a young age, and piano, and we were trained with theory and counterpoint privately, kind of like what would be a European sort of training, private lessons and such, and it was my mother who did all that. But after my father died, my Uncle Lionel, who was the youngest, took over at Fox, and I started going down and visiting with him.

They were all very nice to us and everything. I'd go down and start visiting Lionel, and then I'd start listening to all these reel-to-reel tapes that my father and Ken Darby had worked on. If you watch the late 1950s and '60s movies up until my dad died, he always worked with Ken Darby. In fact for *Camelot*, which is the last Academy Award he won, he and Ken won it. They also worked on *The King and I*, which was also an Academy Award he won. Anyway, Ken was a very technological person, and he had made reel-to-reel tapes of most of those movies from the late '50s and '60s once my father left Fox. I started when I was in college studying violin at USC in Los Angeles. I started listening over and over, particularly to *The Greatest Story Ever Told* and *Nevada Smith*, and I was completely stunned by the incredible art in the orchestra playing—which is entirely another conversation because I think this is something that is so unique to Hollywood of that time, completely singular to the Fox orchestra and their whole group there. It was built over 20 years, so that completely resonated with my aesthetic because I was very much into conducting and classical music; my father was a huge opera and classical music fan. And I have a ton of his scores and things like that. So for me, it was almost posthumous as to when I really learned kind of what Alfred Newman was about.

The other part of it, which I think is unique, is that my father's aesthetic in composing was really tied up in administering a film music department at Fox. I don't know if you know anything about it, but it was the most innovative film department at the time. He pulled in Bernard Herrmann and David Raksin when no one else would work with them because they were so cantankerous and no one wanted to use them. [My father] was a great administrator, a great conductor, and an orchestra person.

So that's kind of the long-winded way of saying what it was like for me. It was mainly posthumous because when he was alive, he made sure that we were classically trained and that we liked school and played sports, and he wanted to make our lives as normal as possible.

ScoreNotes: I want to thank you for sharing that bit of personal history with us because it really gives an insight as to when that moment of becoming a film composer crystallized for you.

David Newman: Right. Thomas, my brother, wanted to compose from when he was a teenager, so he was always writing and working. For me, I played violin and I wanted to conduct, so I didn't really start until I was in my late twenties. Tom and I, and then my sister Maria who is much younger, were trained to do whatever. So after I decided it wasn't some impossible thing to do, because I had been trained to do it if I wanted to do it, I started. That's from my father.

ScoreNotes: That's terrific. Now that we've taken a look at your past, could you fill us in on any future projects that you may have lined up at this point in time?

David Newman: Well, I just finished two projects last year that haven't come out yet [as of January 2009]. One is a project that Tim Allen directed (his directorial debut), a romantic comedy called *Crazy on the Outside*. And I did a film for Playtone, which is Tom Hanks' company, that Donald Petrie directed, called *My Life in Ruins* that will be out next year, which has a lot of Greek music in it with orchestra music as well. And I've been doing the Movie Night in Los Angeles at the Hollywood Bowl each year. This will be the third year that I'll do that. They do a really elaborate movie night that's really serious. They'll either do it with a studio or composer, and everything is synchronized with film, and we do scenes and that kind of thing. And my wife and I are on the board of directors of an organization here called The American Youth Symphony [www.aysymphony.org], which Zubin Mehta's father started 47 years ago. We're doing a Jerry Goldsmith project where for the next three years we're breaking Jerry Goldsmith's career up into three sections...early, middle, and late...we did the early part in December [2008] where we did *Planet of the Apes* and all this incredible music that he wrote.

My daughter is a vocal major at USC but also plays violin in the orchestra, and you know, we have a nice life, doing that. We're trying to pass on the music thing.

ScoreNotes: I do want to thank you for going through some of your recent projects, future projects, and also taking a look back at your past. I really do appreciate it.

David Newman: All right Tom; it's nice to talk to you.

4 *Keeping Score* with Nicholas Hooper

Used by permission.

Nicholas Hooper.

Nicholas Hooper had the unenviable task of following John Williams (and Patrick Doyle) on one of the most popular film franchises going today—the *Harry Potter* movies. In the face of daunting expectations and perhaps some unfair pressure, Nicholas went about his duties and created respectable scores for both *The Order of the Phoenix* and *The Half-Blood Prince*, two soundtracks that represent his style as opposed to that of his predecessors in the franchise.

I caught up with Nicholas during the time of each score release (2007, *Phoenix*; 2009, *Half-Blood Prince*) to talk about the new, more dramatic turns that the music in the *Harry Potter* films was embarking on...

Nicholas Hooper (2007)

ScoreNotes: How did you first become involved with the scoring duties on *Harry Potter and the Order of the Phoenix*?

Nicholas Hooper: David Yates, who is the director, is someone I've worked with for many years; I've done most of his scores. When he took on *Harry Potter*, he wanted to use me as the composer. So he asked if he could do so, and we had to go through quite a long process of giving [the producers] demos, showing them music and eventually persuading them that it would be a good idea. Finally, after a couple of months, we got the go ahead, and off we went!

ScoreNotes: Were you a fan of the novels and/or the film series before you were brought on board?

Nicholas Hooper: Well oddly enough, I was. I read the first *Harry Potter* shortly after it came out and was completely hooked and have been a fan ever since. When I met my wife, I discovered she was a fan and that pulled us together a bit. They are wonderful books, amazing themes which go quite deep, really. Although they seem like children's books, I think they are actually far more interesting than a lot of adult books.

ScoreNotes: Indeed, there seems to be an almost even fan base between children and adult readers. When it came to scoring the films, how difficult was it for you to pick up the series in a fifth installment?

Nicholas Hooper: It could have been difficult, but David's help and the fact he knew the kind of music he wanted made a huge difference. Following John Williams is always kind of a bit forbidding, really, because he is such a great composer, but I had his theme to work with, which I enjoyed doing, too.

ScoreNotes: As far as the themes themselves, what can fans expect from *The Order of the Phoenix*? Will all the famous Potter themes be returning?

Nicholas Hooper: The most famous one will return, which is the Hedwig theme. I used that at the front of the film where you'd expect it, and then during a lot of the important dramatic points in the movie, it appears almost disguised; you just hear it coming in. Otherwise, I'd have to say the music will be different; the mood of the film is darker. There are some very strong characters, like Professor Umbridge, who has her own theme, which purveys a lot of the movie. There is the business of the possession of Harry by Voldemort gradually through the film, and that has its own theme, which again is very different. Dumbledore's Army has its own theme. So the music is different, but the film is different...so it goes with it, really.

ScoreNotes: Was it sort of a double-edged sword arriving aboard a film franchise that already had an existing base of music you had to build off of?

Nicholas Hooper: Yes, although what I would say is that it's not the same as many franchises in the fact that the books develop. So, it's not like this is a sequel to something everybody has heard before. The books are changing, so the films will change. It's a very different feeling from, say, a *Batman 4* [laughs].

ScoreNotes: [Laughing] Very true. Now, going into this project, you were entering one of the premiere movie franchises going today. Did you have a personal strategy on how to manage expectations?

Nicholas Hooper: Well...I thought I did [laughs]. Our plan was to write a lot of music early on, get into it very early, and get a wonderful musical structure that was all working. Things being as they are, the film changed shape, and the music grew and changed shape with it. In the end, it was quite a rush to the finishing post. I had a great team. I think that was one of the important things. I had a team of orchestrators who transferred my MIDI files into music. I had, for the first time, an assistant who looked after all the technical aspects, a fantastic orchestra...just support all the way from the producers to the director to everybody. That was the best strategy of all, I think.

ScoreNotes: I would say that would be the best strategy for any movie!

Nicholas Hooper: Absolutely. We had no trouble in the sense of people interfering and trying to make us go in different directions. Everybody was on board, everybody knew what was going on, and we had nothing but support as a result. I think that's partly due to David Yates, who is just so good at pulling everybody together and making it work.

Nicholas Hooper (2009)

ScoreNotes: What is the direction you steered the music in for *Harry Potter and the Half-Blood Prince*?

Nicholas Hooper: It comes from two places, really. First of all, we came up with an idea, which was a setting of some words by the scriptwriter, both in English and in Latin. We set this for choir and called it "In Noctem." This was going to be in the film but then unfortunately got cut since the length of that particular sequence was too long at the end film. But what we did was take the middle Latin chant out of it, and it became a kind of DNA for the score, and it follows Dumbledore's journey in the film. So that's one big strand of the film. The other one is the reintroduction of the Possession theme from the previous film when Harry is possessed by Voldemort, which again finds its way in subtle ways through the score.

ScoreNotes: What did you find to be the most exciting aspects of writing the score for this *Harry Potter* installment?

Nicholas Hooper: Well, there are quite a few—and exciting isn't quite the right word—the love theme is one. There's more love interest in this [movie]. I really enjoyed writing the sad scene with Harry and Hermione when they're supporting each other in their grief for the people they love going off with others. The other one I loved doing is when Ginny kisses Harry in the Room of Requirements. Those were exciting. The Cave one was also a great moment as the [characters] race across the sea, and the music is building and building to this huge climax as they enter the cave.

The Half-Blood Prince is not what you would call an exciting film in the sense of lots of big action sequences. It's much more of a moving, subtle film. Like when Dumbledore died and they're all raising their wands in the courtyard. That was a very wonderful moment for me to try and get that right and make it absolutely heartrending.

One more that was great to do and interesting was when the dead bodies come out the water. I had a chance to do some very, very dissonant and very unusual music, sort of taking on my experiences of listening to the early twentieth century composers I always loved so much but hadn't a chance to use very much in my own scores.

ScoreNotes: It sounds like there was quite a diverse palette at work in the *Half-Blood Prince*, which must have been a joy to write.

Nicholas Hooper: Yes, it was. But, interestingly enough, there's also more unity of themes than there was in *The Order of the Phoenix*. Malfoy has his theme that runs through. And as I said, so does Dumbledore, so does Harry. So the themes are more constant. But you're right, there is a diversity in it, which made it very exciting to write and very interesting to do. It's a real palette, yeah.

ScoreNotes: What was it like working with director David Yates on this Potter film as compared to the previous installment?

Nicholas Hooper: As always, very creative, huge amounts of input from David. There was a very tight schedule this time, so getting access to him just to talk about things and feedback was difficult. And it was kind of very last minute. But as always, we came up with the goods together. He's a very inspiring man. Just looking at his work in the film, the fantastic acting he gets, it's an inspiration itself before we even talked.

ScoreNotes: One of the neat things I find about the *Harry Potter* series is the consistency it brings with retaining the same acting crew, for the most part, throughout the duration of the movies. How unique is it for a film franchise of today to retain its core talent all the way through?

Nicholas Hooper: I think it must be almost completely unique. I'm not a great expert, but in a series like *Terminator*, I have noticed the complete change except for Arnold Schwarzenegger himself, so in that sense, it doesn't seem to match up. And of course, James Bond changes all the time. So I think it must be unique. And it has, I think, given the actors a chance to develop their characters, which is quite amazing, really.

ScoreNotes: How pleased are you with the results of the soundtrack for *The Half-Blood Prince*?

Nicholas Hooper: Oh, very pleased. A soundtrack is a chance for the composer to maybe pull back some of the things he really liked for the score that had to be missed out or slightly suppressed in the mix because it clashed with the dialogue or whatever. It gave me a chance to make the music really shine and work very well, so I was very pleased with it.

I had a chance to include the choral piece I mentioned in its complete form, and I put it quite close to the front of the CD, although that particular piece wasn't in film order, so that the listener had a chance to hear this theme, which actually purveys the whole score in its original form. So that was exciting. Mainly the CD is in film order this time, which it wasn't last, because it works so well!

There is a piece of jazz quite close to the front of the soundtrack CD that should be great fun for people to listen to that actually didn't make it onto the score. But apart from that, as you get later into the CD, I really get into the development of the music and the way it emotionally pulls you in…which I'm very, very pleased with.

ScoreNotes: The soundtrack sounds like it will make a most excellent companion to the film itself!

Nicholas Hooper: Yes, with a few extra bits and pieces.

ScoreNotes: In a broad sense, what has working on *Harry Potter* meant to your personal development and career opportunities?

Nicholas Hooper: It has meant that I've developed skills, colors, and a type of musical muscle that I didn't have before, I think…and a toughness. It's a very, very tough job doing *Harry Potter*. Going back and doing other smaller things is so much easier and so much more of a joy really, not so much of a struggle. I think it's just pulled me on, really!

In terms of my career, it's difficult to tell yet; it's still early days. It takes years for things to happen in films before they start filtering through. But I certainly have some very good projects I'm working on now. So I'm loving it, really.

5 *Keeping Score* with Andrew Lockington

Photo by Jag Gundu.

Andrew Lockington, *Journey to the Center of the Earth* orchestra sessions, Air Studios Lyndhurst, October 2007.

There are times in the life of a soundtrack fan when he or she will be immediately drawn to a particular style or talent even if the composer is fairly new in the ranks. It took **Andrew Lockington** just one score to win me over.

In the summer of 2008, a surprising bright spot rose up from the busy season of rampaging blockbusters, and that would be Lockington's *Journey to the Center of the Earth*. His campy score was full of pep and wonder, and made for a soundtrack option that immediately stood out as a high-value pick.

Later in the year, Andrew further cemented his status as an extraordinary talent with the music he provided for the underrated family film, *City of Ember*. His score for this feature had a strong fantasy slant to it with its highly memorable themes and heartfelt underscore. Specifically, Lina Mayfleet's theme is a true stand-out! It's a motif that has an honest, innocent charm to it and is completely endearing when heard in the film and on the soundtrack.

In the following interview, taken specifically for this book, Andrew tells us how he got his start in this field, discusses the emerging trends in film composing, and shares insightful background about his recent scores...

Andrew Lockington (2009)

ScoreNotes: Can you please share your background in music and what the deciding factors were that led you into composing?

Andrew Lockington: When I was a little kid I wanted to be a pilot. I was fascinated with everything and anything to do with airplanes. My grandfathers had both been in the U.S. Air Force during WWII, and I'm sure I used to exhaust them with questions about flying. Playing music was a distant second in the occupation race.

Somewhere along the line music took over, though I'm not really aware of when that was. I was always that kid who played piano. I wasn't very disciplined at practicing but had the ability to "lift" music from the radio, television, and movies and play it on the piano. I guess it was a bit of a party trick in public school, and it kind of grew from there.

In high school, I joined a band and got into the rock music world. After playing with a few high school bands, I auditioned for a spot in a professional band. The other members were all in their mid to late twenties, and here I was, barely 15, sporting a blazer with the biggest shoulder pads I could find. Being under 19, I wasn't legally allowed to enter most of the venues we played, let alone work in them. But the other band members looked out for me. More than once, they stepped in when a drunk club patron decided I didn't belong. Playing in the band was a blast, and a dream come true at the time. Though now that I have kids of my own, I can imagine how my parents felt about the whole thing. I remember the drummer would always pick me up in his big blue pickup truck after school, and we'd head out of town to a gig for the weekend. It must have been strange for them to see me go away for days at a time like that.

To this day, I'm convinced they did me the biggest favor by letting me be in that band. I had planned on being in the club scene full time after high school. As luck would have it, the group broke up around the time university applications were due. At that point, I'd been playing in clubs for about three years, and I'd had enough of the lifestyle. The timing was perfect for me to change paths, and I chose to study music at university instead. If they'd kept me from the experience, I surely would have dived head first into that world as soon as high school was over. As it was, I was done with it in time to choose university as my path. Actually, now that I think of it, there was one other career possibility I considered. Being an architect was a dream of mine at one point. I even took all of the architecture and drafting courses that were offered.

In hindsight, the world is probably much safer because I chose music instead of architecture or flying.

ScoreNotes: What were some of the initial challenges that you might have faced as you entered the business?

Andrew Lockington: I still find it funny to think of it as a business. I guess I've never really thought of it as work. Work is physical labor, writing an essay, doing your taxes, rocking a baby back to sleep in the middle of the night.

Music is like those fun school projects you used to have in high school, the one's where you'd get so motivated and excited by it you couldn't believe it counted for marks. Those were the assignments where you'd shoot a video presentation, build a model, make a rocket—things like that. Writing music just doesn't feel like work to me. How could something that's work be so much fun? That's how I think of film composing... even now.

Initial challenges? There were a lot. I remember one of the first films I worked on; I rented $20,000 worth of equipment from the local music store. According to the payment structure of my film contract, I was owed a third of my fee upfront. But the production accountant was very slow and waited the entire 30 days before paying my invoice. At one point, I had so much equipment rented out, the owner of the store called me in to ask what was going on. I explained the situation to him and assured him that I'd be purchasing much of the equipment once my paycheck came in. After considering calling in all of his rentals, the owner decided to let me continue renting his gear. To this day, there's still a note on my store account—it comes up whenever I'm buying something—it reads "seems trustworthy." It's funny to think of now, but back then I was really flying by the seat of my pants.

After four years of university, I was still a few credits short of graduating. I decided to move to the big city and started working as a freelance jingle writer. The money was pretty good, but it just didn't give me the creative outlet I was hoping for, so one day about a year into it, I woke up in the morning and decided to give it all up to pursue film composing. It was a bit of a blind-leap move, but it somehow worked out.

I was very fortunate to convince a successful film composer, Mychael Danna, to hire me as his assistant. For the next six years, I assisted him on his independent and studio films, orchestrated a few projects for him, and we co-wrote a few others. I learned an enormous amount working with Mychael in those six years. It allowed me to experience the film music world from the inside, and acquire valuable music credits along the way. It was by far the most important step in the path that led me into the business.

Among the important things I learned at that time is that having talent is only one part of the equation. There are a lot of very talented composers out there who struggle to make a living in the industry. We all need to be as much business people as composers to make a living, and we need to put at least as much energy into making and keeping relationships with producers and directors as we do into writing music.

ScoreNotes: I first heard your work in *Journey to the Center of the Earth* [2008] and was immediately drawn to your style. Do you feel that this film provided you with a nice opportunity to introduce your thematic writing to the film music world?

Andrew Lockington: *Journey* was a great opportunity to re-visit the style of film scoring that I was exposed to as a kid. The director (Eric Brevig) was looking for a score that would have the same impact as an "Indiana Jones" or an "ET" score would. He had spent many years in Hollywood working with the likes of Steven Spielberg, George Lucas, Michael Bay. He wanted a very thematic score that his viewers would have a relationship with, and hopefully be humming when they left the theater.

Very strong thematic melodies and scores have always been my favorite scores to listen to, so *Journey* offered me an opportunity to explore that in a very unbashful way. While the film is a very modern, present-day film, it didn't hide its relationship to the adventure movies of the past, so that allowed the score to exist in a traditional strong thematic/orchestral way and get away with it.

ScoreNotes: *Journey to the Center of the Earth* was presented as a 3D feature in theaters. Did you have to take any special considerations about the 3D aspect of the film as you wrote the score?

Andrew Lockington: Had you asked me that question two years ago I would have laughed, but it was surprising how much impact the 3D aspect of the visuals had on the score. My studio isn't set up for 3D, so I would write to a traditional two-dimensional visual most of the time. Eric would encourage me to see the 3D version whenever possible, and, sure enough, it would impact what I was writing. I was amazed at how much the visuals would come alive in 3D. Several times after hearing my score applied to a 3D picture, I would take notice of something happening onscreen that deserved to be acknowledged in the score. The 3D viewing sessions proved to be very useful.

ScoreNotes: In general, what is your opinion on the new wave of 3D technology that is emerging within movies, and might this movement affect the art of composing in any way?

Andrew Lockington: I love it. I think over time it will become the norm, especially once technology advances beyond the point of wearing glasses. The scenes in *Journey* that took advantage of the 3D aspect for excitement were a lot of fun, but I must say I was most impacted by the helicopter shots of landscapes or the simple shots of characters' faces. It really felt like you had more of a relationship with the characters in 3D. Eric told me that recent studies have proven watching something in 3D wakes up parts of the brain that normally aren't used in watching a traditional two-dimensional image. I think 3D is definitely the new direction for feature films.

ScoreNotes: When it comes to films that are tabbed as remakes or a re-imagined franchise, do you feel that referencing the source material helps the composer, or is it best to take a fresh approach with these types of projects?

Andrew Lockington: It would depend on the film. For *Journey to the Center of the Earth*, we decided very early on the film would not pay homage to the Pat Boone version. It never attempts to be a remake of that film. Jules Verne's book is even a character in our film. As a composer, I definitely preferred it that way. It allowed me to explore the themes of the story through music without having to work around previous musical ideas.

That said, I recently saw the new *Star Trek* film by J. J. Abrams and found myself listening to the music hoping to hear the original *Star Trek* theme. It finally showed up during the closing credits, which I thought was very appropriate.

ScoreNotes: I'd like to touch on your work for *City of Ember*, a film that I found to be refreshingly fun and heartfelt. Can you comment on some of the various themes that you featured in the score?

Andrew Lockington: Writing the score to *City of Ember* was a very challenging and rewarding experience. I was hired on to that film at the very end of the post-production process. When I signed on, the Abbey Road recording sessions were already booked and only a month away. The first thing I did was call my orchestrator, Nicholas Dodd. The conversation went something like this:

> Andrew: "Nicholas, I've just signed on to do *City of Ember,* but it's a really quick turnaround."
>
> Nicholas: "Fantastic!"
>
> Andrew: "How quickly can you get the score orchestrated?"

Nicholas: "If you can start sending me cues about a month before the session that would be fine."

Andrew: "One month before? That was yesterday!"

Nicholas: "Okay, send me what cues you have right now."

Andrew: "Right now? I just got hired 15 minutes ago."

Nicholas: "Right. Okay. This one's going to be tight."

Orchestrator Nicholas Dodd with composer Andrew Lockington after the last day of recording for *City of Ember.* Abbey Road Studios, London, August 2008.

In the end, I wrote the bulk of the score in three weeks. It must have been floating around inside my head because it came very quickly.

The first thing I did was write three themes. The first theme I wrote was the theme we hear in the opening sequence of the film. I call it the "Ember" theme (I know...not a very creative name). It's meant to establish a dark, ominous, musical soundscape representing the darkness and dread of the city. The second theme is the "Lina" theme, tied directly to the main character of the film. It has a sense of lightness and intelligence and innocence to it that serves to help it contrast with the *City of Ember* theme. The last theme is the "Hope" theme. It gets used the least of the three themes but is a crucial piece of the puzzle. It represents a utopia beyond Ember, both in their dreams and in reality.

The tight writing timeline meant I had immediate access to the producers and director whenever I needed it. The music supervisor, Lindsay Fellows, did an incredible job of wrangling everyone together to review the music. Fortunately for me, everyone was on board with two of the three themes immediately. The Lina theme ended up needing to be rewritten. I was disappointed to have to go back to the drawing board on that one because I'd quite liked the first draft of her theme. But about two hours after the request came to rewrite it, I had a new Lina theme to present that I was even more happy with. I played it for them, and they instantly loved it. It's one of my favorite themes I think, and I'm grateful I was asked to rework it.

It's an important thing to remember as a composer. A good composer can write a great score when given carte blanche by the film makers. But just as often that same composer can write an even better score when challenged by his collaborators. I've lived through solid examples of both scenarios through the years and come to appreciate the potential of the director/composer collaboration much more than I used to.

ScoreNotes: The movie featured a "race against the clock" storyline. How did you incorporate this facet of the plot into the music?

Andrew Lockington: From the beginning, it was made clear to me that this "race against the clock" element was the most important responsibility of the score. I was told "bigger, harder, faster" so often it was written on a Post-it note and stuck to the top of my computer monitor.

One of my first calls was to my programmer, Michael White. I had worked with this amazing synth programmer on *Journey*, and I instantly knew he would be a great asset to me for *City of Ember*. We came up with some analog synth/moog motifs that would bubble and tick underneath the score through much of the film precisely to elicit the feeling of time ticking down, counting down the final days of life of the city's generator.

The generator plays an important role in the story because it is what brings life to the city. It is this gargantuan, almost living, breathing machine that keeps breaking down. The moog rhythms serve to emulate its importance whenever the generator isn't onscreen. One of the reasons it was really important to incorporate this ticking element into the music is that many of the characters in the film are oblivious to the fact the city is dying. Thus, their performances onscreen appropriately lack the anxiousness we as the audience are feeling for them. It was important to give contrast to those performances and keep the "race against the clock" feeling at the forefront of the audiences' minds.

ScoreNotes: Do you feel that *City of Ember* might be the type of film that will emerge as a pleasant surprise to viewers once it makes a run on cable television?

Andrew Lockington: I hope so. I think it's such a fascinating story. I hope more people catch on to it.

ScoreNotes: To further accentuate your productive and impressive year in 2008, you received an award by the International Film Music Critics Association as the "Breakout Composer of the Year." Can you share your thoughts about that recognition?

Andrew Lockington: It was a huge surprise. The other nominees were incredibly talented composers who'd done amazing scores for equally amazing films. I didn't expect to win the award but appreciated being nominated in such good company. Winning was quite a shock.

To be honest, the payoff for me comes in the problem-solving aspect of film score writing. By the time I've recorded and mixed a score, and worked through the challenges that were presented, I already feel rewarded. Having a movie make a quarter billion dollars at the box office and then having the score be so well received is just the icing on the cake.

You know, I have such a personal relationship with my music that I don't think I'll ever understand how others relate to it as well. But as long as they can take something positive away from it, and it helps tell the story of the film, I'm happy.

ScoreNotes: Is it safe to say that you are the type of composer who genuinely enjoys writing strong thematic material?

Andrew Lockington: For sure. I love music that elicits an emotional response—whether that be joy, sadness, excitement, or humor—some music just latches onto our psyche a bit deeper than everything else. For me, strong thematic scores do exactly that, and if done right, provide their audience with enough familiarity with the theme for it to set up an incredibly emotional experience at the end of the film.

ScoreNotes: What are some of the subtleties that go into film music that perhaps the average viewer is not aware of?

Andrew Lockington: I think many viewers are unaware of themes, unaware that they're hearing the same three or four themes through an entire score. I've had more than one occasion where the producers have heard a new cue for the first time and immediately loved it, even hummed along. They couldn't figure out why they liked it so much, and, of course, that was because it was using a theme they were familiar with and had a relationship with already.

In film scoring, building a unique, brand-new cue around a theme the viewer has heard before gives them the experience of hearing something new that they (hopefully) instantly like.

ScoreNotes: On a personal level, how intense does it become for you when you're in the midst of a scoring project?

Andrew Lockington: It gets pretty intense. I've learned to plan my days and hours very carefully. I've learned to really pace myself, breaking the schedule down into minutes that need to be written each day. While one two-minute cue might take a lot longer to compose than another, I always know where I stand in the schedule if I break it down that way.

Someone once told me it only takes two minutes to write a two-minute cue. Most of our time is spent waiting for those two minutes to happen.

ScoreNotes: You have a rather unique setup in that you are based in Canada yet so many films are made in Los Angeles. How has that been working out for you, and do you foresee a time when you might relocate?

Andrew Lockington: I spend a lot of time in Los Angeles, and for sure there will be projects that require me to be physically there for post-production, but so far it's worked quite well keeping my writing studio in Toronto. I'm a morning person, usually getting going in my studio by 5:00 or 5:30 a.m. I find I can often get seven or eight hours of work done before morning hits on the West Coast and my phone starts ringing. Those morning writing hours are very precious to me. I'd have to rejig my schedule to work on the West Coast.

Kaya, Andrew, and Cielle Lockington at a screening of *Journey to the Center of the Earth*.

ScoreNotes: Has your work on *Journey to the Center of the* Earth and *City of Ember* provided any new opportunities or connections for you?

Andrew Lockington: They have. I'm just getting started on Eric Brevig's next film, and I have a lot of friendships with people I met on those projects. I look forward to collaborating with them again soon.

ScoreNotes: As we close here, what are some future goals that you might have set for yourself as you peer ahead toward new opportunities?

Andrew Lockington: I would love to continue to work on new and interesting projects. I know that sounds like a cliché answer, but I truthfully find I'm at my most creative when I'm sailing unchartered musical territory. I love scoring a type of film that I've never scored before, or approaching something familiar in an untraditional way. That's how I do my best work. Most importantly, it has to always be as much fun as it is now. Sometimes I feel like the parents are going to come in the room and break up the party. The minute it feels like work, it'll be time to find another job. Hopefully, that day never comes.

Keeping Score with Marco Beltrami

Photo by Randall Michelson.

Marco Beltrami.

After earning his initiation on the *Scream* films, **Marco Beltrami** has steadily worked his way toward becoming one of the top film composers of today's generation. In fact, the more I hear his work, the more I know that he has a profound sense of what works musically in a film. Marco has the ability of calmly staying focused within the roots of a particular movie's need and not venturing astray. He's disciplined and talented, and that, my friends, leads to success.

Marco was nominated for an Academy Award for his music on *3:10 to Yuma*, a rather successful remake that captured quite a bit of praise all around. In this interview, we discuss what went into that score while also covering Marco's other prominent works including *Terminator 3*, *Die Hard 4*, *Knowing*, and more...

Marco Beltrami (2007/2009)

ScoreNotes: *3:10 to Yuma* received praise as a film that restored a little glory back to the Western genre. What can you tell us about your experience on the film?

Marco Beltrami: First of all, it's one of the most fun projects I've worked on. Though the film was very aware of its heritage, there was no pressure to copy any stylizations of the past. In fact, [director] Jim [Mangold] really wanted to create something new. I tried to approach the score by using only instruments that could have been around at the time the film took place, and then Buck Sanders and I manipulated them to create a more modern setting.

ScoreNotes: How rewarding was it to be involved with a western like *Yuma* in a day and age where Westerns aren't made with regularity anymore?

Marco Beltrami: My dream has always been to work on a Western. In fact, I think I have probably approached many of the films I've worked on as Westerns (sometimes unbeknownst to the filmmakers), in the sense of a lone hero struggling against a forbidding environment. The fact that here I could "legally" pay homage to some of the great traditions that [Ennio] Morricone created was inspiring.

ScoreNotes: What aspects of the film's storyline did you feel offered the peak scoring opportunities for you?

Marco Beltrami: There were a couple sequences that were a lot of fun to work on. There was the scene towards the end of the movie when they're running over the rooftops and having a gunfight and getting away to the train. The momentum of the picture really allowed the music to speak and have fun with some of the thematic elements that had been brewing all along. Another moment is at the end of the movie when Ben Wade rides off in the train. The strong character development allowed the music to have strong, identifiable, simple motives. Ben Wade's theme is just three notes. Simple guitar harmonics comprise Dan's theme. And a manipulated acoustic guitar identify Charlie Wade and the band of thieves.

ScoreNotes: How rewarding a feeling was it to see *3:10 to Yuma* finish at the top spot at the box office?

Marco Beltrami: It always makes you feel good when something you really believe in and invest a lot of energy into receives the attention of others. Sort of a validation I guess. You know, we're sort of an insecure bunch.

ScoreNotes: Moving on to another successful film of yours—what did you enjoy most about working on *Live Free or Die Hard*?

Marco Beltrami: Probably the idea of paying homage to Michael Kamen's scores, but doing so in a way that wouldn't scare the studio. Len liked the idea, but as it was a big-release action movie, Fox wanted to be sure it wouldn't sound too dated, so my challenge was to sort of take this little simple motive that Michael Kamen came up with for the John McClane character and write a modern-day version.

ScoreNotes: How difficult is it to write music for a film that has a built-in blockbuster status as compared to a movie with a modest budget?

Marco Beltrami: The biggest challenge is that usually on a big-budget movie, more people are involved. Working on *3:10 to Yuma,* I dealt with the director and that was pretty much it. And that's often the case with smaller movies. On a bigger movie, there's often different studio executives and producers who come. I guess there is a little bit more fear involved; there's a lot more money that's involved. It's not as easy to take chances with the music as it is perhaps in a smaller-budget film. There's often a temp score that is put down in the movie that has been cut and they know works with the film. There's often a tendency not to stray too far from that for the final score.

ScoreNotes: Do you have a preference, be it by genre or budget, with the types of movies you like to work on?

Marco Beltrami: Genre-wise, I'm not that concerned. I'm more concerned with the movie itself being a good movie and presenting possibilities to me, the composer. I think the only type of movie that I really didn't enjoy that much was a comedy I did awhile back. I'm not crazy about writing musical sound effects and short little tag cues. Other than that, as long as I'm able to explore musical ideas throughout the score and have the chance to contribute something, and the film is good and inspiring, then the type of film doesn't really matter to me.

ScoreNotes: Writing sound effects can't be too inspiring for a composer.

Marco Beltrami: No, it's not. If you have a good sound department, you can work with them and create [sound effects] that work hand in hand together. But when the composer is asked to comment on the action by doing little musical sound effects, that's not that rewarding.

ScoreNotes: What would you say was your breakthrough film?

Marco Beltrami: The first movie I did that really anybody would have seen is *Scream,* back in 1996. That's sort of what gave me the spot with Dimension/Miramax Films back then and gave me an in to work on a bunch of films and sort of cut my teeth. And then I branched off from there.

ScoreNotes: As far as science fiction and disaster sagas go, where would you rank a movie like *Knowing*? I found it to be an underrated, effective film that grew larger in scope the deeper one got into it.

Marco Beltrami: I believe Alex [Proyas] to be one of the great storytellers of cinema and part of that is due to his innovative spirit. His projects are ambitious and require a lot of elements to come together harmoniously. I had heard that there were some who took issue with various visual portrayals, but to me that never detracted from the depth and breadth of his voice. I was hooked in and know many others feel the same.

ScoreNotes: Can you touch on the subway scene in the film, specifically where you have that menacing yet playful melody pacing Nicolas Cage's search for the terrorist?

Marco Beltrami: This is a great sequence from an intensity standpoint. Nick's theme is a 12-tone row, which like his mathematical obsession, sounds like a jumble when the notes are played all together. As they string out, however, they form a multi-meter rhythmic drive that forms the relentless structure for the cue and mimics his confusion and momentum.

ScoreNotes: In what ways does working with a visually inspiring director like Alex Proyas inspire your work?

Marco Beltrami: Alex inspires me to find the crux, or the hinge, that allows the music to work. It's like a puzzle, or the laws of nature, where scientists are always trying to find the one simple rule from which all others are derived. I think Alex does this in his films, and similarly inspires me to. We often joke that finally when we both get it right, his movies will just be one frame and my music just one note. This is the reason to write music!

ScoreNotes: You've built quite a respectable reputation for yourself by the work you've done over the years. Looking ahead, is there anything specific you hope to achieve in your career?

Marco Beltrami: My kids really want me to do a children's movie.

7 *Keeping Score* with Geoff Zanelli

Photo by Suzie Katayam, taken at Paramount's former Stage M.

Geoff Zanelli.

There are some who would say that fully thematic film scores are slowly becoming a lost art. If that is indeed true, thank goodness composer **Geoff Zanelli** is on duty.

Geoff has impressed me very early on with his ability to craft themes that are strong, memorable, and at times quite moving. I also think the further along he gets within the business, the more he will be known for excelling in this thematic vein. I submit that the main theme from *Outlander*, his contributions in the *Pirates of the Caribbean* films, and the love motif from *Hitman* are prime examples of his composing strength and suggest an extremely bright future in the business.

This is a 2009 interview with Geoff in which he talks about the values and challenges of collaborating, the musical contributions to *Pirates*, the fundamentals behind the *Outlander* score, and more...

Geoff Zanelli (2009)

ScoreNotes: You've quietly worked on some of the biggest blockbusters that modern Hollywood has produced. What has the collaborative journey been like for you thus far?

Geoff Zanelli: In a word, enriching. I remember being deliberate about how I'd go about getting things going before I moved back to LA to start my career. I had a lot of peers who were taking the lone wolf approach, maybe going after student films for the experience, things like that, but I took a different road. It occurred to me that the most valuable lessons you can learn as a young film composer were learned in the meetings between accomplished filmmakers. What I was wondering was what do Ridley Scott and Hans Zimmer say to each other when they talk about music? How does Jeffrey Katzenberg or Jerry Bruckheimer talk about film? Without knowing anyone at all in the industry, it took some extra persistence, but I got an internship at Remote Control Productions, which is Hans Zimmer's studio. I was 18 years old on the other side of the door during those big music meetings thinking, "Let me in that room!" I really wanted to know what was going on in there!

John Powell, who had his writing room here at Hans's place, took me on as his assistant, which was a big step for me. That's when I started doing arrangements for John and getting some experience with collaborations like that. After a few years, I was given a writing room of my own and got to collaborate with Hans and the other guys, Harry Gregson-Williams and Steve Jablonsky for instance, and see firsthand how each of those guys works. It didn't take long for me to be in demand as an arranger. Over time, I built up more and more experience on all sorts of films.

ScoreNotes: What would you say are the key factors to a productive musical partnership?

Geoff Zanelli: Trust, mutual respect, and a ceasefire! You don't always get all three, but I've been lucky; nearly everyone I've worked with has a similar desire to collaborate. That's probably the most unique thing about the group of talent I've fallen in with; we're able to work together.

ScoreNotes: It's always a fun test for the fan of a composer to try and pick up on the additional music that was contributed to a film. Are you at liberty to discuss some of your contributions on the *Pirates of the Caribbean* trilogy?

Geoff Zanelli: I am. On the first film, we had a very short schedule, which is why it ended up that there were so many guys on board. Four weeks at most, it might have even been three. For that film, I was mostly doing arrangements of Hans's themes—like the first part of the ship-to-ship sequence was my own re-imagining "He's A Pirate" from the album. "He's A Pirate" is something I worked on, too, actually. Hans had written da sketch of this long suite of themes for the film, which he released in an interview a few years back, and it comes from that. It was in demo form, so the fans who are really curious about this stuff can go listen to that demo and compare that to "He's A Pirate" from the first album. They'll hear the evolution of that piece. So the demo is what it was when it left Hans's hands, and the final is what it is after my arrangement and production, the orchestra's performance, and Alan Meyerson's mix. I fleshed that tune out for the film, and did the same for the sequence when the cursed pirates reveal their curse to Elizabeth and freak her out. We called that sequence "Moonlight Serenade," but I don't think that's the title it has on the album.

When the second film came around, most of us from *Curse of the Black Pearl* were brought back to work on it. This is where I got to write some thematic material for the trilogy. There was a whole sequence on Cannibal Island, and I wrote the piece that plays when we're introduced to that locale. There were also a few Jack Sparrow music moments on Cannibal Island, which I worked on using Hans's theme.

I also did both of the frantic Kraken attack cues. Hans had written a bare-bones collection of riffs and tunes and frantic bits for the Kraken scenes, which we mapped those scenes out with, and then I went in and finished them by arranging them for the orchestra and building up the rest of the arrangement. Some of it was literally just a synth bass and a kick drum when I first got it!

Tia Dalma also appears in the second film, and I wrote her theme as well. She had a relatively small part, and I did a little motif for her with a female vocal when they row to her house in the swamp.

So when the third film came around, that's when I got to go and expand that melody. Tia Dalma becomes Calypso and has, literally, a bigger role in the film. That was great fun, since I hadn't really known that that little motif would have to turn into this giant thematic moment for the third film. That tune plays all over the place in the third film, so in a way, as the series went deeper, I had more and more involvement.

Then I did a few bits near the start of the film, like when we're heading to Sao Feng's place through when Elizabeth is strip searched. Oh! And the seduction sequence, when Sao Feng tries to seduce Elizabeth later on, after mistaking her for Calypso.

ScoreNotes: I first started following your solo career with your work on *Disturbia*. What are some of your recollections about the score you wrote for that film?

Geoff Zanelli: I met D.J. Caruso before he shot the film, so it was early in the process. We hit it off right away and went over our ideas for the score, most of which made it into the film.

Disturbia is about a teenager named Kale who takes up spying on his neighbors while he's on house arrest. So since it had voyeurism as a core part of the plot, there would be some scenes where the audience is watching Kale watch someone. Well, in that case he's pretty passive, just watching, so all the intensity in the film has to come from the music. It has to play the tension that's in Kale's head, so I talked with D.J. about my idea to use the music as the kinetic element for those sequences. That happens a few different ways in the score. When he's watching the cute girl next door go swimming, I'm playing the thrill and mystery Kale feels. Then later in the film, when he thinks he sees a different neighbor kill someone, the music is really doing the subtext there. He's safe in his room, but the music is now playing the panic that's going on in his head.

Another idea D.J. and I talked about was how to handle the love story in the film. It's teenage love, and I thought, well, we can't just go play some romantic orchestral music for that, that's not really being honest with the audience. The music of teenage love comes from a song perspective, almost all of us have our first crushes to whatever the big pop song is on the radio or whatever music we're into at the time. So I thought I'd write a love theme with that in mind, that it should feel like a song in terms of instrumentation and arrangement so it would feel genuine.

ScoreNotes: Is that how you ended up writing a song for *Disturbia* as well?

Geoff Zanelli: That's how it ended up, yes. It was an evolution though. During the process, we screened the film for an audience, and originally there was a song in the sequence where Kale confesses his feelings for Ashley out on his balcony. I remember thinking, "I've done this love theme which plays throughout the film everywhere but here in the big payoff sequence!" So I went and wrote an instrumental piece for that scene and showed D.J. You can see where this is leading...we ended up thinking why not have this be the scene where the score and the songs merge? That's where the approach I'd taken with that theme proved itself. We got a band I'd heard and loved called "This World Fair," showed them the movie, played them the tune I'd written, and they wrote the lyrics and performed the song.

ScoreNotes: I absolutely enjoyed the memorable love theme you wrote for *Hitman*. Can you tell us about the importance of having a softer side, musically, in a film like that?

Geoff Zanelli: Oh, I'm glad to hear that! That's what I liked most about my *Hitman* score, too; you don't really expect romance. It's always great when you can have a real contrast in your score, especially when it's an action film. There's a real danger of being one-dimensional, and sometimes that's OK, but with *Hitman* I saw an opportunity to spread out a little more. It makes the violence more violent, too, actually. If you think about, say, *Kill Bill* or *True Romance*, those both use music in a way to juxtapose something softer against incredible violence. It really resonates when you can do that.

ScoreNotes: When a film spans across multiple locations, as *Hitman* did, what are some of the steps you take to ensure that a score remains cohesive?

Geoff Zanelli: You know, there's a funny thing about writing a score, and this happens to me nearly every time. I start out looking at a blank page, worrying about how I'm going to make this cohesive, yet somehow that concern just gradually disappears during the process. I can't ever pinpoint anything I've done to ensure that cohesion, though, so it's either subconscious or it just takes care of itself by virtue of the fact that every piece has had my hand in it. It could also be that in *Hitman*, the arrangements hint at the locations we're in, but there were two or three underlying motifs that worked their way into most of the cues regardless of the locale.

ScoreNotes: As far as unique projects go, where would you rank *Outlander* on your list of scoring assignments?

Geoff Zanelli: It's got to be right near the top. That's what hooked me in, actually, the unique story. A man from space brings an alien monster to earth, but it's set more than 1,000 years ago in Viking territory! I wondered, "How is this going to work?" You've got to see it yourself, but it holds together well because it's rooted in a classic story, *Beowulf.*

ScoreNotes: At what point did you get involved in the project, and what was your initial reaction to the material?

Geoff Zanelli: It was after they shot the film and had their edit in progress. I went over to director Howard McCain's edit room and met with him, the editor David Dodson, and producers John Shimmel and Chris Roberts. They showed me an early version of the trap sequence with the alien on fire, wreaking havoc on this Viking village, taking heads off of people, and just generally messing things up. I'd been looking for a fantasy film, something imaginative, since I enjoyed working on the *Pirates* films so much, and this was a perfect match. And once you sit down with Howard, his enthusiasm is contagious.

ScoreNotes: Can you tell us about the inspiration behind the key themes that you developed for the score?

Geoff Zanelli: Sure. I started with the Viking music. That's the most "classic" of the themes. It had to be earthly, something to root the score in so I could counterbalance the story against it. It's the most orchestral music in the film. People picked up on the fact that I didn't just go and write a big major-key heroic theme for this, and that was deliberate, too. It still plays heroism, but it's "serious" music; it plays the story about the succession of kings in a reverent way.

There was a theme for the Moorwen, our alien monsters. There's actually two for them—one for the monstrous aspects, which plays during the action, and another theme that is the emotional side of the story. I needed the emotional music for a flashback sequence where we see the Moorwen genocide that Kainan, the spaceman who brings the Moorwen to earth on accident, took part in as a soldier.

And Kainan himself gets other-worldly music. It's more synthetic for him, and a little military, too. The idea is that it's very different from the Viking music for the contrast, different instruments—a different approach altogether. But over time as Kainan assimilates into Viking culture, bits of the Viking theme start to move onto him. He earns it, really; he earns his Vikinghood, and so the Viking instrumentation and eventually the theme itself transfers over to him.

ScoreNotes: How important was it to have a strong main theme as the foundation of the soundtrack?

Geoff Zanelli: Crucial, I think. There had to be this thematic music that anchors the score in something believable and familiar so you can buy into the story. I didn't want the audience to feel alienated from the world; I'd rather draw them in and make them take the journey with us instead of just sitting back and watching a bunch of people go through it on the screen.

ScoreNotes: Can you describe some of the unique instruments that you employed for this film?

Geoff Zanelli: I had a wide palette for this. I wanted to have no limits with what I could use, and Howard was on board with that approach; it's one of the things we talked about early on. So there's the live orchestra, but also a ton of synthesizers, some woodwind instruments from different cultures around the world, a Middle Eastern fiddle, there's a female vocal solo in a few places, an early form of harp called a lyre, and hand drums, which are something we know the Vikings actually played. There's even some electric guitars in there, a few anyway, and some parts where the drums are more like rock drums as opposed to the tribal drums that happen in other parts of the score.

ScoreNotes: Looking forward, do you think that *Outlander* will catch on as a cult classic among sci-fi and action fans?

Geoff Zanelli: There are a ton of people, myself included, who are interested in these types of imaginative stories, so yes, I have a hunch it'll catch on. The response for the limited theatrical release has been very, very positive already. People sought this film out once they heard about it, so that's a good sign.

ScoreNotes: As we wrap up this discussion, can you tell us about some of the projects you are currently working on?

Geoff Zanelli: Right now, I'm co-scoring a miniseries called *The Pacific,* which is a World War II story by Steven Spielberg and Tom Hanks who also made *Band of Brothers.* It's a magnificent show! It'll play on HBO early in 2010. I'm sharing writing duties with Hans Zimmer and Blake Neely on it.

Also, a few months ago I co-scored a movie called *Gamer,* which comes out in September 2009. That one was co-written with Robb Williamson, and we got to be pretty crazy, unconventional, and experimental. Definitely not the kind of thing people have heard me do before! That film has an interesting premise, too. It's about mind control in the future where criminals are used as characters in these live battles, which are then televised around the world—sort of like playing a video game, only you're controlling actual humans. And one of those humans is Gerard Butler, who racks up a huge body count. It's directed by Mark Neveldine and Brian Taylor, the same guys who directed *Crank 1 and 2,* so that should give you some idea of how crazy we got to be.

That's what's keeping me busy nowadays.

Thanks for your interest in my scores, by the way. It's a pleasure talking to you!

8 *Keeping Score* with Tyler Bates

Tyler Bates.

S ince 2007, **Tyler Bates** has made noticeably impressive strides in his career. The composer has, in recent years, worked on such prominent films as *300* and *Watchmen*, while also delivering scores for movies like *The Day the Earth Stood Still* and the *Halloween* remakes. The blend of blockbuster movies and cutting-edge films has proven to be a successful one for Tyler, as are the relationships he's forged with directors Zack Snyder and Rob Zombie. Creatively, he seems to be right at home with these directors and their style of movies.

In this interview, we embark on a brisk journey through Tyler's career, touching on his earlier work and some of the key projects he's worked on thus far in his journey, including the intricacies of scoring a film like *Watchmen*...

Tyler Bates (2009)
ScoreNotes: At what point in your life did you have your first inkling that you wanted to be a film composer?

Tyler Bates: It wasn't until I scored my fifteenth movie or so. I worked with director Stephen Kay on *The Last Time I Committed Suicide*. This was my first score that was gratifying on an artistic level. Working with Stephen Kay was very inspiring to me, and a hell of a lot more fun than touring low-budget in a rock band, eating Del Taco everyday!

ScoreNotes: Growing up, what were some of the movies and film scores that made an early impression on you?

Tyler Bates: *The Exorcist*, *Jaws*, and *Halloween* all left an indelible mark on me. The simplicity of the motifs that were employed to create tension and excitement in those films is obviously very effective. They certainly got under my skin! I also loved Jerry Goldsmith's score for *Planet of the Apes*. Amazing stuff!

ScoreNotes: I'm often curious about the route that composers have to take to make it in the business. Can you describe the type of independent projects you were involved with in the early part of your career?

Tyler Bates: I was willing to work on anything that kept me in music and away from painting houses! Fortunately, I met a few directors in the beginning of their careers who had very limited music budgets, which made me a good candidate to score their films. I did several films for Roger Corman's company as well as Saban. There were so many learning experiences along the way that helped me develop a vernacular in communicating with directors and producers in the context of filmmaking, and yet there was very little I could do to hurt the quality of the films as I was learning the craft of film scoring.

ScoreNotes: Do you miss, in some part, working on smaller scale productions as compared to some of the more prominent features you are now associated with?

Tyler Bates: I don't gauge film projects by "size" or "scale" with regards to budget or profile. I tend to lock myself into my cave [studio] and focus entirely on the task at hand, with the director's vision in mind. Taking into consideration the better part of my first thirty-five film projects, I am happy scoring good films of any budget, if good people are involved. So by all means, I am looking to work on indie films as much as any other.

ScoreNotes: Can you comment on how important it is to have a director who appreciates the nuances and effectiveness of film music?

Tyler Bates: Good directors are mindful of all the details of their films. They know precisely how to convey the essence of the film they are making, and the right composer to help express this. It's also pretty cool when a director understands the time and thought that goes into creating music, especially when you receive your twelfth cut of the movie two days before your scoring dates begin [laughs]!

ScoreNotes: Along those lines, you've collaborated with Zack Snyder on multiple films, each successful in their own right. Did you know early on that he was a director who had a unique vision to offer?

Tyler Bates: I knew Zack was special the moment I met him. He is one of those people that you know is really good at whatever they do, even if you are not familiar with their work.

ScoreNotes: During your early collaborations with him, at what point did discussions about the movie *300* materialize?

Tyler Bates: Zack called me about a month after *Dawn of the Dead* was released [March 2004], to discuss *300*. I began writing music for his initial proposal to studios for their support. I scored an animated short constructed from the pages of Frank Miller's graphic novel that was made to depict the style of film Zack wanted to make. I wrote music for statues, look books, and the test shot Zack made for Warner Bros before they green-lit the film. We even worked up battle cadences to condition the actors in preparation to principal photography. Zack choreographed three scenes to music I wrote along the way. It was an interesting ride, to say the least.

ScoreNotes: Looking back on it, how significant a project was *300* for you personally in your career? Was that your biggest film at the time?

Tyler Bates: *300* was an experience of every extreme one could imagine. I would say that it made me very much aware of the semantics of working on films that become "pop-culture" phenomena. The business, and the process by which large-scale films are made, is really something the average person, or film composer for that matter, cannot completely comprehend unless they have personally been through the experience a few times.

ScoreNotes: I was pleased to see that for Zack's next project, he selected a film that was as ambitious, if not more so, than *300*. What were your first impressions as you started working on *Watchmen* with him?

Tyler Bates: The tone of the film resonated with me as I watched the first cut footage with the editor, Bill Hoy. It was truly inspiring from the get-go. A project such as *Watchmen* is a tall order to deliver, but Zack gave all of us who worked on the movie the necessary support and confidence to put preconceived notions aside when approaching the challenge of making the unmakeable!

ScoreNotes: Had you been exposed to any *Watchmen* material before the film, or was there a bit of research involved to catch yourself up with the background of the saga?

Tyler Bates: I read the graphic novel a couple of times after Zack asked me on to the project. I intentionally insulated myself from the lore of the graphic novel by keeping discussions about the project to a minimum. I felt that I needed to approach the film as I saw it—without anticipating the notions of the *Watchmen*-savvy contingent as to what the score should be.

ScoreNotes: The *Watchmen* are a cast of heroes unlike any the silver screen had seen before. Can you describe the strategy behind the score and, specifically, the approach you took to reference the decade of the '80s in your material?

Tyler Bates: I love all genres of music of the '80s! It was a tremendous mish-mash of acoustic/organic and digital/electronic technology. It is part of my musical DNA, so it undoubtedly bore its head in the *Watchmen* score. Part of my job is to express a feeling and sometimes assimilate the feeling of a particular era, which, like the graphic novel, is evident in the *Watchmen* film. Apart from the obvious, I approached the film from the headspace of its characters. The intent of the score is to express what our characters are unable to say in words, and to do so in such a degree that the audience not only feels the sentiment, but also sees the textural palate of each character's mind.

ScoreNotes: When speaking about "retro" styles, your music for *Doomsday* also had a touch of past inspirations in it. How much did you enjoy working on this project, and was it fun paying homage, in a way, to some of the science fiction films of the past?

Tyler Bates: Nearly all music is a homage of some sort. Neal Marshall is great to work with. His knowledge of movies and pop music is what really made it possible for me to walk the line of what could be cheesy (as opposed to good fun) if handled unintentionally in poor taste. But if you have seen the film, you can see that it was done entirely in "good" taste [laughs].

ScoreNotes: What has it been like working with Rob Zombie on the new *Halloween* movies?

Tyler Bates: Rob marches to his own beat, which I love about him. When we're working together, it feels more like we're making something we like as opposed to being in "the business." I am not at liberty to specifically discuss *H2*, but I will say that no one will call Rob a softie after watching it. It looks incredibly hardcore. And Wayne Toth [special effects make-up] has completely outdone himself. I have never seen more realistic movie blood than this!

ScoreNotes: Does he [Zombie] have stronger input than most directors about the type of music he's looking to use?

Tyler Bates: Rob's films are visually more intense than most I have seen, which in turn has a strong influence over the choices I make when writing a score for him. We created a "sound" for his films with *The Devil's Rejects*. It is not to say that the character of the music I have done for his films will not evolve (or devolve) into something different. It most certainly will over time. Rob and I collaborate based on what we have done thus far as a point of reference when we're discussing new ideas. That said, he is not up in my grill about finite details; however, he doesn't pull punches about what he likes and dislikes. This is one of the things I like best about our working relationship.

ScoreNotes: Are there any challenges in jumping from one genre to the next as a composer, or is that part of the fun for you?

Tyler Bates: It's all part of the fun. But seriously, it's all a bit daunting. I have yet to do a film where I began with the notion that "I got this!" My guess is that the score would be lacking in inspiration if that did happen. I usually begin with the feeling that I have no idea what I am doing! This is probably because of the insanity behind my process for developing the "sound" of each score. I'm not quite sure. For me, the fun is when a project is completed and everyone creatively involved is happy. Of course, when it's too late to make changes, I see my glaring mistakes that weren't visible to me before the dub. But you learn and move on.

ScoreNotes: What is the best thing about being a film composer?

Tyler Bates: As a film composer, you are forced to dig deep and challenge yourself every day. You learn about music of all styles and genres on a continuous basis, and also meet interesting and intelligent people when working in film. Much of my life was spent in rock bands, which are amorphous creatures based on the sum of the creative partners involved, whereas the nature of film scoring is that as an individual, you interpret the vision of a director in the most creative way possible. There are always new stories to experience when working on films, which, as artists, presents the opportunity to reinvent ourselves and expand the scope of our talent beyond what most rock bands can offer.

9 *Keeping Score* with Alex Heffes

Alex Heffes

Used by permission.

Alex Heffes is a composer who has worked on an interesting portfolio of films. At the top of that list are his collaborations with director Kevin Macdonald's *The Last King of Scotland* and *State of Play*, two movies which offer distinctly differing plot themes while providing a similar sense of professionalism in the manner in which they were made.

While I enjoyed the music Alex wrote for *The Last King of Scotland*, it was his effective score for *State of Play* that confirmed my interest in his style. Specifically, I was impressed in how he wrote such varied, compelling music within the narrow spaces of this tightly edited film.

I interviewed Alex circa April 2009, around the time that *State of Play* began its modest run in theaters...

Alex Heffes (2009)

ScoreNotes: Can you tell us a little bit about your background and where you're currently based out of?

Alex Heffes: I originally was classically trained and later played jazz piano. After my formal education, I started trying to put aside what I'd learned and pick up some of the tricks that I found people doing in pop and commercial sessions. That opened up a lot of new ways of working for me. I consider myself very lucky to have had a really solid formal background and the chance to work with bands and artists. I hope this gives me the best of both worlds. I split my time between London and L.A. These days the Internet really has made the world a smaller place.

ScoreNotes: What would you say was your "first break" in the business?

Alex Heffes: Hard to say. I think we all need breaks to continually happen. Sometimes it's the ones that don't seem too important at the time that eventually lead to greater things. Meeting talented people is the best break. I've been fortunate to work on some great quality projects such as *One Day in September*, *The Last King of Scotland,* and *Sweeney Todd*—all of which have ended up in the Academy Awards. Working with gifted people such as Kevin Macdonald and Tim Burton is the best a composer can ask for.

ScoreNotes: I felt that your music for *State of Play* was quite effective and helped guide the story forward in great fashion. Given that it was a very tightly edited film, was it at all challenging in determining the spots that required score material?

Alex Heffes: In a really good picture like *State of Play*, good performances, direction, and editing mean the film already plays very well without music. This is a luxury for a composer because you can actually spot the music where the film will benefit from scoring rather than where it may need "propping up" because of weaknesses in those areas. The scoring process can hopefully amplify and bring out all the strengths that are already there in the picture.

ScoreNotes: Can you share some of the ideas that you and the film's director might have discussed in mapping out the strategy for this soundtrack?

Alex Heffes: I was asked to write some music to the script before shooting, which is quite unusual. I had brought onboard the fantastic British rock producer, Flood, early on in the process, and he recorded all these early jam sessions. We brought in a whole variety of interesting instruments and people in order to create a "palette" that would have a particular flavor. This included the wonderful Crystal Bachet from Paris brought in by Thomas Bloch, some unique sound sculptures and percussion made by Steve Hubback, and the human beatboxer Shlomo. These sessions were a lot of fun and provided many of the rhythmic ideas that came later in the score.

ScoreNotes: There are subtle touches of dramatic influences in the music. How important was it to instill an undercurrent of emotion within the score?

Alex Heffes: You need to engage with your characters to lift your film above just being a plot-led narrative. Russell Crowe is fantastic at being able to convey what his character feels with a minimum of expression. He often says it all with a look. The emotional part of the score comes toward the end where things start to get messy. The relationship between Cal and Steven is what we focused on. In order to do this, I wrote a short theme or motif which comes back in various guises. You hear it on a piano earlier on in the film. Toward the end of the film, it comes back on a "broken" sounding piano—to try and mirror the split in their relationship. When we were recording in the studio, I just happened to open up the Bechstein piano they had there, which hadn't been tuned that day. As it happened, it was well in tune except for a couple of notes, which had a rather interesting off-key sound. So I wrote the main theme of the film there and then around the notes that were "broken" on the piano. Flood had the great idea of recording the theme at half speed an octave lower onto 2-inch tape. When it was played back at the correct speed, it had a slightly fuzzy sound, which is what you hear toward the end of the film to evoke the emotional breakdown of the characters.

ScoreNotes: In the battle of online versus print media, do you think the newspapers will ultimately lose this fight for readership? Or, as suggested in the movie, do you feel there will always be a demand for established newspaper reporting?

Alex Heffes: I think the jury is still out on this one. I guess you'd probably get different answers if you were to pose this question to a child of the Internet generation and someone who was brought up with newsprint on their hands.

ScoreNotes: How captivating an assignment was The *Last King of Scotland* for you?

Alex Heffes: That was a real adventure in all senses of the word. I went to Uganda and recorded a lot of music on location, working with bands and singers we found there. Recording vocals in a disused meat packing factory in the middle of the night in the back streets of Kampala was one of the many memorable events. I rehearsed the choir we were working with in a swelteringly hot store room sitting on oil cans while being eaten alive by mosquitoes. Actually, the malaria there is awful. One of the actors had a bad malaria attack during my stay. It's a very serious problem. We also found a bagpiper who had been in Idi Amin's bagpipe corps in the 1970s. I remember him dusting off his pipes and playing them outside. In moments all the children from the local school came running out of their class to see what on earth was making that noise. They had a ball.

ScoreNotes: Given that the film built up a solid bit of publicity during the Awards season, did the notoriety help put more of a spotlight on your work as well?

Alex Heffes: People did seem very interested in the soundtrack, which is gratifying as we put a lot of effort into it. I still get a lot of mail from all round the world about it.

ScoreNotes: Scanning the remainder of 2009, do you have any ongoing or future projects that you would like to share with us?

Alex Heffes: I'm currently scoring *Shanghai,* directed by Mikael Håfström and starring John Cusack, Gong Li, and Yun-Fat Chow. I'm also working on an album project which has been going for some time. It's an exciting collaboration project with a series of different artists in different locations. More about that shortly!

ScoreNotes: Looking ahead to your future goals, what are some of the accomplishments you hope to achieve during your career?

Alex Heffes: Just keep on going and enjoy—that's the film composers' mantra!

10 *Keeping Score* with Theodore Shapiro

Photo by Stuart Pettican.

Theodore Shapiro.

Some would say that writing music for comedies is a predictable venture. Don't mention that to **Theodore Shapiro**.

Theodore is a composer who has worked on some of the most successful comedies in recent history, including *Tropic Thunder*, *Blades of Glory*, *Marley and Me*, *Year One*, and more. What makes him stand out, in my opinion, is that he writes music on a level above that of standard comedy scores. I've always appreciated the intelligent, thematic approach he takes toward his projects and also the manner in which he raises the bar in the comedy genre each time out.

I had the opportunity to speak with Theodore shortly before the Harold Ramis comedy, *Year One*, premiered in June 2009...

Theodore Shapiro (2009)

ScoreNotes: Can you describe the type of score you developed for the comedy adventure *Year One*?

Theodore Shapiro: The heart of the score for *Year One* almost has a collage-type approach. I took a lot of different elements and put them together to create a sort of unusual stylistic combination. I used drum loops, electric guitars, middle eastern instruments (woodwinds and string instruments), and then an unusually configured orchestra that had a string section that was smaller than the typical compliment and used it more in the manner of a Bollywood or Middle Eastern style string orchestra. That was the idea. I took all these ingredients and threw them into the pot and something came out of it.

ScoreNotes: How enticing is it for you to score comedies that allow for more of a multi-dimensional approach to the music?

Theodore Shapiro: What you're always looking to do is something that enables you to stretch as a composer or find an interesting combination of sounds that engages you in the process and that makes it really fun and exciting. So you're always looking, I think, when choosing a project to do something that's going to give you that kind of expanded palette and an opportunity to go to places that you haven't been before.

ScoreNotes: What were your experiences like with *Year One* director Harold Ramis?

Theodore Shapiro: Harold was completely open. He's just a very wonderful, really intelligent and intellectual guy and a pleasure to work with. The film is a road movie, more or less, in which Jack Black and Michael Cera start the movie as hunter-gatherers in a small tribal village. They get cast out of that village, and then essentially they go on what amounts to a road trip through the Old Testament. At the same time—and Harold as the writer/director was very interested in this concept—the movie traces the arc of civilization. So they start as hunter-gatherers; they encounter Cain and Able and sort of a very rustic, agrarian society. And then they encounter Abraham and Isaac and the Hebrews. . .and then it goes on to Sodom, which is sort of an ancient version of Las Vegas, more or less. Harold was very interested in both the movie and the music tracing this arc that is the pass of civilization. So we talked a lot about that, and although we certainly didn't come up with an approach that is ethno-musicologically correct in any way, shape, or form, I think the music is mindful of that idea. It starts off with an African drumming-type of approach, and then it does enter into a more Middle Eastern language, and then ultimately, when we get to Sodom, there is a little more of a biblical sweep to the music. So it does go on that journey.

ScoreNotes: Can you describe the scope of knowledge a composer has to have to be able to touch on musical influences from around the world?

Theodore Shapiro: [Laughs] I come from a classical background. I went to the Julliard School as a composition student, but I also grew up playing in rock bands and having a wide array of musical influences. I think the training part is really important, but you also just need to have an open ear and keep listening to a lot of material. And a lot of it is just a conceptual notion that you have an idea of something that you want to pursue; then if you need to immerse yourself in that kind of musical language that you're unfamiliar with, you do that.

ScoreNotes: *Tropic Thunder* was another film of yours that played great with audiences. Did you know early on with that movie that you wanted the music to play with a sense of intensity?

Theodore Shapiro: Absolutely. The initial conversations that I had with Ben Stiller were just that; no matter what, we wanted the music to be a completely serious element in the film. Before he started shooting, and we sat down to talk about it, that was the one thing that we absolutely knew. At the time when he was getting started, we were talking about possibly pursuing a more '70s Goldsmith-type approach in keeping with the Vietnam War setting. But then as soon as he shot the film, it became pretty much immediately clear to us that the movie wanted a modern approach. We kept to the notion of the music being serious and intense, and we used a very maximalist, modern approach to the music. It was great, great fun to do.

ScoreNotes: It's not often that one gets to score a Ben Stiller action movie [laughing]!

Theodore Shapiro: That's right; there aren't too many of them. It's just a real thrill to be able to do that. I work on a lot of comedies, but whenever I watch action films like the *Jason Bourne* movies, I always think that I would absolutely love to get an opportunity to write a fifteen-minute action sequence, and this provided me an opportunity to scratch that itch.

ScoreNotes: To follow up that point, you've done a great job with the films you've scored in your career, many of which were comedies. Do you have any interest to branch out to different genres, or is that hard to do after you've proven to be so successful with what you do?

Theodore Shapiro: I would love to work in as many different genres as possible. It *is* difficult to branch out. You do get pretty quickly pigeon-holed in Hollywood as doing a certain kind of thing. And all that said, I absolutely love the work that I do. I find it musically engaging, I find it intellectually challenging, and I don't think a lot of people would think it's a very sad story that I don't get to work on different genres of films. I really love what I do; I'm very lucky to get to do it. If I get to work on other genres, that's great; if not, I'll be happy with that, too.

ScoreNotes: A film that proved to be quite endearing with audiences was *Marley and Me*. Did you have a sense early on that this movie would take off in popularity the way it did?

Theodore Shapiro: I thought there was a chance of that. I'll tell you that the point in which I knew it would was when they had the first preview, and the first time they reveal Marley as a puppy, you hear the whole audience go "awww" at the same time. I just knew immediately that this movie was going to be huge. Dogs touch such a chord with so many people, and so many people have the experiences of having a pet. And the movie, I think, is just very well done; it's very well directed. David Franklin is a terrific director and really knows what he's doing. There's little fat in his films, you know; he just knows how to tell a story. The combination of it being a good movie with the built-in factors of people connecting with the idea of having a pet, loving a pet, losing a pet, and the success of the book—well, I had a sense that it might be pretty popular. I still wasn't prepared for how popular it was.

ScoreNotes: How neat was it for you to mix in some of those Irish melodies that we heard in the score?

Theodore Shapiro: That was great fun! It was nice because there was a main theme for the Owen Wilson and Jennifer Aniston couple, so it was really fun to get to transpose that theme into an Irish tune. That was a really enjoyable cue to get to write.

ScoreNotes: The sentimental value of your music worked to great success in the film, specifically with the final cue in the film. Can you talk about the delicate balance of writing music for emotional scenarios? There's something to be said about music that comes across honestly the way yours does.

Theodore Shapiro: You're referring to the cue "It All Runs Together," and in the film, it's the cue that's playing when they (spoiler alert!) euthanize the dog. My greatest fear was pushing the sentiment too far, but at the same time, it is a moment of catharsis. And ultimately, I think that the cathartic value of that moment is what the movie is about. That moment of release as the dog dies is just so central to the impact of the film. It was a delicate balancing act because the music had to be emotional, honest, and direct, but not too much, and hopefully that's what it was.

ScoreNotes: It absolutely was; I think you nailed it with that cue.

Theodore Shapiro: Thank you.

ScoreNotes: What are some other projects you have lined up for the rest of the year and beyond into 2010?

Theodore Shapiro: I'm finishing a really enjoyable film called *Jennifer's Body*, which is a horror comedy written by Diablo Cody, who wrote the film *Juno*. So it's a really interesting film. It's got the writing style that Juno had, but it is definitely also a horror film; it's very smart and plays around the conventions of that genre. I'm actually writing that score with another composer, Steven Barton, and that's been a really fun experience to collaborate with somebody else. And after that, I'm taking a break. I've had an unusual, busy year.

ScoreNotes: As we wrap up this chat, I would like to say that I like how your music doesn't play generically when maybe it could in a comedy, so thank you for rising to the challenge and giving us soundtrack fans great material to enjoy.

Theodore Shapiro: Thank you so much, I really appreciate it. It's been a real pleasure to talk to you.

11 *Keeping Score* with John Murphy

Photo by Charlotte Murphy.

John Murphy.

J ohn Murphy is absolutely one of my favorite composers to speak with. In our first conversation, the interview for *The Last House on the Left*, he was as personable and informative as any composer I had spoken with before. His wealth of knowledge about the projects he has worked on and the directors he's collaborated with is greatly interesting.

John's not afraid to take chances with his music. As is often the case, his creative contributions have greatly benefited the films he has worked on and makes for excellent listening experiences apart from them. Who can ask for more?

In the following interview, John lets us know what makes him tick as a composer. He also shares his experiences with Academy Award winning director Danny Boyle, and the legendary Guy Ritchie, from his collaborations with both of them over the years.

Overall, this segment offers great insight on one of the top film composers from the U. K....

John Murphy (2009)

ScoreNotes: I'd like to start our discussion off with *The Last House on the Left*. What were some of the scoring opportunities about this film that interested you?

John Murphy: Initially, the thing that interested me was working with Dennis Iliadis. I'd seen *Hardcore*, which was his first film, and thought he'd done some pretty interesting things with the music. So I had a feeling that he wasn't gonna want a typical kind of horror score, you know…that maybe he'd let me try something a bit different. And he had that kind of European sensibility that always gets me. So we met up, and before he showed me the film, we talked about how generic and predictable a lot of horror scores are nowadays compared to how they were in the old days. And then we talked about doing the score in a more organic and melodic way…kinda like a lot of early American horror films were done. You know, like *Rosemary's Baby*.

And when he showed me a few scenes, it was nothing like I expected. It had this kinda cool European pacing, and it just looked beautiful.

For me, the main thing is always the director. If he's gonna be brave with his film, then he's gonna be brave with the music, you know? Which means I might have more opportunities to do something a bit different. And for me, that's the most exciting thing about scoring films…how far we can push it.

ScoreNotes: I read in your CD liner notes that the combination of beauty and dread, elements that are presented in this film, are specific components that you enjoy writing for. What is it about that blend that you find creatively interesting?

John Murphy: I think it's kind of a personality problem that comes out in some of my stuff. I've always tended to lean towards extremes in most art to be honest. I passionately love the really melodic and lyrical stuff by Ennio Morricone and John Barry and Nina Rota…but at the same time, I'm still drawn to the really dark or atonal stuff, you know. With certain films, I just feel that I can bring more to the table when I'm trying to hit those two polar opposites. Because at some point, they kind of become the same thing. You can sometimes see the beauty in something in a more cinematic way if the music is dark and unsympathetic…and sometimes you feel more horror and dread if the music is innocent and lyrical. I like it when scores do that—when the music juxtaposes what's happening on the screen, but actually it's heightening it emotionally. Morricone and Bernard Herrmann were fantastic at doing that.

I think I just feel more comfortable working with those two extremes. I can be in either of those two worlds without forcing it, so it's easier to write that kind of stuff. I don't have to over think it.

ScoreNotes: Does it ever become a bit of a chore or challenge to labor through more of a mainstream project as opposed to a film you're more comfortable with, like *The Last House on the Left*?

John Murphy: To be dead honest, yeah it does! You know, a lot of times, you just don't get the chance to do the films you really want to do. And you can't just sit around and wait for films like *28 Days Later* or *Sunshine* to come around; you gotta pay the bills! So sometimes that means doing something a little more mainstream, but that's cool. It's not like I'm gonna do something I hate or work with someone I know is an a**hole. Though that never stopped me in the past [laughs]. I'm a working composer, and I'll never take that for granted. So sometimes I have to just get my head down and do something a bit more mainstream and just be challenged by that. But yes, it's definitely more difficult. It's just a lot easier for me when I don't feel like I'm out of character, you know? And I feel more in tune with something like *28 Days* later than, say, a romantic comedy or something. The few times I've worked on that type of film, for example like *Guess Who,* I had this horrible feeling that there were 20 other guys within a mile of me who would be doing it better! And nobody wants to feel like they're faking it, you know, even when they are. So yeah, I'm much happier with the edgy stuff. I don't have to think about it too much.

ScoreNotes: Absolutely! And I'm glad you brought up *28 days Later* in your response because I would like to ask you how influential you think that film has been for the modern horror genre?

John Murphy: When we were doing it, as much as we loved it, I don't think we thought it was going to be anything other than this cool, little thinking-man's zombie road movie! And to be honest, when you're working on a film, you're so involved in the making of it, that it doesn't occur to you that what you're doing at that very moment might actually influence other films in the future. You just want to do it as good as you can and get to the finish line in one piece. Then of course, it came out and everyone went crazy, and it kind of rebooted the zombie genre. It's only now, years later, that it's dawned on me how influential it has been to that genre. And I think it might have made a lot of young filmmakers realize that there are other ways to approach films in this genre, and other ways to frighten and disturb audiences without resorting to the usual schlock horror style. That and the fact that it was Danny Boyle…I think it may have given a few new filmmakers a bit more confidence to be a little braver. So yeah, I think it's definitely left its mark.

ScoreNotes: You've collaborated with Director Danny Boyle on multiple occasions. How open is he to expressing new and creative musical ideas when it comes to your work?

John Murphy: Danny's about as open and brave with music as you would ever want a director to be. I think he's the only director I've ever worked with that I couldn't shock [laughs]. You know, he'll talk and talk about how he wants the film to feel, the back-story of the characters, and the themes within the film itself. He'll talk about everything to do with the film apart from how I should do the music. He's never once said to me, "This has to be this kind of track" or "This has to be strings"…or piano or whatever. He doesn't really work like that. After he's overloaded my head with the film, he basically leaves me alone to try things out myself. So when he comes back to hear stuff, he comes in with a completely open mind, never knowing what the hell he's going to hear. And if he hates something, he'll just say it. But when he gets excited about a track, he gets excited! Especially if it's something he didn't expect.

A good example is the end, or the climax, of *28 Days Later*…you know, the crazy blood-fest in the house. Most directors would have been screaming for me to do one of those hundred-mile-an-hour syncopated action things, you know, but we ended up going with this slow guitar groove that went off on this seven-minute grungy crescendo. I don't think I would have had the confidence to play that to any other director. But he loved it. In fact, he went back in and recut the scene longer after he heard it, which is something very few directors will do.

So yeah, to be given this whole level of understanding of the film and the confidence-…and license to experiment and get there in my own way…you don't know how rare that is. That's why my most original stuff has been for his films. He gave me the chance to do what I wanted first. And a lot of composers don't get that opportunity.

Seriously nice guy, too.

ScoreNotes: Another notable director you've worked with is Guy Ritchie. Can you describe what his style was like when you scored his films?

John Murphy: Guy's a one-off, you know, and great to work with in a completely different way. Very dynamic, very single-minded. And he's another one who kind of leaves me to it till he comes in to hear stuff. So he's similar to Danny in that respect, but other than that, in terms of how they deal with music, they couldn't be more different to be honest.

But, you know, there are reasons for that. Guy's films are very character-driven, so it's all about each character having his own theme, his own flavor, as opposed to the film itself having bigger themes. He doesn't really worry about the film thematically as long as the characters have their own musical identity. Which is a weird way to construct a score to be honest, but somehow it works in his movies. For example, there's no main theme in *Lock, Stock and Two Smoking Barrels* or *Snatch*. So it's all about the comedy with him. And because so much of the comedy in his films is in the dialogue and in the rhythm of the dialogue, it's all about the beats in the music, by which I mean the ins and outs and the pauses, not beats as in drums or percussion. And the tempo of the music is critical in his films because it has to groove along with the nonstop dialogue rather than drive it. You don't drive Guy's films…you groove along with them! And I'm totally cool to do that. It's easy to become obsessed with the mechanics of a score and how it's working thematically, you know, but we just don't get into that on his films. He doesn't really care about all that crap. He's very instinctive as a director, so if something feels right to him, then it's right. He doesn't over think it or question it beyond that. So, in that respect, he's very easy to work with.

So it's all about the flavor and the rhythm of the score with him…the tempo, the spaces you leave and where you come back in. And how it all works alongside the comedy, without ever having to resort to "funny music." And somehow it all works.

But you do have to throw the rule book away when you work with him, which is cool with me.

To be honest, I wish we could have done more films together, but I don't hear about it till it's too late, and I'm already on another film. Usually one of Danny's funnily enough.

But Guy's a good lad. And funny. Nothing like the surly, serious guy people think he is.

ScoreNotes: There's something to be said about directors who have a clear vision about what is expected from your music, and I suppose that makes your job easier, too.

John Murphy: Yeah, there's nothing worse than coming onto a film and you suddenly find out that the dynamic director you took the meeting with hasn't actually worked out what he wants the music to do in his film. You play them something, and they're not sure how they feel about it because they're not sure what they want. So at some point, you have to take control and say, "OK…we've got one shot at this. If you know what you want, tell me. If not, let me just do it." And I've been on films where the director has been too nice to just lay out what he really wants, and it's always ended up a mess.

ScoreNotes: Best to be upfront, get it all out, so you can do what you do best.

John Murphy: Yeah, when you have deadlines, you have to be straight with each other from the off…you're gonna have an intense six weeks with this person, and there's just not enough time to be polite with each other. If you hate it, tell me now so I can do something about it before it's too late. Some guys get it, but the guys who don't…well, it usually ends up a disaster.

ScoreNotes: [Laughs] That's not the goal, I'm sure.

John Murphy: No.

ScoreNotes: As we near the end of our discussion, I want to take a moment to compliment you on your portfolio of work and, specifically, your score for the heartwarming film, *Millions*. Can you share your recollections from that film?

John Murphy: To be honest, I loved doing *Millions*. It's actually one of my favorite scores I've done, believe it or not. I love it when I can just sit down at a piano and write simple tunes without having to be ironic or cynical or cool. I just don't often get the chance to do it because I think people see me as the edgy guy [laughs], you know...and there's something about writing from a child's perspective that I love. *Liam* was the same, the film I did with Stephen Friars, which was also from a kid's perspective. I just think you get more freedom to write heartfelt music with this kind of film and not be embarrassed about it, you know. I just don't usually get asked to write those types of scores, unfortunately.

ScoreNotes: Indeed, I do want to compliment you on that score because it is one of my favorite works of yours.

John Murphy: Cheers, Tom, I appreciate that.

ScoreNotes: What does the rest of 2009 look like for you?

John Murphy: The next film out (for me) is *Armored*, directed by Nimrod Natal. It's a cool little heist movie with Jean Reno and Matt Dillon. I got to do a lot of crazy, over-driven guitar tracks, frantic stuff, lots of feedback, and stuff like that. I love doing that. The exact opposite of *Millions*. A pretty volatile little score, but I like it.

ScoreNotes: Has some attitude to it, sounds like.

John Murphy: Yeah. And there's a nice crescendo shape to a lot of the scenes, which is something I obviously love doing. It's a cool little film, very tight and edgy. Nimrod is a pretty exciting young director.

But workwise...and I've got an exclusive here for you Tom...I'm actually going to take the rest of the year off to put out some of my own stuff.

ScoreNotes: Nice!

John Murphy: Yeah, I can't wait. No one knows yet. Just you, my wife, and my guys [laughs].

ScoreNotes: It's a close circle [laughs].

John Murphy: Yeah. I've been promising myself I would do this for a couple of years. I'm actually setting up my label now. And to be honest with you, I think I prefer some of this stuff to a lot of my film stuff. Sometimes you've just got to stop and do something for yourself, you know. As much as you get a lot of creative freedom with this job—and I seem to get a hell of a lot more freedom than most guys I know—you have to give the guys who are paying you what they want. And it gets frustrating sometimes when you have to butcher something you like for the sake of the scene or the film. But that's what you have to do. So I'm taking a few months off to get some of that stuff out my system. So that's what I'm going to be doing for the rest of the year…that, and playing Legos with the kids.

12 *Keeping Score* with Mark Kilian

Photo by Mark Martin.

Mark Kilian.

When composers truly immerse themselves in their projects, it's a type of commitment I truly admire. Mark Kilian strikes me as someone who takes this route with each and every project he takes on, embarking on a quest of discovery with each outing.

In the following interview, originally conducted in 2008 and later updated for this book, Mark explains the different levels he explores when asked to write a culturally rich film score. As you'll read in the interview, Mark goes beyond simple preparation and fully immerses himself to understand the culture that he may be representing with his music. We also discuss traditional Hollywood fare such as *Traitor*, the Academy Award winning film *Tsotsi*, and many other interesting topics in this engaging segment...

Mark Kilian (2008/2009)

ScoreNotes: What were some of the musical directions you explored with *Traitor*?

Mark Kilian: The way I started work on *Traitor* informed the rest of the score in a way. I was in South Africa visiting my folks when I was contacted by the director, Jeffrey

Nachmanoff, to spec up a few scenes. I only had a laptop with me and no sound library at all, so rather than flying back to L.A. the day before Christmas, I decided to build my own library and write with the elements I was able to make. I set about recording a million sounds around the house: tap dripping in the kitchen sink; choir of beer bottles filled to different pitches; different sounds of all my dad's power machines in the garage; percussion played on paint cans, bottles, windows, doors, etc; my old piano and guitar from when I was a child. All these sounds and more became my "orchestra," and after spending a few days building that up, I set about writing music using my new palette. Once I had written the three pieces, I booked a recording session with a vocalist and a guitarist in South Africa and then mixed it back on my laptop (with headphones!) and sent them on. This essentially got me the job. It was a very liberating experience not having my massive sound library with me in that I had to create each and every sound from scratch, and I think the benefit of that was that the textural part of the score became as important as melody or rhythm or harmony. There was a lack of hierarchy in the music in the sense that all the building blocks that make a piece of music were equally important. Of course, much was added to that in the final score, but the initial germ of this idea stayed with me for the rest of the project.

Back in L.A., the first thing I did was organize a massive percussion session with a truck full of rented percussion instruments, including a set of artillery shells, tuned metal plates, Chinese kettle drums, Argentinean Bombos, Roto Toms, the biggest bass drum I could find, and a host of weird and wonderful ethnic percussion instruments. I then hired a bunch of players and then had them play stuff they weren't used to. So the guy who was a great Latin percussion player wouldn't get to touch any Latin percussion, and the great rock drummer would find himself banging metal plates and so forth rather than a rock drum kit. This really helped in getting material that sounded a little more unique as the players were also having a lot of fun and being challenged playing instruments they weren't accustomed to.

ScoreNotes: What aspects of this film's complex storyline did you find to be the most intriguing?

Mark Kilian: The storyline was very multi-layered in that it wasn't a "good guy, bad guy" story. One never really knew Don Cheadle's character's loyalty until the end. Also, I grew up in South Africa where a guy who was locked up as a terrorist and whose organization waged a campaign of terror (Nelson Mandela and the ANC) became the world figurehead of peace and reconciliation and led the country to freedom (and he is my biggest hero!). So the story of *Traitor* resonated with me on that level. The world is not black and white, and this encouraged me to write a score that did not use a thematically divisive approach. In other words, it was my intention to not attach a theme to a character, and I think this helped in allowing the score to not tell the audience who was the "good guy" and who was the "bad guy."

ScoreNotes: When writing music for a character whose intent is not totally clear, does it make it challenging to pick a direction for that individual's representative theme?

Mark Kilian: My themes in *Traitor* are following the events in the story, rather than the characters, so there was a theme for bomb making, and a theme for infiltration, and one for the dissemination of the ideals that drive this terrorist network in the story. I didn't want the audience to care for Don Cheadle in the beginning of the story. Nor did I want them to get excited by the pursuits of the FBI or the fumblings of Jeff Daniel's CIA character. I wanted the audience to have as neutral a perspective as possible so they could go along for the ride and not know who was the "good guy" or the "bad guy" until it was revealed near the end.

ScoreNotes: That's a great example of how every movie is different and how you, as a composer, really need to take an approach that's appropriate for that specific film.

Mark Kilian: Absolutely. One of the exciting things I like about this career is that every film presents a different set of obstacles, opportunities, and ways that you get to explore the telling of a story.

ScoreNotes: What kind of a timeframe was involved in developing and recording the score for *Traitor*?

Mark Kilian: I would say it was somewhere around three months, and it felt like a really good schedule. I was brought in fairly early in the process, while they were still editing the director's cut, so I got to work along with them and get stuff into the temp score before they started doing previews. The earlier the composer is working on the film, the better. Temp scores are helpful in telling the composer how the director would like a scene to feel, but they can affect the outcome of the score in a negative way, as the composer is often battling with replacing something that the filmmakers have been listening to over and over as they edit the film. This usually does not contribute to the originality of the score.

ScoreNotes: One of your scores preceding *Traitor* was the evocative *Before the Rains*. Can you tell us how that score differs from your work on *Traitor*?

Mark Kilian: *Before the Rains* is a very different kind of film. That was a film where there was much more of a traditional thematic approach to the score. It was an absolutely beautifully shot period piece set in Kerala in the south of India. It was directed and shot by Santosh Sivan, and when I first saw the opening few minutes, I just walked over to the piano and wrote a few themes, as I was so inspired by the beautifully shot opening. I got to explore traditional Indian music, which I've studied at university and have always loved. I went to India to record and work with the filmmakers, and it was a very exciting experience for me to immerse myself into another culture for a while.

ScoreNotes: Do you find that being able to work with diverse cultures in film offers unique creative opportunities for you and your music?

Mark Kilian: Most definitely. I'm most proud of the moments where I've been successful in taking the musical essence of a culture and weaving it into a tapestry that is my own. It is so tempting to write a score that is a drone with an ethnic instrument wailing away on the top, but that is less interesting and can do the film a disservice. *Tsotsi* and *Rendition* are definitely ethnic scores, but as much as they are attached to the story, they have their own unique world of sound that is drawn from a much broader experience than just the physical place where the story takes place. *Before the Rains* is a little different in that it was a period piece. I tried to be more authentic with the sound palette I was using. It was in essence a classical Indian score, but I did use some African percussion and made some electronically manipulated soundscape material.

Traitor was an ethnic score, too, but as the story moves from place to place, the score is somewhat devoid of ethnic authenticity. I used a host of interesting instruments like the Hang Drum, Duduk, Oud, Bass Ruan (Chinese "smiley face" guitar) Egyptian Saz, electric violin, and Ney flute. Along with the Seattle Orchestra and the crazy percussion stuff I had recorded, I used production techniques more akin to electronica to put the score together. I also used a lot of bends in the strings and played with major/minor tonalities throughout, which gave the string writing a more "ethnic" feel to it without being a typical "Middle Eastern" string sound.

The last two films I've done since *Traitor* have both been ethnic stories in a way, but both are set in America. One is an African-American story called *The Least Among You,* and the other one is a Latino story called *La Mission.* They both offered me the same opportunity of going into another culture, learning what I can and then trying to write a score that draws from this, but is not dictated to by it. *La Mission* was my first real experience working with Latino music, and I bought all these instruments online and from local music shops, some of South American origin and some not. I used a double ocarina (bass) to make some of the low drones and pads, and the Swedish door harp to make some of the tension textures, and the triple Native American flute to make some higher pads. For the melodies and counter melodies, I used the Contra Bass Native American flute, the Charango (string instrument from Bolivia), the Chinese Hulusi (bamboo wind instrument with Gourd), and the Jarana, a smaller guitar also from Mexico.

The film I'm working on now is *North by El Norte,* a Mexican film about a young man from Tijuana trying to cross the border into the United States. For this, I'm using a Bass Harmonium, which I had custom built for me in India, an Igil from Tuva (two-stringed bowed instrument), electric mandolin, African bass Kalimba, and so on. I'm also using some Mariachi brass, which I've sampled and resampled and mangled to make some of the interesting rhythmic and textural material.

ScoreNotes: It seems like quite a bit of independent, extensive research is necessary to really capture the authentic sound of a culture to represent it well. I felt you successfully delivered that authenticity with *Before the Rains,* a score that I easily recommend to others.

Mark Kilian: Thank you. I try to live this role where I sort of see myself as a bit of a "method composer." You have to do the research, but you need to actually live that culture a little bit and try and immerse yourself in what makes that culture tick. I think that's important. I know it sounds a bit silly, but when I'm working on an Indian movie, for example, all I have on my iPod is Indian music, and I eat Indian food wherever possible! When I started work on *La Mission,* I started to learn Spanish and am still taking courses. Working on *North by El Norte* now, I'm listening to all the new stuff coming out of Mexico as well as the traditional folk stuff. I'm also taking trips down to Tijuana just to feel the "vibe" there, so a tiny bit of it might inform the score. I think anything one can do to live and breathe the culture is helpful. Once you understand the cultural aspects of the music better, it is easier to play with moving away from the generic and expected palette associated with that culture and still remain true to the culture somehow. Scoring movies is very much like cooking: once you know exactly how each ingredient tastes and how they cook, it is easier to deviate from the recipe and create your own custom-made dishes.

ScoreNotes: Becoming engrossed with the culture can only help the scoring process.

Mark Kilian: Absolutely. I grew up in South Africa, which had apartheid when I was a kid, so I was always fascinated by the other side. I was about 19 when I had my first real conversation with a black person, even though we had lived practically side by side not 10 miles away my whole childhood. There were a lot of Indian people in South Africa, too, and I never really got to meet any until I was much older because of apartheid. My folks used to play an Indian music program on Saturday mornings on the radio station, and it was just such a fascinating and different sound.

ScoreNotes: How satisfying was it for you to have played a part in the Academy Award film *Tsotsi*?

Mark Kilian: Very! We were all very proud of it, and it was even more fulfilling because it was a great honor for South Africa to win that award and for the film to represent a side of the country that you don't see too often.

ScoreNotes: Indeed. The beauty of film is that one can explore issues and people that one normally wouldn't encounter. In that sense, *Tsotsi* was an important film as well.

Mark Kilian: Absolutely. Almost every film coming out of South Africa up until that time was dealing with apartheid or some legacy of apartheid. *Tsotsi* was a new world for the audience to experience, and one which black South Africans live every day. It is a story about the lives of the new "lost" generation of township dwellers seen through their eyes, and not the experience of the white people or the international community. Very refreshing.

Tostsi Oscar photo.

ScoreNotes: In addition to your score material, *Tsotsi* also featured multiple songs in it. Did the song and score components prove to be difficult to blend into the soundtrack together?

Mark Kilian: Actually, Paul Hepker, who co-wrote the score with me, and I unofficially filled the music supervisor's role. So we were quite involved in the choices and editing the music and trying to make it fit. It was actually great! I've always had a great time working with songs, and I love movies that have songs in them. It was a big discovery for us learning about the new rap-influenced Kwaito music of the young people in South Africa, and we wrote that score in South Africa, so we had a wonderful experience learning and researching. We got to meet a lot of the artists and producers who made those songs, and it was a discovery of a whole different world we knew very little about, as we'd lived in the U.S. for over 10 years at that point. Even though our score doesn't sound anything like the songs, I think what we encountered working with that material informed us a little bit about that world, and it got to "seep" into the score in some way. The songs and score I feel work very well together for this reason.

ScoreNotes: At this current point in your career, is it important for you to choose projects strategically to ensure diversity for your work?

Mark Kilian: I think so, because I really don't want to be pigeon-holed, and I'm not overly concerned about climbing up this ladder super quickly. I love the process; that's why I do this. I'm happy to be working on films that are interesting to me rather than films that may not be so interesting to me and make a lot of money. If I spend the rest of my career doing interesting films and learning about new cultures along the way, I'll be very happy.

ScoreNotes: I've spoken to many composers who are conscious of being typecast to a specific genre or style, which becomes a tough mold to break out of.

Mark Kilian: I've been extremely fortunate. I don't have that many films under my belt yet, but so far they've been quite varied. *Traitor* is an action-thriller, *Rendition* was a political film, *Before the Rains* a traditional period piece—so I've been very lucky. And I really enjoy that. I don't think I would be very happy if I were getting the same kind of calls all the time.

ScoreNotes: Since your accomplishments in 2008, what has transpired for you thus far in '09, and what might you have lined up for the near future?

Mark Kilian: I have a few interesting projects coming up and am very excited about my new album I will be finishing in a few months. This will be my second solo album under the name "The Gravy Street," and I'm exploring many of the cultural worlds I've been talking about. Writing music outside of film is at once daunting and liberating, and I really enjoy having that "extra mural" activity to keep me on my toes.

13 *Keeping Score* with Ramin Djawadi

Ramin Djawadi.

Ramin Djawadi emerged on the commercial film scoring scene in full when his music for the first installment of *Iron Man* landed in theaters in 2008. As with any high profile project, there's a bit of a double-edged sword awaiting the composer at the end of it with fans and peers each wanting something a bit different with the score. Critics and expectations aside, I personally feel that Ramin's work was quite respectable in the film and featured a few high-flying moments that were perhaps a bit underrated by the film score pundits of the world.

The following interview was captured in 2008 and subsequently updated in 2009 for this book. In addition to discussing what it was like for Ramin on *Iron Man*, we also get into some of his other work, including his contributions for *Prison Break* on Fox, his score for the charming, *Fly Me to the Moon*, and more…

Ramin Djawadi (2008/2009)

ScoreNotes: First off, congratulations on your work for *Iron Man*. Given the immense pressures of writing a score like this, were you still able to have fun writing music for the *Iron Man* universe?

Ramin Djawadi: It was a lot of fun, but I have to admit it was also a lot of hard work, obviously. It's a big movie; it was a lot of pressure…lots of conceptual changes and experimenting until we finally got to the point where we were all happy.

ScoreNotes: By that experimentation you're referring to—did you hash out a great number of different themes for the director [Jon Favreau] to listen to?

Ramin Djawadi: Yeah, there were a few different ideas. Mainly the issue always was how many guitars we were going to have. Originally, I was going way more orchestral actually, and then we decided to go into the whole rock and roll direction. So that's why we changed around quite a bit.

ScoreNotes: And that was actually going to be one of my questions—at what point in the process was it determined that a rock element should be used for the character?

Ramin Djawadi: Well, it was fairly early on. The trailer was a big part of that…the Iron Man song, the Black Sabbath song. I have to give credit to Jon Favreau, actually. He always, once we really started talking about what it should be, said that he didn't want it to be a traditional orchestral superhero kind of score. He wanted to try something different and do a rock and roll score. I thought that was a great conceptual idea to do something like that.

ScoreNotes: Were you surprised by the record-breaking box office numbers that the movie debuted with?

Ramin Djawadi: Yes, I was. I mean I knew that it was a good movie. By the hype that it had, I had a feeling that it was going to do really well. But I did not expect the record-breaking opening at all. I was amazed. I was so excited.

ScoreNotes: It was really wonderful for Marvel Studios as well because they had a lot riding on it.

Ramin Djawadi: Right, absolutely, yeah. It was their first own production on a feature like this. So I'm sure they were thrilled to see those numbers.

ScoreNotes: Absolutely. Now, were you a comic book fan going into this, and if not, are you one now?

Ramin Djawadi: No, I was already one before. I don't so much read comics now, but when I was a kid, I did. I've always been a big fan of any of the comic book movies. That's why actually when Hans did *Batman Begins*, I approached him and said, "Look, let me just write one scene with Batman in the picture." And then I ended up working on the entire project with him. So when I heard about this *Iron Man* movie, I got really interested in that one. I am a big comic fan.

ScoreNotes: Nice. Did your experience on *Batman Begins* help you out on this project?

Ramin Djawadi: For sure. Yeah, obviously that was a big project, too. And just working with Hans in general—it's good to see how he handles projects like that. I think it's always hard to put music into something that's only known on paper, so it's not easy.

ScoreNotes: And along those lines, given that *Iron Man* is a bit of an unconventional superhero movie, did you find it challenging to find the right moments in the film to unveil the main hero theme?

Ramin Djawadi: Definitely, especially because there are so many different moods or moments I want to say. There are the moments where he's really being almost aggressive and destructive. When he breaks out of the cave for the first time or when he flies to Gulmira. And then there are moments when he's just having a good time. When he tries out the Mark II and he just flies out of his house and he's almost being a little kid trying out super-fast cars. He has his different moods. It wasn't easy to always have something that would accomplish both.

ScoreNotes: Sure, and most superhero movies do have some snazzy opening titles where the composers could lay down the groundwork for the theme, and that didn't really happen with *Iron Man*. It kind of just jumped right into the action.

Ramin Djawadi: Exactly, and this one opens with AC/DC. So in a way, it does lay the groundwork for the style because we tried to continue in that rock and roll vibe. So what I was really left with, rather than lush themes, was going after riff-based rock things. The difficulty I was facing was that if I tried to play melody on the guitars, I was afraid that it would sound too dated. So I fell back onto rhythmic and thematic ideas.

ScoreNotes: Now, what type of working relationship did you have with the director, Jon Favreau? Did he have a keen ear towards the music that he wanted in the film?

Ramin Djawadi: Yeah, he was very involved from the beginning. We constantly talked on the phone. The cutting room was just down the street, so he would come by as much as he could, and I would play him anything I had, work-in-progress kind of things.

I didn't have picture in the beginning. I just kind of played with ideas without picture. Once I had picture, even though it was never really locked until the very end, he gave me input as much as possible.

ScoreNotes: In taking a look at the movie, is there a particular scene that you really relished scoring? Is there one that really stands out for you?

Ramin Djawadi: Let me see. Well, definitely the one when he flies off for the first time with the Mark II. I thought it was a terrific scene just how the camera pans around to see, and you see the face for the first time, and he sort of flies out and tests his suit. That was always a wonderful scene, I thought.

ScoreNotes: Yeah, and I agree. I thought the music jumped out successfully during that sequence, and it really kind of brought the origins of *Iron Man* to life in that one sequence. That was well done.

Ramin Djawadi: Cool, thank you.

ScoreNotes: Now, are you still doing work on the television series *Prison Break*?

Ramin Djawadi: Yes, I am. We're going into a fourth season, and I think it's set to come back in the fall [2008]. I'm not working on it currently.

ScoreNotes: Personally for you, what is the biggest difference between television and film scoring?

Ramin Djawadi: Well, the turnaround in TV is much, much faster, and the involvement in the feature is much different. There are many more changes, and the scenes are more analyzed. It's interesting that the process for the feature is longer, even though I try to treat *Prison Break* as if it were a regular feature. I wrote themes for the characters and for plotlines, and I'm actually trying to carry that through the show.

ScoreNotes: And just to touch on that point, when you say film scenes are analyzed a lot more closely, is that a little more pressure for you as a composer? Is there a little more weight on it?

Ramin Djawadi: Oh sure, of course, yeah. Just because there is more time, it happens a lot that there will be multiple versions for a scene. You'll write one scene, and it is successful, and then everyone will agree to put it aside. It works. For two weeks, that scene will be okay; then all of a sudden, you'll write the scene after or before, or there will be a picture scene, and then conceptually things don't line up anymore. And then that scene needs to be adjusted again. That happens all the time. So there's definitely a lot more pressure.

ScoreNotes: I guess being creative is one thing, but being flexible is also another key component to being a composer these days.

Ramin Djawadi: I think it's a must. I always say if I write something and my director or producer doesn't like it and I like it so much, I can put it in the car and listen to it all day. But if they are not happy with it, then it just needs to be adjusted until everyone is happy with it. This attitude is really important to me.

ScoreNotes: And it sounds like you can't take things too personally with the critique that comes out.

Ramin Djawadi: Yeah, not at all. Obviously, you can raise your opinion, and it can be discussed, but the key word is that it is a collaboration. You have to try and make everybody happy. You can't just say that what I just did here is absolutely perfect and can't be changed.

You have to be open-minded, absolutely.

ScoreNotes: Now, do you foresee a point in time where you might exclusively focus on writing music for films?

Ramin Djawadi: Possibly. In fact, that's actually what I've done more than television. *Prison Break* is really the series that just kept me in there because it is so successful. But overall, I've done more work in film than in television.

ScoreNotes: I always like to ask the composers this type of question: Are you happy with the soundtrack release for *Iron Man*?

Ramin Djawadi: Oh, very happy. Yeah, for some reason some of my other features that I've done didn't have a soundtrack release. So it's always exciting when the CD actually comes out.

ScoreNotes: That's good to hear. I do think that you did a wonderful job on scoring the picture. I know there's a lot of pressure and that there was a lot riding on it, but I think everyone came through.

Ramin Djawadi: I'm glad to hear that; thank you very much. My fear was always that I would be criticized for not delivering a traditional score that everybody was expecting. I think either way, I couldn't win. If I did that, I would have been compared to the other one. We went so different that I think it was a fresh idea...going for the rock and roll kind of thing.

ScoreNotes: Absolutely. Every superhero is different, so they can't all have the same type of theme.

Ramin Djawadi: Exactly. I totally agree.

ScoreNotes: In what ways has your career changed after having worked on such a high-profile project like *Iron Man*?

Ramin Djawadi: I'm definitely trying to be more selective about my projects. I like the variety of styles. I enjoy doing an animation movie after a big live-action feature.

ScoreNotes: After the intense experience like *Iron Man*, did an animated movie like *Fly Me to the Moon* feel like a relief to work on in some ways?

Ramin Djawadi: I actually like the intensity. It pushes you to new limits. Every movie has its own challenges. *Fly Me to the Moon* was actually already completed before I started with *Iron Man*.

ScoreNotes: What were some of the thematic and classical inspirations that went into *Fly Me to the Moon*?

Ramin Djawadi: This movie had a much more traditional approach. The idea here was to split the score into three different categories. The humans, the flies, and space. Most of the score is traditional orchestra except a few synth elements in space.

ScoreNotes: Shifting gears to your work on *The Unborn*—what were some of the techniques you employed to amp up the fright factor in the film's score?

Ramin Djawadi: The main elements other than orchestra and electronics were a solo voice and solo electric violin. I did lot of experimenting with it.

ScoreNotes: Having explored a few different cinematic and television genres, can you tell us what new and exciting adventures might be ahead for you?

Ramin Djawadi: I'm currently working on a beautiful animation movie, *Around the World in 50 Years*. It's about little sea turtles traveling the world and experiencing how humans affect nature along the way. It's a very moving and educational film that hopefully will appeal to everyone.

ScoreNotes: I thank you for joining us today, and I sincerely hope we may be able to catch up again sometime in the near future.

Ramin Djawadi: Absolutely. I would love to.

The Bonus Interviews

The following two interviews are included as bonus segments so that we may see what's new with veteran composers Bruce Broughton and Craig Safan, two of my personal, all-time favorites (and two of my favorite interviews that I've conducted on ScoreNotes.com).

The contributions by these composers to film and television music are substantial, and I feel that if the movie producers of today can reflect back to recent history, they'll find that composers like Bruce and Craig stand ready to deliver unforgettable scores as they always have. Just imagine, if you will, a Craig Safan score for an *Incredible Hulk* movie or Bruce Broughton's take on a *Narnia* sequel. I tell you, we would be in for a grand experience if such scenarios came to pass in the future.

14 *Keeping Score* with Bruce Broughton

Used by permission.

Bruce Broughton.

Some of **Bruce Broughton**'s fantastic, well thought out contributions in film include scores for *Silverado*, *Young Sherlock Holmes*, *Tombstone*, and *Lost in Space*. He has an ability to write memorable, thematic work that sticks with you for quite some time after you've heard it. There is also a sense of great timing and patience in his style. The underscores Bruce often writes fit the needs of a film with great precision. This discipline also paves the way for an even bigger payoff when his main themes are fully realized. In short, what you're getting with Bruce Broughton is a veteran composer who simply knows how to deliver well-rounded, highly effective film scores that have pleased filmmakers and fans for many years.

I had a great time speaking with Bruce for this interview. He shares an insight and knowledge about film music I think most of you will find to be in-depth. There are also compelling "behind the scenes" commentaries that Bruce shares about the composers of today, the challenges of staying active in the current Hollywood system, and what it is about being a composer that he enjoys most.

This interview was originally recorded in 2007 and later updated exclusively for this book...

Bruce Broughton (2007/2009)

ScoreNotes: In general, what do you enjoy most about writing music for film?

Bruce Broughton: The thing I like the most about film music is that I like the chance to wear different hats, sort of like being an actor. Sometimes you're a cowboy, sometimes you're a space dude, sometimes you're a cop, and whatever. I like being able to take on different characters. I like being able to figure out emotionally what's happening in a story. I like being able to write specifically. I like the opportunity to be able to work with different combinations and practice my craft, particularly with orchestration, because you find on every picture you're working with a different ensemble, a different group. Sometimes you're working with synthesizers, sometimes you're working with strings, sometimes you're working with brass, sometimes you're working with all of them. You're working with them usually in different ways so that even if you had the same combination for two or three different shows, you wouldn't be doing them the same. So, you get a chance to wear different hats and expand your craft and technique.

ScoreNotes: That actually ties into the next questions I'd like to ask. Your impressive body of work spans many genres and themes. Now, if we're talking about wearing different hats, which hat do you like to wear the most?

Bruce Broughton: I really like them all. I don't like to do too much of the same thing for too long. There was a time, particularly when I was doing a lot of television series; when I was doing soap operas, I was sort of like the soap opera king. Then I got onto westerns, and then I went to cartoons. You can be associated with one or the other and find that you're getting a lot of the same kind work. I actually like to be a moving target. As I look back, there are a few things that I've done a lot of. I've done a lot of Americana-themed shows; I've done a lot of children's shows. Someone asked me one time whether it was intentional that I had done a lot of cult films, and I said, "I have?" He listed a whole bunch of things like *Ice Pirates*, *The Boy Who Can Fly*, and such. He asked if that was intentional, and I said I wasn't even conscious of it.

I like to actually do a lot of different things. I think the hardest things to do are when you're really asked to do very little, when you're asked not to say too much. In these days, film scoring has become rather cool emotionally. Not cool in terms of its hipness factor, but just cool in that it doesn't want to say a lot. So sometimes music is just sort of there as an alternative to sound effects, and those kinds of things drive me nuts. Those are very hard to do.

ScoreNotes: When music is treated as an afterthought that really irks me as well.

Bruce Broughton: It's also…boring! I don't like to write boring. That's the other thing about film; you really get a chance to get out and say something. That's one of the things about film music that is very different than other kinds of music. Film music is done almost entirely as a work for hire, meaning that you're basically writing on behalf of somebody else. The producers, the legal author of the work, the director, or the studio can tell you what they want and how much of it…whether they like this or whether they don't like that…whether they like trombones or they don't like trombones. They can ask you to take things out and/or put things in and go up or down. That kind of music is very specific, and sometimes it gets to be very, very difficult, particularly when the people in charge are not in agreement as to what they want.

ScoreNotes: Yes, I suppose that would pose quite a few creative challenges.

Bruce Broughton: Yes, mostly political challenges. I mean, how can you keep all these people happy? One time, I had 12 people in my room listening to my music, and I couldn't even figure out who they all were.

ScoreNotes: Yes, it's daunting enough to really create something that fits a movie, but when you're mixing in all these different personalities that you have to please, I can imagine that it gets quite difficult.

Bruce Broughton: It's difficult, but you figure…all the film scores that have been written have always tried to please some creative point of view. In film particularly, you're basically working with or for a director, one person who put this film together from the concept to the idea, or at least from the script, all the way through. From the casting to choosing the location manager, the cinematographer, the lighting person, the greens person, and the costume person has all been a creative process…all these things add to this person's vision of what the film is, what the story is, and how the story should be told. Then he or she brings the composer in. The composer is sort of the last chance to really add something and to be part of that creative team. So it's a very specific and important function that we do, but it's definitely a collaborative thing; and for that, you have to listen to instruction, get ideas, and sometimes you have to argue and put your ideas across and have them come back at you and find middle ground.

ScoreNotes: Do you ever find that some directors turn the reins over to your sensibilities as a composer to find what feels and sounds right, or are they generally more apt to impose a steadfast vision?

Bruce Broughton: Yeah, directors are human beings, so they come in all types. Some people are not very knowledgeable about music, and some people are more knowledgeable about music. I actually prefer people not to be too knowledgeable about music. I'd rather talk about drama, their film, more than I want to talk about music. Some directors have a lot of confidence, and they'll basically leave you alone and walk away. Although not so much these days as in prior days because now with synthesizers and computers, the directors want to hear what they're getting. So they are much more involved now in the working process than they used to be 20 years ago. They'll come over and listen to the piece, talk about it, and make suggestions. Some people are more hands-on than others. Some directors—this hasn't happened to me, but it's happened to some friends of mine—some directors actually sit in the room while the poor composer is writing music, and as the composer puts his hand on the keyboard, the director shouts out, "No, no, not that chord!"

ScoreNotes: Oh my goodness! Talk about micromanaging.

Bruce Broughton: Yeah, but that doesn't happen a lot. It can. It can run the whole gamut from somebody saying, "Well, I'll see you in a couple of weeks, and then you can show me what you've got," to someone saying, "I'll see you tomorrow. I'm going to be camping out here, and what's for lunch."

ScoreNotes: Well thankfully there are some directors who do let the composers do what they specialize in, and a lot of times things work out wonderfully. I'd like to know what your response is to the appreciation that the fans continue to show toward your scores, such as *Silverado, Young Sherlock Holmes*, and *Tombstone,* to name a few.

Bruce Broughton: Well obviously I'm always happy to have my music appreciated. You like to have your music appreciated. I think that sometimes the fans get confused in separating, how can I say this, in separating too much the music from the film. The music in the film, no matter what it is, was placed there by common agreement. It was placed there because the director or the producers liked it or wanted it or thought it was appropriate. I've read comments fans have made about certain scores, such as "Oh the music was this or the music was that" and "He shouldn't have done this or should have done that," without realizing that it probably wasn't the composer who made that decision. The film and score was the way that it was because it was done under instruction. And it really doesn't matter who the composer is. Whether it is John Williams all the way down to the newest guy on the block, all the music is there because it's gotten past the director. It's been approved by the director, the studio, and all the people.

I think fans sometimes get so wrapped up in the music that they wish the music could do this or that, but it really can't. Sometimes also the music can't do this or that because the film doesn't permit it. Like in some films, you have a great theme, and you never get a chance to use it. But in those films that you mentioned—*Silverado, Young Sherlock Holmes*, and *Tombstone*—those are particularly emotionally rich scores. The one I get talked to about most often is probably *Tombstone*, because it's so over the top. People ask me to write music or a concert piece and say, "Well we really liked *Tombstone*. Could you write something sort of like that?" Meaning can you write something which is emotional, something that has emotional content, which will get us moving, will get us feeling something…will get the audience interested in what the music is. Which I think is a valid request.

ScoreNotes: Do you suppose that part of the reason why we hear such similar sounding scores in films today is a result of the director wanting to get something that closely matches what he or she has as a temp track?

Bruce Broughton: Yeah, that's a very specific problem in film these days. A couple of years ago, a friend of mine who knew a lot of my music, called me up and sang me a theme. He said, "What's this theme, what movie is this?" And I said, "Oh this is easy. It comes from a movie I did, *Honey I Blew Up The Kid*." He said, "No, it's not." "Of course it is!" I said. He insisted it wasn't. "No, I wrote it…I should know," I said. He told me that it wasn't and that I should go see this particular movie that he had heard it in. I went to see the movie, and my theme was used. It was very similar, obviously very similar. As I sat and watched the entire movie, I could hear all of my music that had been used as the temp track. It had been refashioned, moved around so that it wasn't exactly the same, but it was definitely the model.

It was sort of like the girl that used to be a brunette that is now a redhead. She used to wear green, but now she's wearing blue. It's sort of like that, you know. That happens a lot. There are a few reasons why it happens a lot. Temp tracks, the idea of putting temporary music in to see how it's going to play, have always been a problem. It used to be done years ago for scenes like montages or chases where the editor needed to get a sense of timing and motion, so he or she would grab a piece and put it in there to see how it would fit…to get a sense of how the scene played. But in the last 15 or 20 years, since the world has become digital, it's very easy to find any piece of music and be able to cut it down to fit almost any scene.

You see these films now that have not an original score, but only a temp track, a temporary score…that's going in for marketing, to get audience previews to get impressions as to how the film will play. But the music, to an unsophisticated ear, sounds as though it's finished. It sounds like a score because it's so technically perfect in terms of the editing. But it's actually a Frankenstein, a piece from this, a piece from that. As this temporary score remains in the film, everybody gets used to it. The director likes it; the studio likes it. Even when they don't like it, they get used to it. And when it's gone, they miss it. So the pressure becomes upon the composer to do that. Some composers will do that. They'll write a piece that's very similar to it, enough that they won't get sued. Or they'll use it as a jumping off point for an original score. But it's harder and harder to come up with really original material when the temp tracks are so heavily in the film and there is a lot of pressure to not change the music. And they just don't want to change the music because if the film is marketing well and it looks like they're going to make a lot of money when the film goes into general release, they don't want the music to suddenly twist it around and lose 20 percent of their earnings.

ScoreNotes: The composer is going to be trapped if the music makes it all the way to test screenings and the people love it. You'll then have to make the score that the people who hired you want in the movie.

Bruce Broughton: I won't mention any names or scores, but there are some very, very, very famous and very well-known soundtracks over the last 20 years that were based on other pieces. We probably all know what they are. But they were a result, surely, of a temp track or a piece of music done by composers who have a lot of technique and ability. It's just becoming more and more prevalent because it's a practice that isn't going to go away. There's too much anxiety in films. If a film costs $20 million, that's a lot of money! If it costs $100 million, that's *really* a lot of money! If you are going to spend $100 million, you're going to want to make back $100 million and more so you can make a profit. Most films don't make their money back.

There is a lot of tension on directors who have the responsibility for this huge budget to keep the studio happy. They themselves want to be creatively and artistically happy. And of course the composers want to make an artistic and a creative statement, too, but they want to please the directors and keep working. Everybody wants to keep working. If a young director comes out and has a major failure, he can disappear. So, he's going to be very cautious. And making big-budget movies tends to be a very conservative affair. People aren't going to make any crazy moves because they don't want to take the whole ship down. There's a lot of money. So there are a lot of things at risk. There are a lot of careers at risk. If a studio has too many flops, the guy who runs the studio will be looking for another job, whether it's his fault or not; that's just the way that it goes. Hollywood runs by the fickle finger of fate. Sometimes you're a big hit, through an accident, sometimes you're not, through an accident, sometimes people like what you do, and sometimes they don't. That's all a matter of taste. I'll give you an example.

When *Silverado* first came out, it was not a big hit. It was in the theaters for a while, and then it went away…but it never went completely away. It went immediately into videos and people started renting it. And then once cable television came on, it started showing on cable, and pretty soon it was on television. Well, now it's on television all the time.

You could hardly pass a week where you couldn't find *Silverado* somewhere. People say, "Oh, that was a big hit!" No, no it wasn't; it just never went away. A lot of movies are like that because the taste of the time was not ready to take on a new version of an old fashioned genre.

ScoreNotes: I'd like to thank you for taking the time to chat with me. Your candor was very refreshing.

Bruce Broughton: Thank you, I appreciate the opportunity to talk to you.

15 Keeping Score with Craig Safan

Craig Safan.

Most of you will know **Craig Safan** from that little pub in Boston called *Cheers*. And why not, he wrote the music for the episodes as well as the show's theme song, which is perhaps one of the most popular in television history (it's probably popping in your head even now as you read this). It's quite an iconic accomplishment for sure. However, I know Craig for another reason, and it's not for the music he wrote for that local tavern. It's his music from a film that takes place just a little further away from Massachusetts...*The Last Starfighter*.

You see, when I was growing up, Safan's majestic theme from *The Last Starfighter* was as influential to me as that of *Star Wars* or *Raiders of the Lost Ark*. It was the type of fanfare that inspired me greatly and, in fact, was one of the key factors that led me to appreciate film music the way I do. Needless to say, I was thrilled at having a chance to interview Craig, and, as it turns out, I was not disappointed.

In this discussion, Craig catches us up to date with what he's been up to, shares news about a sequel to *The Last Starfighter*, and reflects about his work on *Cheers*. He also shares candid opinions about just what is wrong with some of the film music being written today.

This interview, originally entitled "Into the Starscape with Composer Craig Safan" was recorded in March 2009…

Craig Safan (2009)

ScoreNotes: Can you please catch us up to date with what you've been up to recently?

Craig Safan: I've been spending less time on films the last few years and more time developing theater. I started out as a theater composer when I was in college, and in my mind, I always thought I would be writing for musical theater, and somehow I ended up in this film career. As that has tended to slow down in the last few years, I've gotten more and more into my original desire, which was to write theater. So I've been living half time in New York and half time in Los Angeles. I have three musicals that are now in development.

ScoreNotes: I'd like to touch on one of your notable and prominent works, *The Last Starfighter*. What are your recollections from that film as its 25th Anniversary nears?

Craig Safan: First of all, it was an extremely exciting project. At the time, it was a pretty big movie, and it was nice to get a larger movie after having done a bunch of smaller movies. And I love working with Nick Castle, whom I had done a movie with previously called *Tag: The Assassination Game*. We've done a lot of movies together over the years, but that movie was exciting because it was a big jump for both of us. I loved the idea of working with a giant orchestra and of finding a way of trying to make it mine. I mean, there was no way you could write outside of the sort of late romantic, John Williams model. There was no way the studio would ever accept that. So I had to try and find a way to make it mine, and hopefully I did. It certainly has lasted and keeps being re-recorded all the time, whether in Prague or in London or wherever. It was just great fun to do. A lot of work, a lot of notes [laughs]…a lot of music.

ScoreNotes: Are you aware of any special plans surrounding the anniversary of it?

Craig Safan: Well, I know there's going to be a 25th Anniversary DVD released. And I know there's a special section of it that's going to be interviews with various people involved. I was interviewed about a month ago on camera. They interviewed [the director] Nick Castle, [the writer] John Betuel, and Catherine Mary Stewart. I'm sure they got Jeff Okun; they got all the computer guys. But the guy who is doing it is trying to sort of put it together in some sort of inventive form, almost like an action comic book, so it isn't just talking heads. I know there's going to be some screenings here in Los Angeles. I hear there's going to be a big screening at the Arrow Theater, which is this small independent theater in Santa Monica that does a lot of premieres and a lot of special shows.

ScoreNotes: Does any part of you wish *The Last Starfighter* could be made with today's technology, or might that ruin the charm of it?

Craig Safan: Well, the film was definitely of the period that it was made in, as every film ends up being. And that was what was happening then. That was cutting edge then. Now…it's passé. It's something you can do at home on your laptop. I can almost do the score at home on my laptop [laughs]. The other thing is that there are plans for a sequel. There has been a script written, it's been storyboarded, and I think they're just sort of waiting for the final go. At least as far as I know, I've been asked to be involved in that. That would be exciting, and that will be done, obviously, with contemporary methods.

But you can't really go back. Every show has its own look. You still can see some of the great films like *The Day the Earth Stood Still* or *Invaders From Mars*. I mean, those effects are great. They're some amazing effects that were done in the '50s. You wouldn't want to redo them; it would be sort of silly, I think. And a lot of the CGI today…it looks, at least to my eyes, over the top. They're trying to do too much. I felt that some of the later *Star Wars* films were just too complex. You lose the beauty of the focus. I think people are now backing off and only using it where you really need to or using it in ways that are sort of subtle and you don't quite realize it's being done.

ScoreNotes: I do agree that special effects are at their best when they're blended into the makeup of the film.

Craig Safan: I mean *Starfighter* is quaint because there's so much variation in terms of the level of the execution of the special effects, just because there was a limitation of time and technology. So there are some scenes that really look a little cartoony and other scenes that seemed to look a little better.

I would be scoring it, and I would look up on the video screen and there would just be a little white dot going across a black screen, and they would say, "That's the Kodan warship." You'd have to imagine it was this huge thing so that you could write this gigantic score and assume eventually the visual would come up to the size of the score, and it did. But it was a fun process with a lot of levels. You'd see the spaceship, then you'd see the background, then they'd start adding layers of atmosphere, which was fog and mist. All that was added layer by painstaking layer to make it feel like a reality.

ScoreNotes: In some sense, I guess it's like acting against a blue screen in the manner in which you were asked to compose it.

Craig Safan: You have to just sort of go with the script and imagine it…and assume the director knows what he's talking about and go for it.

ScoreNotes: Moving on to another medium, and specifically the television arena, can you tell us about your time on *Cheers*?

Craig Safan: When I got the call for *Cheers,* I was friends with the producer and director, Jimmy Burrows, and he called me up and said he was doing this new series and wanted me to work on it. I read the script, and I said, "Let's make it sound like you wandered into this bar, and it's like one o'clock in the morning, and Woody Allen is sitting there with a little band, and he's like not very good, but he's playing clarinet, and all the notes are somewhat sour. And let's just stick with that. Let's just make it slightly weird, off key, and not quite good." And we stuck to that, and from the very first episode, it had that sound. That stuck with the show the whole time. It was always just a little off, a little weird. Kenny Wild, who played the bass on a lot of those sessions, used to call it the "bar band from Mars." But the sound of the show was from the very first episode, and we just pretty much stuck to it.

I really believe that an important aspect to doing any film scoring, and especially television, is coming up with a very specific palette of sound. You don't just want to go in and say, "Okay, I can do everything I want to, every sound I want to." You sort of give yourself limitations, and then you have to work from that, and you end up being more creative because you're stuck. It's like a painter saying, "Okay, I'm only going to paint in yellow and blue today." So I believe that's a really good way to approach a score.

ScoreNotes: And we can use that as a segue into what television and film scoring have evolved into. I would just like to get your thoughts on what you think about the current state of film and television music.

Craig Safan: I don't follow it as closely because I feel like I'm sort of a little out of it right now. But a lot of what I hear is just very standardized, which is sort of boring to me, although I'm sure I wrote a lot of standardized music, too, especially in all the TV movies I did over the years. There's occasionally a show that I really think is terrific. You know, I like the music a lot to *Revolutionary Road* and to *Wall-E*. I think that Tom Newman is doing just really interesting music. But a lot of music is just to me really sappy and over the top and just really, really obvious.

In terms of TV music, the big change that happened—and it certainly happened when I was working too—was that whereas you used to meet other players, you now really don't. That's been true since the mid-'80s; it's like you can pretty much do a full television score in your garage studio with one or two players. All the reality shows sound like they're all library shows, although I know they all aren't. It's just like endless rhythm and weird sounds, which have their place; but I guess at this point in my life, it's just not that interesting. It's very rare that I hear anything musically that's really interesting. In fact, in TV, I'd have a hard time naming something that's musically interesting.

ScoreNotes: From my perspective, I've grown numb by the generic scores that are put to use.

Craig Safan: It's the same thing over and over and over. It's sort of boring at this point. Even the movies, too. That's why I think *Slumdog Millionaire* won for best score. I mean at least it was a breath of fresh air. I think a lot of those other scores, even the nominated ones, are technically great, but they're just musically boring. They've been done so much. You know, like *Benjamin Button* to me was a boring score. I know people liked it, but it's like I've heard it a million times, and it's like how many ways can you slice that apple? Which is why I liked *Wall-E,* because I thought it was very restrained and didn't have to be, so it was a very intellectual score. I loved *Slumdog Millionaire* because it put a smile on my face. It was fun, it was inventive, it was silly. It was just a great score that fit with the film absolutely perfectly.

ScoreNotes: Indeed, I felt it had a great charm to it.

Craig Safan: It was absolutely charming because there was a certain naiveté to the whole movie. If you just think of it in story terms, it was a pretty tough movie with a lot of really, really dark scenes. But the whole movie was almost kind of played like a fairy tale so that the darkness was like a fairy tale darkness in a way. So, yeah, I absolutely loved that movie and thought the score was great and totally deserved the award. But I thought the other really good score was *Wall-E,* in terms of the nominees.

ScoreNotes: With your theater projects currently ongoing, might you look to a sequel to *The Last Starfighter* to get you back into scoring film?

Craig Safan: If it happens, it happens. It's sort of a fickle business. I guess I can't really complain; I worked almost non-stop for 30 or 35 years. I never was out of work. But it's a business that when you get to be at a certain age, you just don't get hired as much because the people who hire you aren't working very much and the young executives want to bring their own people in. I think that's just true in all of the aspects of film business. There are always a few guys who keep working, but most of the people start to fade away. I just think it's the nature of the business, so I'm realistic about it. Obviously, if you have a movie and it's a hit, suddenly you're hot again. I can remember I used to be friends with Elmer Bernstein; he helped me start in the business, and he was sort of unemployed. Suddenly John Landis came around and remembered how much he liked Elmer's music and hired him for *Animal House*. It revitalized his career when he was in his 50s. So, you know, it can happen, but we'll see.

ScoreNotes: I guess the level of frustration for me, if you want to call it that, is when you know there are so many talented composers available and you hear some of this new crop of composers essentially delivering the same type of style and technique. It really makes you long for the heroes you grew up with to come back.

Craig Safan: Well, you know, you've got to go out and make a movie and hire me.

ScoreNotes: [Laughing] There ya go...

Craig Safan: I think it's just the reality of the business; you can't be bitter about it. I can remember when I was starting out being on these panels at AFI or ASCAP, or whatever, and being with a lot of the older guys at the time; you know they had the same complaints. It's the nature of the business. For better or for worse, it's not a business that necessarily will take you into your later years...even though you may be a much better composer. I think I'm a much better composer now than I was when I was working a real lot in the '80s and early '90s. But, you know, I'm doing other things and that's fine. I did very well and certainly have a lot of projects I'm proud of. It's just the nature of it. You can't dwell on it too long, and it's sort of out of your control, because as much as you rant and rave, that's not going to get you work.

ScoreNotes: That's certainly an even-keeled approach you've adopted.

Craig Safan: Well, you really don't have much choice...[chuckles]

ScoreNotes: Speaking of projects that you're proud of, what are some of the hallmarks that stand out for you as you look back at your career?

Craig Safan: Well, *Cheers* and *The Last Starfighter* are the ones I'm best known for. The other ones I that really like...I love the music to *Mr. Wrong*, even though the movie didn't do very well. I just think that was a really, really fun score, and it had a lot of elements that had to be pulled together. The other one I like a lot is *Stand and Deliver*, which was a very early electronic score. It just works well with the picture, and I love the picture...and I know the picture has touched a lot of people because people still come up and talk to me about how much that film has changed their lives. And it was a very small score, unlike *Mr. Wrong* and *Starfighter.* I liked *Stand and Deliver* because it was just a very, very low budget, good score, and I loved working with those guys.

I still like *Remo Williams;* that's a fun score and fun to listen to. Again, that was a really, really complex thing to put together. We were on a whole bunch of 24-track machines all slaved together. We had a full orchestra; we had a Korean band, probably about a 12- or 15-piece Korean group, that could not possibly play in time or in tune. And then, of course, I had the Synclavier going full blast on that, too. So putting all that stuff together was Dennis Sands, who was the mixer on that, and who did a great job. It's very, very difficult, and this is pre–Pro Tools, to make all that stuff work and to make it all feel like music. That was complicated.

ScorcNotes: Well Craig, it's really been an honor for me, as a long-time fan of yours, to be able to talk film music with you. I hope we can catch up again in the future.

Craig Safan: Absolutely, I would love to. It's always fun to talk to you.

Interviews with Today's Top Television Composers

16 *Keeping Score* with Murray Gold

The music from the BBC's modern *Doctor Who* series is some of the best ever produced for the small screen. While that may be a rather ambitious claim to make, I know of no other way to introduce **Murray Gold**, whose music for the series has left an irreversible, positive impression on me. In fact, it's the type of music that sparks my imagination through its diverse palette of colors and unending charm.

When I'm asked to make general soundtrack recommendations, the Season 3 and Season 4 soundtracks of *Doctor Who* are at the very top of my list. My hope is that after you read this interview, you'll set out to discover what it is that has me so excited about the work of Murray Gold...

Murray Gold (2009)

ScoreNotes: How would you best summarize your experience of working on the *Doctor Who* series?

Murray Gold: It's been a bit of a blur, actually. I sort of changed countries halfway through and carried on doing the same job from New York. It's been interesting seeing the changes in the storytelling and the new ideas that come through. To me, it's been pretty much a steady meat and potatoes job, in a way.

ScoreNotes: Well, I have to tell you—those are some gourmet meat and potatoes, because I would stack your work from Seasons 3 and 4 with any soundtracks that have been released in many years!

Murray Gold: Thank you, Tom.

ScoreNotes: How pleased are you with the *Doctor Who* soundtrack releases from Silva Screen records? Also, was it difficult to select and arrange the cues that finally made it onto each disc?

Murray Gold: It's always a nightmare to get them done. They're not a vanity project, but if I don't do them, it's not like the world is going to end. I've normally got a million things in November that I'm doing, and that's also the same time that people are saying

115

I need to get the album together and mastered. This is obviously the third one to come out, and this time I called Jake Jackson, who is the mix engineer on *Doctor Who*, and he actually flew to New York to help me choose what was going to go on the album, and that made it a bit easier. In the middle of that month, I was writing a movie soundtrack and also doing the *Doctor Who* Christmas Special and also scoring a four-part British period drama called *The Devil's Whore*. So I had my work cut out for me.

ScoreNotes: That's taking multi-tasking to new heights!

Murray Gold: I'm very monogamous when it comes to writing music. I actually like to have one thing in my head, and I like to obsess about it. I like that every idea I have goes to that one thing. I like to know that my head is just doing one thing. But yeah, that was tricky, actually, doing three or four things at once. And a lot of Hollywood composers do that (scoring three or four movies at once), but it's just a nightmare doing that for me. You know, you want one protagonist that you're trying to write a theme for, and you want to develop that.

ScoreNotes: With all that's going on, do you have any plans to remain active on the spinoff series, *Torchwood*?

Murray Gold: Well, there is a *really* big five-parter coming up, but Ben Foster is scoring that, and he's doing a great job on it.

ScoreNotes: And can you describe the collaborative relationship you have with Ben?

Murray Gold: Well, he's a friend, really, and he's a great musician. I sort of installed him in *Torchwood* and got him the job. I sort of started off the series by writing the theme and the first and fourth episodes and some other stuff later on. He's really gone out on his own with it now. It's exciting for him because it gets a lot of exposure, and it's good for him.

ScoreNotes: While listening to *Torchwood*, a lot of positive things really came out of it, such as Captain Jack's bold and rousing theme. Do you like working within that context, writing thematic material that shifts from one episode to the next?

Murray Gold: Yeah, I think that's the puzzle part of it. I think you can have infinite variations of the same thing by changing the background, context, and style, which is a really good way of working. I think it's really important to make a decision about what materials you're using and just to stick to it. For example, in *Doctor Who* and the *Cyberman*, there are like six notes, nothing particularly unusual about it, and nothing particularly creative; but I just said, "This is the *Cyberman*." Eventually, you just play it over and over again, and essentially it becomes sort of iconic.

ScoreNotes: Can you describe the evolution of certain cues? For instance, might you touch on how the track, "All the Strange, Strange Creatures," became the featured cue for the trailer?

Murray Gold: It wasn't supposed to take over the role that it did. It was just written for one episode; I think it was written for *Gridlocked*. I think *Gridlocked* was on the slate early. Obviously, we get a few episodes finished before the season actually runs on air. *Gridlocked* was one of the ones that was done before airtime. I think the mill got hold of that music and ran it as the trailer. I never intended it as the trailer; it was just some music for that episode. It took on more of a kind of important role because it had been identified as the trailer music, which made it very fore-grounded.

ScoreNotes: A destiny of its own, as they would say.

Murray Gold: Yeah, there are so many different ways that the music becomes important. Sometimes by putting it on the album, it becomes important. Sometimes, it's just that one little bit of music that was in an important position in one of the episodes becomes important because it turns up on YouTube and people start wanting it. Sometimes you just can't help noticing that it's popular.

ScoreNotes: Right, the power of YouTube.

Murray Gold: I actually watch a lot of stuff on YouTube. Some of it I get really bummed off at because people upload the whole album and slap each other on the back and think they're doing a really good thing. It's kind of annoying. Silva Screen takes the trouble, and you know they don't work on a very high profit margin, and does a very good service in releasing the film scores. Then someone sticks it on the Web the day that it's released. That's kind of annoying.

ScoreNotes: Oh yes, absolutely. In those terms of making it available for people to just grab, that's bad ethics.

Murray Gold: I don't think the people that do it really realize that it's harmful to the record company. It's not that much for one person to pay for one record; but if someone puts the music up, it means that 100,000 people can take it. Eventually, it means that companies like Silva Screen, that don't work for huge profits, won't put it out. We need them to put this music out; otherwise, it just won't come out. Then there would be nothing to rip off.

ScoreNotes: That's a good point. Especially with Silva Screen actually packaging the CDs the way they do, with such great care, as well as the extensive liner notes. You can tell that there is a passion involved for the music.

Murray Gold: It's a total passion. They love it and are passionate about film music. They do a lot of rerecordings and reissue a lot of the stuff that people have asked for, and they are very conscientious about responding to their audiences and their market. So if there's stuff that people want to hear released, and they can't get a hold of, Silva Screen is the kind of company that will listen and do a release of a record, a CD, later on. So I definitely support them.

ScoreNotes: Now in looking ahead a bit, do you foresee wanting to stay involved with the *Doctor Who* series for an indefinite amount of time? Have you put some sort of timetable in your head as far as your involvement with this?

Murray Gold: No, not really. Everything is up in the air and is up for debate.

ScoreNotes: What do you think are the biggest differences between writing music for television versus writing scores for movies?

Murray Gold: I think with film you don't get a chance to test out your themes. You don't get an episode one. You've got to make your point and show your journey within 90 minutes to two hours. And that's the only journey that you're going to take; there's no revisiting it. So you must be very bold from the beginning and confident that you know exactly the route that you're taking through the material. With television, especially long-form television, you're dealing with a six-month work process. Like on *Doctor Who*, the first two or three episodes of the series are a kind of testing ground to a certain extent. They may be a chance to try on familiar themes, and the ones that stick can come back later on, but you already know that you built up an audience for them. But with a film, the audience is only there for an hour and a half. You have to say what you have to say. You have to smuggle the new themes into their subconscious. You want them to come out and hear that music again and immediately think of that material and that movie. It's harder in a way to do that.

But the feature film I'm working on right now [*Hoodwinked 2*] is the one...I've never thought I'd do a film where you'd get as much variation as you do on *Doctor Who*. This film I'm working on now is an animation that really, really moves fast. It's very interesting because every single frame is being drawn. If you watch drama and an actor does something cool, you want to score it. But here, everything, the way they walk and talk, every frame has been thought about and drawn, so you really want to do the best thing you can for it. It's very interesting.

ScoreNotes: So I guess it sounds like you really have to take a close and tight look, almost minute to minute.

Murray Gold: Frame by frame. You just want to hear everything. You want to hear as many cue points, and then of course you want to back off and sort of make sure that you aren't being too busy or exhausting the audience. You do have to watch for that as well. Comparing *Doctor Who* with this feature animation, television executives especially are always concerned about losing their audience because of the flip button. You really want to make sure that it's impossible for them to leave. You can't carry on that way in a movie. You can't be at the audience all the time. You have to back off. With an animation, especially one like this with a ninety-minute car chase, you have to avoid the pitfalls of exhausting the audience. But it's really good fun.

ScoreNotes: With the restrictions of writing for film, would that sway you from pursuing writing scores for movies in the future, do you think?

Murray Gold: I get a kind of relish about certain projects which is really independent of whether they are film or TV, or whatever they are. I don't do adverts as a general rule, but otherwise everything is up for grabs. Sometimes it surprises people the things I get excited about. I don't predict it either. There's always a certain type of music that I want to get paid to write. I want to be paid to write stuff that is adventurous and fun and exciting and that communicates my love of music. And those kinds of projects don't come along all that often. Nearly all the ones I choose have that quality about them. I'm allowed to write that kind of music.

ScoreNotes: As we wrap up here, I'd like to say that if I were to ever travel the cosmos, your music would be what I would take with me. That's how much I enjoyed listening to your material on *Doctor Who*.

Murray Gold: Wow, that's a huge compliment.

ScoreNotes: Keep on doing a great job, Murray!

Murray Gold: Thanks, Tom.

17 *Keeping Score* with James Dooley

James Dooley.

Used by permission.

James Dooley knows no bounds! He's successfully written music for "The Big Three" (movies, television, videogames), and he isn't looking back.

For this interview, I mainly centered our discussion on his fine work for the imaginative television series, *Pushing Daisies*. The music that he so enthusiastically wrote for it made him an Emmy Award winner in Season One and also gave him an increased visibility in the industry. Not to be outshined, however, is James's accomplished work in both videogames and film, where he has composed music for significant titles like *inFAMOUS* (videogame) and the 2009 box office hit, *Obsessed*.

We explore the facets of each of these notable and varied projects in the following, informative segment...

James Dooley (2009)

ScoreNotes: Did taking the reins of a television series seem daunting to you in any way?

James Dooley: *Pushing Daisies* required a massive amount of music. Each episode contained approximately forty minutes, and the schedules only allowed for six days of writing time. I spent every waking moment writing. A show like *Daisies* really puts on the pressure, but I wouldn't have had it any other way. The stress and the time constraints were a part of *Daisies,* and I loved dedicating myself to the show. Where else are you going to be able to write music for a fairytale-esque, romantic comedy based on death that includes odd instruments like harpsichords, finger snaps, and music boxes?

ScoreNotes: The music in *Pushing Daisies* truly has a memorable, playful charm about it. What aspects of the overall concept did you find to be the most inspiring?

James Dooley: The characters, themes, and the subtext in *Pushing Daisies* were all very inspiring musically. Each character also had their own theme, and when they interacted, their musical themes interacted as well. Each character's theme was defined instrumentally. Olive was defined by a saxophone and strings. Emerson had this crime jazz motif, which was an acoustic bass with finger snaps. This way, when a character came onscreen, they had much more of a presence.

The show revolved around the two main characters, Chuck and Ned, and their relationship. The music for the show was often driven by this love theme. Their love was never fulfilled, so I wrote the music to reflect both hope and sadness at the same time. There was also a childlike quality to it, because they are children when they first fall in love.

The musical subtext of *Daisies* was very fun to write. The music was never really playing what you would see on the screen because there was so much going on in each scene. We also had to mislead the audience with the music. There was a murder on the show every week, so I had to write the music to insinuate that each suspect was in fact the murderer.

ScoreNotes: Looking back at your Emmy Award for *Pushing Daisies*—please tell us what your initial reaction was when you found out you had won.

James Dooley: When I heard them announce that I had won the Emmy, I experienced the greatest sense of relief. The Emmy holds this great sense of significance, and once you are nominated, there is a lot of pressure to win. I was so glad that I didn't have to hear anyone say, "At least it was nice to be nominated."

ScoreNotes: For a series that had so much talent associated with it and so many positive accolades bestowed upon it, do you feel that it could have gone on for a much longer run than it ultimately did?

James Dooley: Absolutely. The show was in a very sustainable place. If the writer's strike had not occurred, I believe the show would still be on the air. We were doing very well, the ratings were great, and we had the support of the fans and the network. It was an unfortunate event.

ScoreNotes: Aside from your impressive work on *Daisies*, can you tell us about some of your recent projects in other mediums?

James Dooley: I just finished the videogame for PS3 called *inFAMOUS*. It is about a modern-day superhero who has to make the choice between right and wrong. I also just finished the film *Obsessed*, starring Beyoncé Knowles and Ali Larter. The film has a *Fatal Attraction*–like quality. I just started working on the videogames *Nerf* for the Wii and *Jax and Daxter* for the PSP.

ScoreNotes: How does composing a videogame like *inFAMOUS* compare to the assignment of scoring a television series? Is one more challenging to manage than the other?

James Dooley: *Daises*, having an abnormally large amount of music, contained about forty minutes of music per episode. A videogame like *inFAMOUS*, on the other hand, usually contains three hours of music. A large amount of music is required for videogames because you have to write music for each place the character goes and the different actions he does. With *inFamous*, I started with the trailer for the game and spent quite a while perfecting it before moving on to the score. I would say that the most challenging part of scoring *inFAMOUS* was keeping track of all the elements that my fellow collaborators and I created.

ScoreNotes: What was your experience like working on the film *Obsessed*?

James Dooley: *Obsessed* is a romantic thriller starring Beyoncé Knowles and Ali Larter. I went straight from working on *Pushing Daisies* to scoring *Obsessed*. The two pieces couldn't be more different. *Daisies* had a large amount of thematic material. *Obsessed*, on the other hand, had a basic musical theme that ran throughout the film and drove everything forward.

ScoreNotes: For its budget, the movie did quite well at the box office. What was it about the film's formula that attracted audiences the way it did?

James Dooley: I think audiences were attracted to *Obsessed* because it is a very contemporary and emotional movie. We decided to go in an emotional direction with the music for the film. The piano sequence that plays in the beginning of the movie is the main musical theme. It is repeated throughout the film, but changes subtly as the film progresses. It eventually becomes distorted as Ali Larter's character becomes crazier and crazier.

ScoreNotes: As a modern era composer who has found success in movies, television, and videogames, what would you say is the key factor in being able to write effectively in all three mediums?

James Dooley: To understand the different nature of each medium, you have to be aware of the timeline of each project. For example, film and television runs on a fixed timeline. Films play without interruption. The music in these mediums generally builds over time as the story progresses. In videogames, there is no fixed timeline. The music needs to reflect the things that the characters choose to do and the things that they interact with. The main focus in composing videogames is making the experience interesting for the gamer.

ScoreNotes: How has your style evolved from your first feature film, *When a Stranger Calls,* and what was expected from you as a composer from the industry in general?

James Dooley: When I scored *Stranger,* everyone really liked the temporary music that was added to the film, but everyone had a different opinion on how to change it for the film. I basically revised the score over and over again until they ran out of time.

With *Obsessed,* I went in a different direction from the temporary music, and I was able to bring more to the table. I added more finesse to the music in *Obsessed* and could write it more in a romantic way. I would probably have been afraid to write like this when doing *When a Stranger Calls.*

18 *Keeping Score* with Christopher Lennertz

Christopher Lennertz.

Used by permission.

Christopher Lennertz is a dynamic talent in the composing business. Truthfully, his portfolio is so versatile that I could have slotted him into any of the parts in this book. After all, he's a young but accomplished film composer who has achieved success in television, in movies, and in the arena of game music. In fact, one of my all-time favorite videogame scores is the music he provided for *Medal of Honor: European Assault*, a score that unlocks the dramatic impact that game music offers (and it's one of my favorites from the series). However, I ultimately decided to place him in an area where he has received perhaps his most notoriety, and that would be for his superb work on the television series *Supernatural*...

Christopher Lennertz (2009)

ScoreNotes: Can you describe your experiences as a film and media composer thus far in your career? Have there been any surprises along the way?

Christopher Lennertz: I've had a very fortunate and amazing ride in the business so far. Most importantly, I've been able to work with some amazing artists like Basil Poledouris and Michael Kamen. I learned so much watching them and being part of their process that when I branched out on my own I really felt ready to continue and follow in their footsteps. I think the only surprise has perhaps been the vast importance of the business side of this career. There are so many wonderful composers out there, but one really needs to also get the importance of personality and how that plays into the equation as well.

ScoreNotes: You have composed music for television, movies, and videogames. Which medium do you find to be the most appealing to write for?

Christopher Lennertz: I prefer to consider all mediums under the category of dramatic music, and am happy writing for all of them. As long as the story or situation is compelling, then I will definitely enjoy lending my musical voice.

ScoreNotes: Have you had any situations in which you were composing for different projects during the same time frame? If so, how were you able to juggle the workload in a situation like that?

Christopher Lennertz: I often have a few projects at various stages of the composition process going on at the same time. Most of the time, I've been fortunate to have a wide variety of styles and genres to compose for, and that allows me to move between the projects with little difficulty. It actually keeps everything fresh and exciting.

ScoreNotes: You've received accolades for your work on the television show *Supernatural,* including an Emmy nomination. How positive an experience has working on the show been for you?

Christopher Lennertz: *Supernatural* has been an amazing experience from the very beginning. A close friend of mine from film school, Eric Kripke, created the show and asked me to be involved. I had scored many of Eric's films before, so we had a great shorthand in communicating about music. The show itself is fantastic, weaving scares, mythology, and emotion through the entire arc of the series.

ScoreNotes: What do you feel are some key elements of the show that has made it a success?

Christopher Lennertz: I think the strong chemistry of Sam and Dean, the Winchester brothers, is what really makes the show work. They are great and very believable together. Along with this, Eric's vision and scope really set the show apart. It has grand themes, but is always presented in a very real way through family drama.

ScoreNotes: Shifting over to your work on videogames—what did it mean for your career to have been involved with the *Medal of Honor* series?

Christopher Lennertz: It was amazing. To follow Giacchino and work on a series that Spielberg created was an absolute dream. The great thing about *MOH* was that it had such a vast and powerful historical perspective from which to draw upon, in a musical sense. You already had this amazing back story of World War II that could influence and guide the emotions of the musical score. It was fantastic.

ScoreNotes: Did you confer with the composer of the first installments, Michael Giacchino, at all during your time on this game series?

Christopher Lennertz: Yes, I spoke with Michael as soon as I was hired. I knew I had huge shoes to fill, and I wanted him to know that I was a fan and would try to continue his musical legacy on the series. He was incredibly gracious and offered me great advice and support whenever I might need it.

ScoreNotes: We often see game-to-film adaptations of fantastical, fictional fare but rarely for historically-driven material. Do you think a film version of the *Medal of Honor* series would be feasible?

Christopher Lennertz: I think that in many ways, *Saving Private Ryan* was the inspiration for *MOH*, so I'm not sure that it would make sense to go back to the theaters. Plus, there are so many amazing, true stories in the history of the war that the best idea might be to use one of those as a storyline.

ScoreNotes: On the topic of movies—can you recap some of the key film projects you have worked on?

Christopher Lennertz: Well, my most recent film is called *Adam;* it's a drama with a comedic touch that Fox Searchlight is releasing this July. It's a wonderful love story in which the lead character has Asperger's syndrome. Other than that, I'd say I've become known for both my comedy and family work, such as *Alvin and the Chipmunks*, *Meet the Spartans*, and *The Perfect Holiday*, as well as my Horror work on Clive Barker's *Saint Sinner* [in addition to my ongoing duties with *Supernatural*].

ScoreNotes: In *Meet the Spartans*, the premise was predictably silly, as intended. Your score, however, was not. You created a soundtrack that intentionally played it straight, so to speak. Can you talk about the impact a score has when it plays opposite of the comedy onscreen?

Christopher Lennertz: That is an approach that I learned firsthand from the master. I was fortunate enough to study with Elmer Bernstein, and no one has ever scored comedy as well in my opinion. He was a true genius, and his timing was perfect. He always said that a straight score will actually enhance the humor on the screen, much like a straight man in a comedy sketch. It actually highlights the comedy. I know *Stripes*, *Caddyshack*, and *Animal House* by heart, so that musical palette definitely influences my comedy scoring. Those were the classics!

ScoreNotes: Do you think your music for *Meet the Spartans* might pick up some consideration for you the next time someone in Hollywood sets out to make a fantasy epic? It really is an excellent, stylish score that packs a bit of a punch!

Christopher Lennertz: Thank you. I hope so...but I doubt it. We'll see, perhaps if it gets temped in the right film and no one mentions where it came from. I certainly am very proud of the score, but sometimes producers want to pigeonhole creative people a bit. I like to think that I can do anything though.

ScoreNotes: When you reach your top goals in film composing, will you maintain an interest in television and game scores?

Christopher Lennertz: Really, my top goal is to be able to write great music to support a great story...that, and work with people whom I like, respect, and admire. The medium really doesn't concern me too much. I'm thrilled to be writing music and telling stories. That, to me, is the perfect situation, regardless of where those stories exist...in a theater, in a living room, or on a computer.

ScoreNotes: Besides composing, what are some of your other passions in life?

Christopher Lennertz: First and foremost is my family. I have a wonderful wife and an adorable baby girl as well as siblings and parents who are all very close. Besides that, I'd say cooking, sailing, skiing, and since I'm currently training for my first triathlon, let's add swimming and cycling as well!

19 *Keeping Score* with Michael Levine

Michael Levine.

Michael Levine is an explorative composer who isn't afraid to take a chance. It's this approach that has led him to the success he's enjoyed, I feel. In the following interview, Michael discussed a bevy of subjects with me, including his music for the mega-popular television series *Cold Case*, his rather diverse and open musical interests, and how it was that he got his first break in the business, courtesy of a one Hans Zimmer...

Michael Levine (2009)

ScoreNotes: Unlike some shows that feature a perpetual storyline throughout, *Cold Case* offers up a stand-alone story—or case, as it were—each week as its focus. Are you regularly asked to write music that represents the different decades that the show shifts back and forth from? Also, does a dynamic timeline like that keep things interesting for you on a creative level over the long haul of television series?

Michael Levine: Actually, I rarely write period music *per se*. The period is usually evoked by the licensed songs that are used in the flashbacks. Often, though, I will allude to the period through an instrumental color or harmonic idea. And, yes, that's part of the fun. The challenge is to make it still feel like it belongs in the *Cold Case* sonic vocabulary.

ScoreNotes: What was the overall tone that you were looking to establish for the series when you first started scoring the early episodes?

Michael Levine: *Cold Case* differs from other "procedural" shows in that the story is not as much about the mechanics of solving the case but about learning the victim's story and how they were important to the people around them. So, the tone is more emotional than similar shows. [Executive producer] Jonathan Littman once said, "I write an opera every week. But the emotion is rarely explicit, instead lurking just below the surface."

ScoreNotes: Which episodes do you feel showcase some of the best examples of your work from the series?

Michael Levine: Hmm, six seasons—that's tough. But some of the standouts include *Our Boy Is Back*, which includes "Carl's Recollection," the favorite of *Cold Case* creator Meredith Stiehm; *Saving Sammy,* for which I created music that serves as an analogy to the central character's autism; *Beautiful Little Fool,* an episode about a songwriter for which I wrote songs with episode writer Liz Garcia; *The Letter,* one of the most romantic scores of the series; and *The Good Death,* just because I think it's a good tune.

ScoreNotes: How does the collaboration with the show's directors typically work for you? I imagine the spotting process is quite different and faster paced than that of film sessions!

Michael Levine: TV is a producer's medium more than a director's. There's no time to spot with anyone other than the post-production team. The editor's choices for temping [placeholder music] are invaluable. As soon as I can, I submit cues for approval from the show runners [executive producers].

ScoreNotes: Can you comment on the rather enthusiastic fan base that has developed for *Cold Case* as well as some of the feedback you have received from viewers?

Michael Levine: The fans are an inspiration in good times and a life-saving spirit boost when things aren't going well.

ScoreNotes: How gratifying was it to have received the multiple ASCAP awards for your work on the show? Can you share your sentiments about the honor?

Michael Levine: What I love best about the ASCAP awards is that it gives me a chance to mingle with my idols. You have to realize that I started out as a fan, and I still am one. But when you get an award, you're a fan with *access!*

ScoreNotes: Now moving off of *Cold Case*, I'd like to ask some questions about your musical style. First, how vital is it for you to remain open-minded as a composer?

Michael Levine: I have about as eclectic listening habits as anyone I know. My iPod contains pop, rock, rap, jazz, classical, world, avant-garde, spoken word, and even some film music. It's always set on shuffle. Where I live in Topanga Canyon, AM radio is a lot more reliable than FM. And AM is stranger than FM. I might listen to the American Songbook, Persian pop, and Norteño all on the way into work.

All of these things influence my musical style, but I hope my voice is distinct no matter what the context.

ScoreNotes: Spanning all the projects you've worked on, can you describe some of the innovative techniques that you've employed during your career that readers might find interesting?

Michael Levine: I am immodestly proud of the chances I've taken with concert music. I wrote the world's first pedal steel guitar concerto; composed a piece for musical saw and strings in which the strings were divided into one group tuned ¼ step sharp and the other tuned to true pitch; and wrote an electric string quartet that borrowed from my rock 'n' roll experiences, incorporating distortion and ring modulation. I also wrote the book, lyrics, song, and score for *Orpheus Electronica*, which was, possibly, the first "rave opera."

ScoreNotes: What would you say is the most exotic combination of sound effects and musical instruments that you've brought together for a piece?

Michael Levine: *Orpheus* included highly manipulated samples, sound design, strings, vocals, and spoken word over an electronica bed. An early commercial I did for Mitsubishi Eclipse included animal cries, world drums, and an opera singer—rule-breaking in 1989, and much copied after.

ScoreNotes: As far as your early days, is it true that you wrote the jingle for several TV commercials, including the catchy Kit Kat spot? If so, did any particular jingle ever become too popular for your tastes, or do you remember it all in good fun now?

Michael Levine: At one point, I was vaguely embarrassed that, after a degree from music school, pieces performed at Lincoln Center, commissions from dance companies, playing on dozens of records, and appearing on MTV, my best-known contribution to Western culture was a 30-second encomium to a quadra-furcated candy bar. But now I'm happy that anyone remembers *anything* I do.

ScoreNotes: How important was it to get your start by working on television commercials? I assume it opened up a few opportunities for you?

Michael Levine: It gave me invaluable musical, production, and business training. But most of the opportunities that writing for commercials opened up were to write for more commercials.

ScoreNotes: What would you say was the key moment in your career that cemented your transition to television and film?

Michael Levine: An agent once told me I was unhireable because my reel was *weird*, and even worse, *it didn't sound like film music*. The following day I gave that unlistenable CD to Hans Zimmer who left me a message the next day, which went, "Michael, I just listened to your reel and it's incredible. Most people, I tell them their stuff is [crap], but yours is incredible. Here's my home phone number—if you give it out, I'll have to kill you." He has definitely wanted to kill me more than once since, but he has been an awesomely generous help to me countless times.

ScoreNotes: With regards to movies, can you touch on some of the film projects that you've worked on and some of the composers you have worked with?

Michael Levine: *Misconceptions, Columbus Day,* and *Adrift in Manhattan* are independent films I've scored in the past two years. I also helped out Hans Zimmer with *The Simpsons Movie* and Hans [Zimmer] and James Newton Howard with *Batman: Dark Knight*. Other composers I've aided and abetted include Rupert Gregson Williams, Harry Gregson Williams, and Cliff Martinez.

ScoreNotes: Looking at your current and future portfolio, can you tell us about some of the other television shows or projects that you have going on through 2009 and into 2010?

Michael Levine: *Cold Case* will be back for a seventh season. I will probably continue to contribute to the next album of [Nickelodeon/Columbia artists] The Naked Brothers in some capacity, although probably not as involved as I was in producing their first two albums. I hope to score a movie or two and will probably do bits and pieces of work for Hans. I also have a slew of art music projects I am eager to do as time permits.

ScoreNotes: In your opinion, where do you think the future of television music is headed? And is it headed in the right direction?

Michael Levine: TV and the Web appear to be becoming one thing. Is that good or bad? Probably a bit of both.

20 | *Keeping Score* with Nathan Barr

Nathan Barr.

Used by permiss on.

When it comes to choice scoring opportunities, you'd have to say that HBO provides composers some neat chances. Case in point: the (relatively) new series *True Blood*, which is quickly becoming a widespread hit on the cable network. This modern-day vampire tale offers the type of intelligent writing and dramatic twists that fans of HBO entertainment have come to expect from its programming.

Onboard to write the music for the show is **Nathan Barr,** an accomplished and gifted composer who is literally hands-on when it comes to his work (he often plays his own instruments). Having worked on *True Blood* for two seasons now, Nathan was kind enough to tell us what goes into the musical score for a show about vampires coexisting with humans in modern-day Louisiana...

Nathan Barr (2009)

ScoreNotes: To begin with, how fulfilling has it been for you to work on a series like HBO's *True Blood*?

Nathan Barr: *True Blood* is one of the most, if not the most, fulfilling projects I have worked on in my ten years in the business. For one thing, everyone involved in the production is a pleasure to work with. Alan Ball is very involved in the musical process every step of the way, and one of the aspects of working with him that has been so gratifying is the way he has allowed me to explore the musical world of *True Blood* without too many rules. With this kind of trust, it has really inspired me to do some of my best work to date. There are so many eclectic characters that are beautifully portrayed by the actors, which means thematically I have a lot to work with. The tremendous success of the show is also exciting, as it means all the work we do is being listened to, watched, and appreciated by many.

ScoreNotes: When you were first introduced to the show's Gothic premise, how interesting and different did you find the overall concept to be?

Nathan Barr: My introduction to the show was screening the pilot in preparation for a meeting with Alan and his creative team. I remember thinking how polished and cinematic the pilot looked. I was also impressed at how the show approached the age-old legend of vampires with a fresh eye—no easy task! Learning that Bill was over a century old, that Sookie was a mind reader, and that the story was based in the South immediately excited me because of the musical possibilities. It's an excitement that I still carry with me as I approach the finish of Season 2.

ScoreNotes: How would you describe the general style of music from the show, and what are some of the various instruments you use to deliver it?

Nathan Barr: I would describe the score as very organic, very acoustic, with a strong emphasis on cello, guitar, and piano. These three instruments are the heart of the score. At times the score is Appalachian, at times folksy, at times hymn-like, and at times modern-classical with the various string effects. I think it has a very unique sound as far as composition for television is concerned, and I am very proud of this.

ScoreNotes: Does the timeline of working on an HBO series differ from that of a typical television production?

Nathan Barr: Thankfully, working on an HBO show is rather relaxed in terms of schedule when compared to that of network television. The least amount of time I have ever had to turn a show around is one week, and the most amount of time is closer to a month. I've never had more than 35 minutes in a single episode, and in a couple of episodes, I've had only 10 to 12 minutes of score.

ScoreNotes: Overall, what would you say are some of the key elements that have made *True Blood* a success with viewers thus far?

Nathan Barr: A great show all starts with the writing. Alan is a brilliant writer and has hired a team of brilliant writers to help bring Charlaine Harris's incredible world to the small screen. The show is particularly effective with its use of cliff-hangers, surprise twists, and the complex emotional journeys of all of the characters. I also think there is at least one character that everyone can relate to in one way or another, and so audiences become emotionally invested in the story and that particular character's journey. Add blood and sex and the supernatural to these strengths, and you have a very potent mix of elements to entice audiences.

ScoreNotes: How involved does the series creator, Alan Ball, become with the music you develop?

Nathan Barr: Alan is very involved with all the music in the show. He encourages his team of writers to pick out songs while they are writing to help them set the tone of the episode. In terms of score, Alan and I meet and go through every cue in every episode a couple of days before each dub. He has an excellent understanding of how score enhances picture, and his comments are always driven by the story—making sure the score is doing everything it can for each character' moment in the show.

ScoreNotes: After taking a look at your background, I see that you were exposed to many diverse cultures, musical styles, and instruments as a youth. As a composer today, what are some of the methods you employ to stay innovative in your craft?

Nathan Barr: For me, one of the methods that keeps things fresh is to add new instruments to my collection on a regular basis. Before I started *True Blood*, I added a bowed electric guitar and an upright piano, sawed in two, to my collection. The addition of these two instruments to my collection guaranteed that there would be textural elements in this score that I had never worked with before, thus sounding fresh. Speaking from a melodic standpoint, I really rely on the strength of the story and its characters to inspire strong melodic components from me. In the case of *True Blood*, I have composed some melodies—particularly that of Bill and Sookie—of which I am very proud. Coming up with that melody in particular was fairly effortless because the writing and acting are so strong.

ScoreNotes: In your opinion, how open is the movie and television industry to the use of unique instruments and "out of the box" approaches?

Nathan Barr: It depends entirely on who holds the creative reins for the project. With someone like Alan Ball, if it works, he doesn't second-guess it. It could be bagpipes and pipe organ, and if it's doing what it's supposed to be doing for the scene, then we're good to go. More generally speaking, so long as the instrument doesn't sound too out of place for the world of the movie or television show, then I find people are open to it. If, for example, a movie takes place in present-day Manhattan, having instruments that evoke a strong Middle Eastern flavor would be out of place unless our story has Middle Eastern elements in it that we are trying to accentuate.

ScoreNotes: Might you please update us on how your movie projects are proceeding? Are there any upcoming projects you can mention at this time?

Nathan Barr: I am starting on two film projects as soon as I finish up Season 2 of *True Blood*. One is a horror film called *Cotton*, produced by Eli Roth, whom I love working with in any capacity. The other is a dramedy by a director I have worked with before named Barry Blaustein and starring Rainn Wilson, Sarah Silverman, Michael C. Hall, among others. Both are projects I am looking forward to.

ScoreNotes: As we wrap up here, who would you say has been the biggest creative inspiration(s) in your life?

Nathan Barr: There are so many it is hard to point out just one. But the music of Bach and Richard Strauss certainly inspire me on a daily basis.

21 *Keeping Score* with Bear McCreary

Photo by Andrew Craig.

Bear McCreary.

The innovative approach of **Bear McCreary** is something to behold. His imaginative approach to scoring the modern *Battlestar Galactica* series offers a type of science fiction soundtrack experience unlike any I've heard before for a television series. While there are times when unique, experimental visions fall short, McCreary's output is rare in that it succeeded in establishing a completely unique style while also delivering music that is a pleasure to listen to both within the show and on its own—a success on all levels.

The following interview was conducted soon after *Battlestar Galactica* concluded its run on the SyFy Channel. In the piece, Bear shares his engaging perspectives on what it took to bring the music of *Galactica* to fruition...

Bear McCreary (2009)

ScoreNotes: As you look back at the work you've done on *Battlestar Galactica*, how proud are you of the success that the show has achieved?

Bear McCreary: I'm extremely proud of the work that all of us have done on the show. But I can't say I'm extraordinarily surprised. I knew when I saw the very first episode that I was involved with something very special, and my instincts proved correct.

ScoreNotes: Can you talk about how your work on the show has helped you grow as a composer?

Bear McCreary: It's had a huge impact on me creatively and artistically. One of the first things I learned was how to work on a small budget, even though that's not really the case anymore. The initial seasons of *Battlestar* were relatively low budget, and in fact, even the last season was still on a much smaller budget than any kind of network show (like *Lost* or *Criminal Minds*, for example). And so I originally had a very small group of musicians at my disposal. Other composers in my position would have probably opted to hire no musicians at all and actually make some money. But instead, I tried to create a big sound with a handful of people, and I learned to use them effectively and efficiently.

I decided we shouldn't emulate a big orchestral sound. This was an important decision at the time that was not made just by me, but also the producers involved who didn't want to go through the old *Star Trek* and *Star Wars* musical gestures. So we ended up doing something a little different, and it was both inspired creatively and financially. As the show has gone on, budgets have gotten bigger, and we started using orchestra, but I still kept the core lessons I learned in doing the show with just a handful of musicians. And it's forever changed the way I think about music and the use of soloists and the use of a very small ensemble to create very big, powerful sounds. Ironically, it's made me a better composer of larger-scale music by working on a small scale for so long.

ScoreNotes: Sometimes we need to take a smaller approach before the larger ones open up.

Bear McCreary: Absolutely! If I had been given a huge budget from the beginning of *Battlestar Galactica*, it wouldn't sound the way it does now. My approach back then would have been very different. I've learned a lot, and I'm very grateful for the way it worked out. I feel that I made the best out of each season and created a sound that is very unique.

ScoreNotes: I suppose that you and the production team knew very early on that the score would be influential in defining the tone of the show?

Bear McCreary: One of the interesting things is that the score was the most different part of the [new] show from the old show. And this goes back to the work that Richard Gibbs did on the mini-series—which I was involved in as a composer, but I was not *the* composer. Richard started off with this really minimal sound that was very different from the orchestral bombast of *Star Trek* and *Star Wars*, which is the language in which Stu Philips wrote his excellent score for the classic show. But the ship looked basically the same. The characters had the same names. A lot of it was recognizably *Battlestar Galactica*. There was only one part of it that was entirely different—and I'm not talking about Starbuck being a woman [laughs]; I'm talking about the music. Definitely, everyone knew that it would always be an important part in establishing the tone of the show, the identity of the show, and distancing it from the original, which was an issue in the beginning.

ScoreNotes: What are some of the unique instruments that you used along the way in *Galactica*?

Bear McCreary: The entire score is performed by relatively unique and unusual instruments. One that you've heard frequently is the Duduk, which is an Armenian woodwind instrument that has a very melancholy, dark sound. Another interesting one is the Erhu, which is like the Chinese violin, or the Chinese cello, as it's sometimes called. It's an instrument that has a very vocal quality; often times it sounds like a soprano singing, but it's in fact a string instrument. And there is a lot of interesting percussion. Taiko drums, frame drums, tabla, chang-changs, dumbeks. Any kind of percussion instrument from around the world. Those are the main instruments you hear a lot of.

ScoreNotes: I can imagine part of the fun for you is to set out to discover the different types of instruments that are out there that can help you achieve the sound you're looking for?

Bear McCreary: Absolutely. Again, this goes back to my Season 1 experience when we had a relatively small budget to work with and I couldn't afford a 50-piece string section at that time. So instead, I thought I should find some interesting instrumentalists. For example, I called Chris Bleth because he played Duduk, and I asked him, when I met him, what else he played. And he brought Bansuris, Shakuhachis, Chinese Membrane flutes, and all these other things that I had never even heard of. Likewise, I hired Eric Rigler to play the Uilleann Bagpipes, and those have a very characteristic sound, but I also asked him what else he played. He brought out the Great Highland Pipes, which are the big bagpipes you see in parades, and he also plays Irish pennywhistles and a lot of unusual ethnic instruments that we've used from time to time, including the shofar, conch, and sipsi. It was really an exploratory process for me.

ScoreNotes: From your perspective as a composer, which episode from the series stands out as your favorite?

Bear McCreary: From a compositional standpoint, no episode could rival my experience on *Someone to Watch Over Me*, which was toward the end of Season 4. The music was involved with every aspect of the episode. The writers called me before they even wrote the story. I did extensive interviews with them talking about my musical and creative process, and that became the character of Slick, who is a struggling composer/pianist that Kara encounters. I was on set while they were shooting it, writing the music that he would be playing on the piano. Then I was of course involved in editorial and obviously ended up scoring the episode as well. So that was an episode that I was involved with from beginning to end, which had never happened before for me. In fact, I think it's extremely rare in television scoring that you would have an episode that deals with music in that way.

The other thing that's interesting is that this episode is the one where the score became a character in and of itself. The music was actually introduced into the world of the characters, which is extremely weird and kind of hard to wrap your brain around. There's a theme that the audience of *Battlestar Galactica* is familiar with because they've heard it in the score for an entire season. And then you have characters in the show that actually become aware of this music. So it's like this really weird breaking of the fourth wall. I would have never guessed from the beginning of the series that we would go into this bizarre musical territory. But it was extremely rewarding and exciting, and I got to write some of the best music I've ever written for that episode.

ScoreNotes: Very innovative. It's almost as if the music melds into real time.

Bear McCreary: I'm very honored to be a part of it. I think that the writers, David Weddle and Bradley Thompson, and the director, Michael Nankin, probably wouldn't have chosen to do a story like that if they didn't know that they had me as a resource. It was interesting, because I felt like I had a real influence on the story.

ScoreNotes: With *Caprica*, the series shifts back in time to an earlier point in *Galactica* history. Did you have to adjust your approach with the music to reflect this?

Bear McCreary: Yes, the music is extremely different than *Battlestar*. In fact, there are very few musical connections, which I think makes the musical connections all the more powerful because the rest of the score is a very different tone, a very different mood and language with different instruments playing them.

And I took my cues from the series itself. The show feels very different than *Battlestar*. It takes place in a very polished society that is at its decadent and opulent peak. It didn't have any of that frantic tribal, primitive conflict that *Battlestar* had. So the music was very different but the approach is the same. That's really the connection, the approach to scoring long arcs instead of individual characters. I'm writing themes that can be identified in the pilot and brought back as the series goes on, to be manipulated and changed. So the thing that's most interesting to me is that these little threads in the music that connect us with *Battlestar Galactica* can become more prominent as the show goes on. My goal is that, as the series goes on, the score becomes more and more like *Battlestar*. So that theoretically speaking, if this show narratively goes all the way up to the beginning of the *Battlestar Galactica* mini-series, the *Caprica* score, which started out very different, will transform slowly into the *Battlestar Galactica* score.

ScoreNotes: In your opinion, and in general terms, is writing music for a "prequel" a bit more challenging than writing a score for a sequel?

Bear McCreary: It's challenging in different ways. To follow up any project with another one that's related is difficult. And if you think about it, many of my projects have fallen into that category. For example, *Terminator: The Sarah Connor Chronicles* is a sequel of sorts to *Terminator 2*. My score could inevitably be compared to the masterful scores that Brad Fiedel did. So I had to find ways of identifying myself and also recognizing where I was coming from. *Battlestar Galactica* is a different story compared to the old show, so I had to do my best to do something completely different and obliterate all those references. So *Caprica* was really more like *Battlestar* where I wanted it to sound totally different [from its predecessor]. So it did present some challenges, because I've been doing *Battlestar* a long time, and the show is so similar that it's tempting to use a lot of the same techniques, and, really, I've had to develop some new ones.

ScoreNotes: What has the fan reaction been to your work on *Battlestar*?

Bear McCreary: Fan reaction seems to be positive and passionate. I've been continually amazed at the intelligent discourse that happens at my blog (BearMcCreary.com/blog). It's been great to interact with the fans and talk with them and get their opinions. But most of all, it's been really rewarding hiding things from them and seeing if they'll find it. When I realized how perceptive the audience is, it really did have an impact on what I wrote. I always put a lot of thought and care into my scores, but I must confess, in Seasons 3 and 4 of *Battlestar*, I put in even more, because I realized there's this audience out there that was paying attention, and it was more rewarding.

I've done a lot of live concerts, and I've always been stunned at the audiences that come out and see the *Battlestar Galactica* score performed live and how well they know it, how much they respond to it, and how much they understand it, both in connection with the series and separate from the series. Ultimately, I always feel like I am writing music, and it works well with the series, and I feel like my soundtrack albums work well as albums. And everything that I've seen from the fans would point to the fact that they agree with that.

ScoreNotes: I really like how you take the music straight to the fans. When did you first have the idea to do something like that?

Bear McCreary: The first time was with the release of Season 2 on CD. We did a show in 2006 at a little club here in town called The Mint, the capacity of which is about 120 to 150. It's like a little jazz club, and we rocked the hell out of it. But that was the first time that I ever thought doing something like this might be something people would be interested in. And I must confess, I was amazed that anyone showed up at all!

Then in 2008, we booked The Roxy Theatre in Los Angeles, which holds about 600. It sold out so quickly we had to open up a second night. And *that one* sold out so quickly we ended up turning people away for two weeks. I was astonished at the interest in it! People flew in from Malaysia, Canada, London, and really all over the world just to see this music in concert. That's when I realized there was something really special happening here. You couldn't do that with the score to a typical cable television show and have that kind of response.

ScoreNotes: Do you feel that a theatrical version of *Battlestar Galactica* is just a matter of time before it happens?

Bear McCreary: Frankly, I think you have a better chance of the moon crashing into the planet and killing us all. My answer is twofold—creatively there's no need for it. The show is not like *Star Trek* because it came to a conclusion. But then also logistically, it's a complicated franchise. It's got movie rights tied up with different people than the television rights do. I must admit as a fan, I think it would be great, but just having what little experience I have with the business side of it, my gut instinct is that the rights to the feature film side of it are infinitely more complex than the television side.

ScoreNotes: I have a feeling that if the rights weren't such a tricky issue, they would probably reboot it, even though *Galactica,* in this incarnation, is a recent series.

Bear McCreary: I think a reboot would happen before any kind of movie with this cast ever would. Because obviously the story is done; we got to the end of it. You can't do *Battlestar Galactica: The Next Generation.* I feel strongly that Ron Moore and the other writers/producers really wanted that kind of closure. That's not to say that some other producer or developer might not reboot it again. The window between franchises getting rebooted seems to be getting smaller and smaller these days, so who knows. I just feel like we collectively, as people having worked on *this* version of *Battlestar*, we're done. Our version of the story is finished.

ScoreNotes: How fulfilling was the time you spent working on *The Sarah Connor Chronicles*?

Bear McCreary: It's been a dream come true. It's been a chance for me to play around in the *Terminator* universe, which is basically where I grew up. Those first two films were among my favorite movies and were literally the reasons why I wanted to get involved with the movie business in the first place. So I leapt at the opportunity to be involved in the universe. But beyond that, I think that the show was so loyal to the [James] Cameron films and did all the right things and created these fascinating characters, beyond the characters that were in Cameron's movies. I mean that's what my interest was in the beginning, as it was with everyone else. But it was the new characters that really roped me in.

Overall, it was just an incredible experience. I got to write a really lyrical, beautiful theme that I'm very proud of. The album that we did out of it turned out wonderfully. It was a great show. I must confess that I am very sad that it is no more.

ScoreNotes: From the fans who were watching it, they seemed to really enjoy it. So it's a little confusing why it got eliminated.

Bear McCreary: Well, at the end of the day, there just weren't enough of them. And in many ways, *Battlestar Galactica* has always been an underperforming show by [SyFy Channel] standards as well. It's all about expectation. If *Battlestar Galactica* had aired on Fox, it would have been cancelled in three weeks. So, it's funny that *The Sarah Connor Chronicles* didn't survive, even though routinely it got more than twice as many viewers as *Battlestar* ever did at its peak. But it's all about expectations and network ad revenue. You know, it's financial decisions made by financial institutions. And it was a great show. I know that we would have just kicked [butt] on Season 3. Hopefully, one day there will be some chance to continue that.

ScoreNotes: For a franchise like *Terminator*, how important was it to keep the music associated with the movies?

Bear McCreary: Well, I think it's incredibly important to a point. I think the music has to take its cue from the film itself. And I am not a fan of *Terminator 3*; I've never pretended otherwise. And I was very happy when I saw the pilot episode of *The Sarah Connor Chronicles*—when they were considering hiring me—and how loyal they had stayed to the tone of *Terminator 2*. I'm not even talking about the timelines or the chronological placement of the story—I just mean the tone of it. The tone of it was very much in line with Cameron's films. And I knew the music had to acknowledge it.

With *The Sarah Connor Chronicles*, they couldn't afford to use the *Terminator* theme all the time. We only had it on the title card, so I was given the choice to do something new and totally different or to try to keep it in that same musical universe. I did my best to make the score feel like it belonged in *Terminator 1* and *2*. So as a fan of the franchise, I think it matters very much. If you're talking about doing a big franchise reboot and want to go a different direction, it becomes a different scenario.

ScoreNotes: I find it interesting and a bit worrisome about the manner in which all these reboots are coming to pass.

Bear McCreary: The franchises themselves are evolving in such ways that you realize they are becoming myths and legends. Every generation has a version of it that means something to them. They'll just probably continue to be remade, and that's good because there's a new generation of kids that are discovering the movies that I loved when I was a kid. I'm happy if some kid goes and discovers *Terminator 1* or *2* because they saw the PG-13 *Terminator 4*. I think that's great. But at the end of the day, you wonder if we do this for 30 or 40 years, who's going to be making anything new? Obviously, that's the extreme end of the argument, but you do wonder.

Bonus Interview

This interview, included as a bonus segment, features the composers of the new and *classic Battlestar Galactica* in one compilation. While the styles of the two series differ, it's interesting to see how the torch was passed from one composer to the next.

22 *Keeping Score* with Stu Phillips

Stu Phillips.

As a youngster who had yet to realize that film and television scores could function apart from the screen, **Stu Phillips's** work really fueled my imagination when I was growing up. To me, he belongs in a hall of fame for composers, if such a place existed. He is responsible for some of the most popular themes in the history of television, including the original *Battlestar Galactica, Buck Rogers, Knight Rider,* and many others. His work entertained me then, and it still does now.

I am happy to present this nostalgic and rather candid segment with one of the most popular composers the small screen ever had the pleasure of hosting...

Stu Phillips (2007)

ScoreNotes: Looking back on your career in television, can you share with us your most rewarding contributions from the variety of projects you've worked on?

Stu Phillips: Boy, it goes back a long time. Actually, my television career goes all the way back to when I did some specials in New York City for ABC. It went from there to the *Donna Reed* television show for about three years and the *Monkees* on into *McCloud* and *Quincy* and *Switch* and the *Hardy Boys, Galactica, Buck Rogers, Knight Rider,* and the *Fall Guy.* My career in feature films is a little less than that, but the picture which I guess I am most identified with at this point is *Beyond the Valley of the Dolls,* which has become some sort of a cult favorite.

ScoreNotes: Well, the interesting thing about your work is that a lot of your television themes played like music you would hear in the movies.

Stu Phillips: Yeah, I mean the obvious ones would be *Galactica,* which was like a feature film every week...a short feature film. And it was a classically-oriented score. *Buck Rogers,* a little different. It wasn't in the same vein...a little more pop music. *Knight Rider,* oh I don't know what you'd call that. It was one of the first of the electronic scores on television. It preceded *Miami Vice* and a few other shows that were geared that way.

ScoreNotes: And I guess it had to be an electronic score because you had a talking car.

Stu Phillips: Well, actually, the theme was electronic. The early scores were basically orchestral with just a little bit of electronics on them. They didn't really want to go that wholeheartedly, synth-wise. Then when I left the show and went over to 20th to do *Fall Guy,* another composer came in with another producer...another whole new crew of people, and they decided they wanted to do more in the electronic vein. So the following years that the show was on the air, it was more electronic than when I did it.

ScoreNotes: Now, that must have been interesting back then, comparatively speaking, with the electronic resources that we have now as compared to then.

Stu Phillips: Oh yeah. I mean we were in the early days. Actually, my use of electronics, which I did at the last seminar, was a picture I did in 1968 with the original Moog synthesizer that Paul Beaver had, which was about 15 to 20 feet wide, about 8 feet high, and it was just a whole bunch of bays with patch cords going in. I brought a picture of it [to the seminar] to show to the people there, and they were really amazed because they had never seen something that big that is now the size of a keyboard.

ScoreNotes: [Laughing] Sounds like the size of NASA's first computer.

Stu Phillips: Yes…well, NASA had all those backup reels spinning and everything else for memory. This didn't have any memory. Basically, Paul Beaver just played it, and that was it. There was no memory involved. But it was quite something. It was very unusual. I experimented a lot in the '60s with some of the electronic things that were available in those days. I feel like I'm a bit of a pioneer—not a lot; there were other people doing it as well, but I enjoyed that part of it. It was interesting. I can't say that I'm a great lover of the electronic music sound, but I used it all through my career…whenever it was necessary and it made sense.

ScoreNotes: Sure, and with a lot of your opportunities regarding science fiction, the setting is in the future, so it kind of goes hand in hand I suppose…the fitting of the electronics.

Stu Phillips: Yeah, it's kind of a natural thing. It just seemed to work with that genre of film. Nobody knows what music would sound like if we were in the year 4000 or 3000. There's no way of knowing, so it's certainly a sound that works for the genre. However, it lacks the emotional content of an orchestra, which is why your more successful science fiction [projects] have been orchestral, like *Star Wars, Star Trek, Galactica*.

ScoreNotes: Right, and I was going to ask you your opinion on the music of the new show. The new show is a success, but I'd be curious as to what your opinion is of the musical soundtrack.

Stu Phillips: Well, I don't like to give opinions of fellow composers, and Bear McCreary is a very lovely man, and we're good friends. Actually, in one of the episodes, he and the producers decided to use the old *Galactica* theme. I was kind of worried. He called me up and said, "Oh Stu, we're going to use the old *Galactica* theme." I kind of shuddered a bit and wanted to know what part. He said, "Oh, I'm not fooling around. I'd like to come over to your house and look at the scores. I want to sit with you for an hour, talk about it." He said he didn't want to do it an injustice. That is very nice for a composer to do that, especially when he's coming over to somebody who did the original. And he did come over here, and we spent quite a long time together. He did a magnificent arrangement of it, which they did use in the show. I'll just say this. He's a very nice man. He does a wonderful job with what he's doing. I'm not a big fan of the show, though. So we'll put it that way, okay?

ScoreNotes: Surely. If we could just talk about the show itself—what specifically doesn't work for you?

Stu Phillips: I can't buy half the cast in business suits and a tie and the other half of the cast in some kind of space outfit. It just doesn't work for me. I don't know exactly what it is that they are trying to say, if they're trying to say anything. If it's supposed to be a comparison [to modern events of] today, I don't really know that [it's working]. A few of those things kind of disturb me. I'm not sure what their direction is or what they're doing, whereas in the original Galactica, you knew what they were doing. It was simply a fairy tale, a western in space…it was a space opera. They made no bones about what it was meant to be. There were a few things in it that tried to make comparisons between [current events of the time], but it wasn't as politically oriented as the one is now. I am not a big fan of the show at this particular point. But it's a good show.

ScoreNotes: Yes, the production value is great. What gets me personally is something as simple as shaky camera movement. It seems that everything is filmed with a hand-held these days.

Stu Phillips: I don't know. I haven't been up to Vancouver. I don't know how they are doing it. A couple of episodes that I did watch…it doesn't knock me out. And that's about as far as I'll go. But I do want to comment and say that the [Bear] is just a lovely man and a good composer. He does what he's been instructed to do by the producers and director, as I have been through most of my career. You very rarely get the opportunity to just go out on your own and have no one direct you in what they want to hear from you. So, he's in the same boat as I was in. We do what we're told and make a living.

ScoreNotes: Sure, at the mercy of the director and producers.

Stu Phillips: Yeah, pretty much.

ScoreNotes: Now in your opinion, why do you think television itself has shied away from the type of thematic music that worked so well in the '70s and the '80s? Is it because the world has evolved and TV has evolved with it?

Stu Phillips: I think limiting it just to television is not right. Film and television have gotten away from a lot of content. The only thing that I can see is that it appears as though producers and directors, or let's just call them filmmakers nowadays, whether it be television or theatrical film, seem to feel that melody is corny. That having a love theme with a sweeping feeling during a love scene is extremely corny, and they don't think that they want to have that. However, basically your average moviegoer and television watcher *is* corny [laughs].

ScoreNotes: That's why we're tuned in!

Stu Phillips: Yeah, your audience is basically that way. Why they want to avoid it, I don't know. It seems to be an intellectual approach now. Everybody feels like, we just don't want to hit anything on the head. We don't want to be obvious about it. At times, it's fine. A lot of composers all the way back to the '30s and '40s also occasionally would treat scenes—maybe not whole movies, but scenes—where they would not hit it on the head so that it would have a vague quality about it emotionally…let the audience feel it. But other times when it was necessary, hey, let's go…let's hit it! Now, it seems that people want to hold back on it. I feel personally that the scores don't have continuity anymore in some of the major films. They're just a slap dash of an hour and twenty minutes worth of music, but there's no continuity because there's no theme to draw from. Fortunately on *Galactica*, I had a producer who liked thematic music. Everybody had to have a theme! I wrote the main title so that there were almost six different elements of the theme that I could pull out of it at any given time to do something in the scene. But that doesn't seem to be what they're looking for now.

ScoreNotes: Hopefully, those days will return.

Stu Phillips: I certainly hope so too.

Interviews with Today's Top Videogame Composers

No longer a side note, the scores from today's videogames are as prominent and well made (in many cases) as the film soundtracks of modern cinema. As soundtrack enthusiasts around the world are discovering, music from games is no longer simply just an alternative; it's a downright viable, creatively rich option for grand, dramatic, and colorful music.

In the following chapters, you'll have a chance to meet some of the award-winning composers in this field as they share their experiences about writing innovative music in a technically complex medium.

23 *Keeping Score* with Marty O'Donnell

Marty O'Donnell.

When the conversation is about videogame music, **Marty O'Donnell** deservedly takes his place near the head of the discussion. O'Donnell, along with co-composer Michael Salvatori, helped shape the musical identity of the medium's more popular franchises with their work on *Halo*. The signature sound created for *Halo* is, in my opinion, one of the more recognizable themes ever created in modern gaming and was often featured on the front lines wherever the title was promoted. Oddly enough, I never played *Halo* at any point in my life, but after experiencing the soundtracks for each installment, I somehow felt like I had. That is a testament to the writing talents of O'Donnell and Salvatori (and Stephen Rippy for *Halo Wars*).

In this interview, Marty takes us into the world of *Halo* by discussing the rather interesting blend of thematic inspirations that fueled the score...

Marty O'Donnell (2009)

ScoreNotes: At what point, do you feel, did the use of orchestral game music first become a serious consideration for game developers?

Marty O'Donnell: I believe that the first game developer to use music in a truly serious way was Cyan in 1993. Robyn Miller, the composer for the game *Myst*, used a film scoring approach rather than the traditional game scoring approach that was common at the time. He used recordings of oboe, strings, and orchestral percussion samples to score the mood of the game rather than real-time midi. The interesting thing for me was that his score wasn't limited to the cinematics but was also used during gameplay. Instead of a simple bed of music that looped non-stop during a level, the music came and went based on location or to enhance some task that the player had chosen to perform. When I played *Myst,* I felt that music in games had come of age, and I was intrigued enough to try composing for them.

ScoreNotes: Can you provide an overview of what your current responsibilities are at your studio, Bungie?

Marty O'Donnell: I'm the Audio Director/Composer for Bungie. Anything and everything that emanates from the speakers of all Bungie games gets my attention. I work with the designers, artists, and engineers from the beginning of every project to help cast the audio vision for every game. Then I, along with Jay Weinland (Bungie's Audio Lead), C Paul Johnson (Bungie's Senior Audio Designer), and Mike Salvatori (my long-time writing partner at TotalAudio), produce the audio. I've also used many outside musicians, actors, engineers, and other talented people over the years to accomplish that task.

ScoreNotes: Might you please describe some of the inspirations that led you more toward this field of composing?

Marty O'Donnell: I started as a piano performance major but switched to composition because I wanted to write original music for a prog-rock band I was in during my conservatory days in the late '70s. I received my Masters in Music Composition from USC in the early '80s, and while there I took a composition for film class with David Raksin. After that I started a company in Chicago with Mike Salvatori mainly writing music for commercials and film. I always enjoyed playing games, but after hearing and playing the game *Myst,* I got in contact with Cyan and was hired to produce the audio for *Riven,* the sequel to *Myst.* I love the music of Bach, Beethoven, Brahms, Debussy, Barber, and Vaughan Williams; the film scores of Jerry Goldsmith and Thomas Newman; and the bands Jethro Tull, Gentle Giant, Led Zeppelin, and Yes. Besides Robyn's work on *Myst,* I also was attracted by the work Nobuo Uematsu did with the *Final Fantasy* series. The most important element that attracts me to composing for games is the interactive, adaptive nature of the music's performance. The music plays back differently almost every time you play any one of the *Halo* series. It's designed to adjust to each player's choices as much as possible.

ScoreNotes: Can you talk a little bit about the types of themes that were written for the *Halo* series, and specifically, some of the inspirations behind them?

Marty O'Donnell: In 1999, when we first started talking about music for the *Halo* series, the three words that stuck with me were ancient, alien, and epic. I was hoping to write a single piece of music that might capture those feelings for the listener. My first instinct was to use the sound of monk chanting to evoke "ancient" and decided to get that right up at the beginning. The musical feeling for "alien" comes from some of the creepier sounding musical effects and also the Qawwali style voice that sings in the middle sections. It might not sound alien to people from the Middle East, but for most westerners, it seems to work. I got the "epic" part by using orchestral strings and percussion and a driving, exciting rhythm. There are lots of other themes throughout the *Halo* games that are inspired by the emotional content of the story. I used full orchestra, synths, solo instruments, piano, harp, choir—whatever it took to communicate the right emotions.

ScoreNotes: At what point during the game development process does the composer usually get involved? For example, when did you first get underway with the development of the music for *Halo*?

Marty O'Donnell: I prefer to be in right at the beginning if possible. With *Halo*, I was already at Bungie finishing up *Myth 2* when the first concepts for *Halo* started coming together. I began working on the sound design for the game and then soon afterwards got some early musical ideas into the mix. I was able to record live orchestra and singers for the MacWorld 1999 unveiling of *Halo*, which was almost two years before we released the game on Xbox. The earlier a composer is exposed to the story, look, and feel of a game, the better.

ScoreNotes: How satisfying is it to see the music from *Halo* be recognized so positively in both the gaming community and in the general soundtrack world?

Marty O'Donnell: *Halo* seemed to fall just at the right time and the right place. None of us thought it would become as popular as it has, and I'm personally thrilled to see so many people taking notice of the score. I've always believed that a good game score should have the same chance to be accepted as legitimate music as any other medium for which music has been composed. It still represents "functional" music as opposed to purely "art" music, but that's a distinction I don't care all that much about.

ScoreNotes: How much further do you think game music has to go before it is embraced at the same level as film soundtracks? Is it simply more about awareness than anything else?

Marty O'Donnell: I think that fans have already embraced game music, so we just have to wait for the rest of the public to catch up. A lot of the folks who determine categories for the Grammys or other music awards aren't necessarily gamers, and so they just haven't been exposed to the kind of music that has been composed for this medium yet. I think that is changing, and we'll see how it goes over the next decade or so.

ScoreNotes: Hypothetically, do you think that writing a score for a *Halo* movie would be an enticing opportunity? Also, how well do you think the game could translate to film?

Marty O'Donnell: I would love the opportunity to score a *Halo* movie. I also believe that a great movie (or more than one) could come out of the *Halo* universe. Whether or not that will ever happen or anyone would ask me to be involved are decisions out of my control.

ScoreNotes: I am a big supporter of music being applied to any and all works of art. Do you feel that there can be room in the entertainment universe for book scores (music "inspired by the novel"), or is that concept a bit too far-fetched?

Marty O'Donnell: Programmatic music has been around for a long time; there's nothing far-fetched about it. Just about all the great composers have done something like that at some point in their careers. It might be cool to have interactive music along with the Kindle. Hmm, I should call someone about that.

ScoreNotes: As you look ahead, what has you most enthused about the future of game music?

Marty O'Donnell: I think the future is bright for game music. Better technology, better composers, better music is happening each new year. Games are a great place to be creative.

24 *Keeping Score* with Winifred Phillips

Used by permission.

Winifred Phillips.

Ever since she emerged on the scene, **Winifred Phillips** has entertained gamers and soundtrack enthusiasts alike with the keen, insightful music that she composes. Truly a unique "voice" in the game music arena, Winifred's talent shines through with each of the scores she develops, often contributing an intuitive component that enhances the gaming experience.

In this Q & A, she enlightens us about her background in the arts, talks about some of her notable scores, and tells us what it's like to be one of the few female composers in a male dominated industry...

Winifred Phillips (2009)

ScoreNotes: Might you please tell us about your musical background and what some of the key drivers were that led you into composing?

Winifred Phillips: Music has always been a huge part of my life. I'm classically trained across a range of musical disciplines, from instrumental and vocal performance to composition and theory; and from a young age, I'd dreamed of being a composer. Writing music for videogames didn't occur to me right away, though. I got my start as the sole composer for a drama series on National Public Radio called *Radio Tales*. The series presented fantasy, horror, and sci-fi dramas based on world-famous works like *Beowulf, The Pit and the Pendulum*, and *War of the Worlds*. Each drama required non-stop music, so the experience served as a great training ground. The series ran on NPR for about six years; then it moved to Sirius XM Satellite Radio, where it still airs every week. I was with the series until 2002, and then I switched gears and began to pursue a career as a videogame composer.

ScoreNotes: What is it about writing music for videogames that first triggered your curiosity?

Winifred Phillips: I remember the first time a piece of videogame music grabbed my attention—it was really startling. For most of *Final Fantasy VII*, the music presents the usual synthetic texture that we're all used to. Then, during the final boss battle with Sephiroth, suddenly a live choir breaks through. I remember how immensely surprised I was, and how enormously important that last battle felt with the choir singing the villain's name. My heart leapt into my throat, I forgot to breathe, I played that boss battle like my life depended on it. . . . I felt like I was going to have a heart attack! I think the worldwide popularity of that song, *One Winged Angel* by Nobuo Uematsu, is a testament to the shared experience that we all had playing that boss battle and hearing the expressive force of the full choir urging us on. Years later, when the idea of actually writing music for videogames occurred to me, I remembered *One Winged Angel*, and that memory was a big part of why I actually took the leap into videogame music.

ScoreNotes: Do you find that game music offers the composer a chance to be more explorative as compared to film or television projects?

Winifred Phillips: I think that videogame music offers the opportunity to experiment in different ways, within the restrictions of the medium. Videogame music is interactive by nature, so there are technical and structural considerations that impose limits and strict requirements on the compositions. That being said, videogame music plays a more dynamic and integral role in the experience as opposed to the music of film and television. It is rare nowadays to encounter a sequence in television or film in which the score moves center stage. My last memory of such an occurrence was from *The Truman Show*, when the music of Philip Glass would suddenly surge forward during the movie and arrest the audience's attention in those dramatic moments when Truman began to realize the truth about his world. But those sorts of moments are a rarity in modern film and television, whereas in videogames, music serves this function constantly.

In writing the musical score for *The Da Vinci Code* video game, I was able to create vocal motets in a liturgical style for puzzle sequences, action tracks with bombastic orchestral flourishes mixed with contemporary rhythms, and a cinematic underscore that was nearly operatic in nature. This music occupies much more of the gamer's attention, because it serves to keep the gamer immersed in the world of the game, while still solving a puzzle or navigating an action sequence to its successful conclusion. Videogames offer many more opportunities to create ambitious music, and I have found this to be very inspiring.

ScoreNotes: How long have you been collaborating with music producer Winnie Waldron, and what are some of the reasons why you two make such a good team?

Winifred Phillips: We started working together at National Public Radio on the *Radio Tales* series. We both continued with the series when it transitioned to Sirius XM Radio, and when I jumped ship and plunged into the videogame field, she jumped with me. Winnie Waldron has a multitude of amazing talents. In addition to producing my music for *Radio Tales,* she was also script editor for that series, so she has a thorough understanding of what makes a good story. In our videogame work, she constantly stresses that the music must serve the best interests of the story and fuel its momentum. Winnie and I have a very close working relationship, and she is frequently present while I'm composing. Her guidance and feedback are invaluable to me. In the tradition of the best music producers in the field, Winnie has an instinctive and profound understanding of what the listening audience will enjoy, and what will turn them off. Working with Winnie has been and continues to be one of the most satisfying collaborations I've ever experienced. I can't imagine ever working without her.

ScoreNotes: When you write scores for videogames based on movies, are you typically asked to account for the style of music heard within the film itself? Or are you generally given a good bit of breathing room to develop a stand-alone score?

Winifred Phillips: It has been my experience that the style of the upcoming film's score is a complete mystery to the developers, which means that I'm given freedom to create music for the game in a style that makes sense to me. It is my understanding that, while the developers would like to incorporate the musical style of the film into the game, it isn't possible in the majority of cases. For the game to be ready in time to launch alongside the film, the music composition for the game must begin long before the film composer has written a single note. I've heard that there are some exceptions—most notably for film sequels in which the musical style of the series has been firmly established—but I haven't worked on projects that are part of a series.

The most information I've ever had about the upcoming film's score is the identity of the composer, and that really isn't much help. For example, I knew that Michael Giacchino would be creating the music for the *Speed Racer* film, but his work is quite varied, which meant that I had no idea what his choices would be like for the film. So I went ahead and scored the videogame in an eclectic, retro-futuristic style that I thought would best accentuate the glossy, neon fantasy world that the Wachowski Brothers had created. When I finally went to the film and heard Giacchino's score, it couldn't have been more different from what I'd done. But it's perfectly fine for the game score and the movie score to be different. A game and a movie are unique mediums, so why shouldn't their music be unique, too?

My experience was the same for the *Charlie and the Chocolate Factory* project—I knew that Danny Elfman would be scoring the film, but his style can be very divergent from project to project, so I went ahead and scored the game in a way that made sense to me. And it turned out that my approach was radically different from Elfman's, so the experience was much the same for me as it was on *Speed Racer*, but with one exception. It turns out that Tim Burton (the director of *Charlie and the Chocolate Factory*) is an extremely hands-on director with every aspect of his projects, including the associated games. He personally approved every track I wrote for *Charlie and the Chocolate Factory*. That was a tremendous thrill for me, and even more so when I heard how different Danny Elfman's score was from mine. It goes to show that two different composers can have two very different musical approaches to the same subject matter, and both can be equally appropriate.

ScoreNotes: Can you touch on the rather innovative approach you took to create the organic score for *SimAnimals*?

Winifred Phillips: With the *SimAnimals* project, I started with the main theme. Arriving at a style for the theme took some experimentation, and the development team at Electronic Arts was very helpful during this time. Once the main theme was written, the rest of the track flowed very naturally from it. The main theme has some post-minimalist elements in its composition but is also highly dynamic, with a strong emphasis on melody. *SimAnimals* is a member of the simulation genre of games, in which many things are happening at once in a large environment that the gamer can influence but never completely control. It was my goal that the music should reflect this sense of simultaneous activity, while still conveying the warmth and the upbeat attitude that have always characterized games in the Sims franchise.

ScoreNotes: You created a simply wonderful track entitled "Go Mario" on the Game Music compilation album, *Best of the Best*. Was that a one-off assignment that you approached with great enthusiasm? It's quite a catchy rendition!

Winifred Phillips: Thanks very much! I enjoyed working on that track. The assignment for the album was to create a unique rendition of a classic videogame song, with the goal of paying tribute to the original piece, while still bringing a fresh approach to the work. Winnie immediately suggested the theme song from *Super Mario Bros.* It is such a part of videogame history and culture, and I was thrilled that she thought of it. I performed a nearly cappella vocal version of the main theme from *Super Mario Bros.*, adorned with classic 8-bit style sound effects and kazoos. The whole purpose of the approach was to convey the fun of the original game. I knew it was a risk to perform a cover version of a song that was so well loved, so I was very happy that my version of the song was so well received. I'm glad that you liked it!

ScoreNotes: Staying on the topic of game music—can you please touch on some of the awards you've either won or have been nominated for?

Winifred Phillips: My first project as a videogame composer was *God of War.* As members of the music team for that project, Winnie and I were honored to receive the Interactive Achievement Award from the Interactive Academy of Arts and Sciences, four Game Audio Network Guild awards (including Music of the Year), and many "Best Original Music" awards from sites like GameZone, GameSpot, and IGN. I've also been nominated for a G.A.N.G. Award for the music I wrote for the *Shrek the Third* videogame, and I received a nomination from the Hollywood Music Awards for the music I wrote for the *Speed Racer* game.

ScoreNotes: Your impact on the videogame music industry has been quite positive (as the recognition you just mentioned attests to). I feel your work is impressive both within the context of the games and as stand-alone soundtrack experiences. Do you think this is a field more female composers may choose to enter based on your success in it?

Winifred Phillips: Thank you very much! I'd certainly like to think that the participation of women like Winnie and myself may help reduce the gender gap in some small way. There are significant quality-of-life issues that continue to be a greater hindrance to women than to men in regards to working in the videogame field, but recent improvements in working conditions may open doors for women to join the industry in greater numbers. More specifically, however, women are still a very small minority in the field of music composition for media of any kind, whether it is in films, television, or videogames. I don't know exactly why this is, and I suspect that there are many and various reasons for the current state of gender unbalance. While organizations like the Women in Games Special Interest Group at the IGDA are helpful for issues regarding the industry as a whole, I think the barriers for female composers are probably unique. I'm actually heartened by the story of Marin Alsop, who made history at the Baltimore Symphony Orchestra in 2007 by taking up the baton as the first female conductor of a major symphony orchestra. I think the image of a woman standing at that highly-visible conductor's podium could help the cause of female composers in America by showing a woman in a position of authority in the world of orchestral music.

ScoreNotes: Aside from composing, what are some other creative interests that you enjoy being involved with?

Winifred Phillips: When I have free time (which has become a precious rarity), I enjoy creative writing, specifically in the fantasy genre. I've had short stories published in the *Sword and Sorceress XX* anthology and in Marion Zimmer Bradley's *Fantasy* magazine. I have a great passion for fantasy and mythology and would love to create music for a fantasy role-playing videogame in the future.

25 *Keeping Score* with Inon Zur

Used by permission.

Inon Zur.

Inon Zur is a stalwart of the game music industry. His music can be heard in such popular games as *Crysis*, the *Prince of Persia* series, *Lineage II: Oath of Blood*, and more!

In the following interview, Inon takes us into the studio of a game composer for a fascinating discussion about the unique aspect of scoring videogames. As you'll read below, writing music for videogames is a world apart from film music and presents a whole new set of challenges that are foreign to the cinema!

I think you'll enjoy this conversation with someone I consider to be among the top composers in this industry…

Inon Zur (2009)

ScoreNotes: When you were first starting out in the composing field, did you ever anticipate having a career in the videogame arena?

Inon Zur: Definitely, no. We have to remember that most of my musical knowledge as far as studying was concerned was done between 1980 and 1992; during this time videogames were mostly electronic sounds. I was really surprised when I was approached by my agent later in 1996, and he asked if I wanted to compose for games. He started sending me orchestral scores that were written for the medium, and I was like, wow, I didn't know this type of music was needed for games, and if this is the deal, then why not.

ScoreNotes: What were some of factors that lured you into game music?

Inon Zur: When a composer is writing something, he either writes it to the picture or he writes a symphony. In videogames, it's actually both. You're not locked to picture, but you do need to write for a defined story with a certain goal or path. The motions, emotions, and all the factors are already built in there, and you have to fill it with the musical emotion. So it has both worlds inside it, which makes it very intriguing and quite interesting.

ScoreNotes: Can you take us back to your work on the *Prince of Persia* videogame series and tell us about some of the different themes and motifs that powered those soundtracks?

Inon Zur: Overall, *Prince of Persia* is a fantasy, so that is one component about it that the composer needs to understand before he starts composing. The second thing is that *Prince of Persia* embodies an ethnic quality to it. Both factors influenced me a lot, so the way I orchestrated and composed it was in a storytelling style rather than something that sounds modern. I also used a lot of motifs, instruments, and scales. These two factors were pretty much the most influential elements with the creative writing process.

Now, the world of *Prince of Persia* always had the human versus something that is not very human and usually very evil. Generally, the emotions in *Prince of Persia* and the challenges that exist in the world are very humanlike, but overall the outcomes were always in an exaggerated proportion that is a fairytale-*ish* style. So the trick is to get very up close and personal when it comes to the actual Prince and what he feels, yet get really grand and emotional when it comes to the large battle. So you have to sort of play within these two arenas, and this is true to all *Prince of Persia's* games.

Now, each one of them is very, very different from the other one. First, in the *Sands of Time*, which I did not compose, the Prince was very young, and it was more ambient/

Middle Eastern. With the second, third, and fourth, the Prince is growing up, and with it, the music also matures. Maturing meant more orchestral music, more serious themes, more use of complicated music rather than rhythms and melodies. I can say that the last one [*Prince of Persia*] really brought it to a new climax because of the very emotional romance that was going on in the storyline. So we had to address this issue, too, which actually opened a lot of opportunities for interesting music.

ScoreNotes: Does a project like *Lineage II: Chronicle V: Oath Of Blood* stand out as a special project to you? I felt that the score for this title was particularly moving and dramatic!

Inon Zur: It was special because I was basically given a free hand to do whatever I wanted. The most interesting thing about *Lineage* is that most of the cues that I wrote had one or maybe two words that described what I needed to do. Love…deception…intrigue…evil. That's it! Write the cue!! [Laughs] But it allowed me to basically exercise one of the more free-writing styles that I ever did because I really had almost no description of what's going on. They just wanted the emotion, period. It was a very interesting approach, so yes, that was a lot of fun.

ScoreNotes: Can you comment on the use of the haunting and dramatic vocals heard on some of the tracks?

Inon Zur: Vocals always evoke different emotions. When you hear a vocal, it's easier to identify. Sometimes it doesn't even matter if you understand the lyrics or not. Just hearing the human voice evokes some emotions that sometimes do not occur when you don't use it. So it could be very effective when we're talking about the most delicate and sensitive human emotions.

ScoreNotes: As we all know, there are high levels of complexity and thought put into the development of game titles. What would you say are some of the toughest components to juggle while scoring a videogame?

Inon Zur: I liken it to movies where composers write the music to the picture, and he or she really cares that the music will address what's going on there. Period. In games, that's about 50 percent of it. The other 50 percent are the different cues of the music in the game, because you're not writing music for a certain specific thought. You write music for a level, a map, an area. So lets say a minute and a half to a two-minute sequence of music needs to serve an area where the player spends a good 45 minutes on that level or environment. So there starts what we call the *implementation state*. As a composer, you have to be very aware of the fact that the music has to serve a place where it wouldn't necessarily hit every point, sword hit, or gunshot, etc. It should be there and, again, evoke certain emotions and describe what's going on in a general way. But if you write it with a certain approach and the music just loops and loops and loops, the player will usually get tired of it after 10 minutes and will shut it off. So here comes the next part.

The next tactic is how you compose in a way that you can take what you've composed and actually pull it apart, break it down to different stems, loops, and elements, and play them separately in particular spots so you won't feel that the music is repeating itself again and again. This is the basic idea. Now, if you are progressing further, such as going from fighting single enemies to tens of enemies, then maybe you want to increase the intensity of the music. How do you increase the intensity when all that you have in the budget is enough to compose two minutes? Well, there are a lot of methods to do it, and I don't want to really get technical here, but these are some of the components that composers in other media don't have to worry about, but it's part of our method.

ScoreNotes: Have you ever had an experience when you were playing a game you had worked on and you notice that the music was not used in the manner that you intended it to?

Inon Zur: Oh, sure. It happened a lot during the early stages when the process was all a bit more, let's say, primitive. But also it sometimes has to do with people who were not as professional as I expected them to be. I'm trying to be involved as much as I can with the implementation part, but sometimes they just say to me, "Don't worry about it; we'll take care of it." And then I really start to worry.

ScoreNotes: In some respects, much like a film composer hands off the music to the director, sometimes you don't know just exactly how it will be used.

Inon Zur: That's true.

ScoreNotes: Can you comment on just how much more serious and intense the gaming experience has become thanks to the use of these well thought out, often orchestral, scores?

Inon Zur: Games are looking to be closer and closer to movies (with the interactive component), and it's not all about the challenge of winning or losing in games. It's about the way the game looks, the way the game feels, and the emotional impact that the game has on the player. For example, when people are playing *Fallout*, many of them have told me that they had to stop playing after 15 minutes because they were too scared. So, basically, in this way, the music has a lot to contribute. I think that the increased awareness in the last five or six years about the importance of it and the attention that is being directed to music in games, has definitely created a very unique and much higher quality product.

26 *Keeping Score* with Cris Velasco

Cris Velasco.

omposer **Cris Velasco** has paid his dues. In the process, he's essentially proven a classic point that if someone wants to succeed badly enough, and has the talent to do so, then there is a path forward.

In this segment, Cris takes us back to his early days of composing and shares some rather interesting recollections about what he had to do to earn his stripes in the business. Now one of the premiere composers in the videogame industry, Cris has worked on such top titles as *God of War, Beowulf, Clive Barker's Jericho,* and more...

Cris Velasco (2009)
ScoreNotes: Can you describe to us what it's like to be on the front lines of the emerging and dynamic videogame music scenc?

169

Cris Velasco: I definitely feel very lucky to be here. I probably just got into the business at the last possible second while people were still not convinced that game music would be anything noteworthy. I started, I think, five years ago, and it went from where it was, just a complete rarity, to actually having a live music budget; and even then, we just brought a few soloists into the studio. Now, almost every project I'm doing is getting at least a 60-piece orchestra. I've definitely, firsthand, seen it go from small to large in just a few years.

ScoreNotes: Before you became engrossed in game music, what were some of the projects you had worked on during the earlier days of your career?

Cris Velasco: I started out doing some orchestrating for Disney and did the odd short film here and there. I actually knew pretty early on after graduating from UCLA that I wanted to get into the gaming industry. It took a long time; I definitely paid my dues. It's almost embarrassing to say, but it took me like eight years to go from graduation to actually making a living writing music.

ScoreNotes: Often times, we hear about the up and coming film composers who have to work on small, independent projects to make their mark. Is there any type of a parallel trajectory in the world of game music to "make it" in the business?

Cris Velasco: Yeah, kind of. My very, very first project, that I don't often talk about just because it didn't feel like my "real" first game music experience, was in the mod community, which is short for modification. A lot of times kids who want to be programmers or somehow work in the game industry will get together with some other like-minded people that really don't have a lot of professional experience and will work on mods. They'll take a popular game like *Half Life,* for instance, which is the game I worked on, and will take the source code from the real developer, which allows them to get inside the inner workings of the game and change things around and essentially make their own game out of it. I did a *Half Life* mod called *Gunmen Chronicles.* It started out with just a bunch of kids having fun, and I was looking for an opportunity to score a game even if it wasn't going to pay anything. I just wanted to build up my chops for writing. It just so happened that I picked an excellent one to work on because this mod seemed professional enough that Valve, the original creators of *Half Life,* discovered it and decided that they wanted to fund this thing and really get it up to speed. It was actually picked up between Valve and Sierra and was released. You can still go to Best Buy today and find this game there. That was sort of my first "music for games" experience.

After that, nothing happened for a while. It didn't really give my career a shot in the arm I was hoping it would. But, after a lot of weird, odd jobs, musically speaking, I finally got the opportunity to write a few minutes of music for the *Battlestar Galactica* game five years ago. That was with Vivindi Universal, and they liked what they heard and hired me to write more and more for that game. I went on to do four more games for them, and after that my career just took off.

ScoreNotes: Thank you for sharing how you got your start in the business. This is the kind of background that I think many readers would be interested in reading about because there is a lot of sacrificing that goes on behind the scenes.

Cris Velasco: It's funny. I have a lot of friends that are also composers, and it's always better when you can rise up the ranks with your own friends and sort of leave no man behind. But it doesn't always happen that way. So I have a lot of friends who have asked me for pointers, and I tell all of them my story about working with mods and just getting a feeling for writing for games and the mechanics of game music, about how it has to loop and getting it more interactive with the game play. But I always stress to everybody to work on mods to get their feet wet. And almost everyone turned their noses up to that because it's not sexy, there's no money in it, and they just want to go 0 to 60 just like that.

I had one friend who took my advice. I sort of laid out a plan for him and advised him to look at all the different mods being made in the community and find two or three that are really good and then do a professional sounding demo for them and just get on board. You're not gonna make money, but if those guys are any good, they'll eventually get picked up by some big gaming company, and if your music is good, they're going to remember you, and that's sort of your in to a bigger company. Nobody did it but this one guy, and today he's an audio director for a company.

ScoreNotes: Sometimes there are no shortcuts, and you really do have to get in there and grind it out.

Cris Velasco: There's a very, very small percentage that gets really lucky and just makes it happen almost immediately. But for the rest of us, it's kind of a grueling process. Like we said, paying your dues, honing your craft, and making connections. If you're tenacious enough and have talent, I really think that eventually it will happen.

ScoreNotes: Can you please tell us about some of your contributions to the *God of War* series?

Cris Velasco: I would never say that *God of War* single-handedly made my career, but it definitely played a big part. I'm not the only composer on it, of course . . . there are four to five composers working on each one, and we all kind of take the credit for these scores. But the first one kind of really came out of nowhere. I had a friend, Victor Rodriguez, over at Sony in Santa Monica at the time who was telling me that he had a new game coming up and felt that it had potential to be huge and wanted me to demo for it. He kind of described it, said it sounded great and would be something that I would love to work on. I submitted a demo for that, and luckily they liked it and brought me on board along with everyone else. That game turned out to be such a monster hit for them, and it was the same for the composers. It really meant a lot, even though there were four or five of us, to say that you were on the composing team for *God of War*. It instantly gave you some street cred [laughs].

ScoreNotes: When you talk about a group dynamic, such as the team of composers on this project, did you collaborate amongst yourselves to develop the material?

Cris Velasco: No, the guys at Sony managed all of us, and there wasn't, at least for my part, interaction between composers. I'd just get a call from someone over there (with instructions on what level I had to work on). They would make sure that each composer was writing within the style guides of *God of War*, sort of how we had determined what that music was going to sound like.

ScoreNotes: Can you take us a bit behind the scenes and tell us about your time spent working on *Clive Barker's Jericho*?

Cris Velasco: *Clive Barker's Jericho*, and I've said this before in other interviews and it's still completely true to this day, was a dream project for me. I've been a huge Clive Barker fan since I was a kid. Even as a much younger kid, I would go to my friend's house, and every single weekend we'd rent the first two *Hellraiser* movies and watch those over and over again. I've continued to be a fan throughout my whole life, pretty much.

It's funny. To show you where my head was at with Clive, I started out as a huge fan even before I was in music—I got a pretty late start in music, like in my early 20s—and so I went from just being a fan. I would show up with my book when he was doing book signings in Los Angeles and would feel nervous about meeting him in person and shaking his hand. When I eventually went to college and got into composing a few years later, I'm still going to book signings to meet the guy, and now he's seen me over and over and over throughout the years, so he's starting to kind of remember me. So I transitioned into telling him that I was a composer and that one day I would be working with him. I told him it's my dream that this is going to be happen and just to be on guard [laughs]. He was super nice about it and encouraging.

Maybe a couple years later, when I had my first demo CD, I brought it to him at the signing, and I was very nervous about handing it over to him because I respected him so much, and if he hated it, it would crush me. But I gave him the CD, and nothing really happened from there. I was waiting in line at another signing, and his assistant was there, and I asked her if he had listened to the CD yet. She said, yes, that they listened to it on the way back in the car after I had given it to him, and he really liked it. That gave me the encouragement to go talk to him again. And this is like over 10 years of meeting this guy at book signings. Finally, we got to the point where he actually called me up at home and said, "Hey, Chris, I've got this videogame I'm doing (*Clive Barker's Demonik*), and I'd be really honored if you would think about writing music for *Demonik*. And you know, I flipped out, of course. I got under contract, and I went to meetings at his house about it, and the developer was there as well. It was unbelievable. And then a couple weeks later, the whole game got cancelled. I was just devastated.

So after that, like a year later, I was talking to him on the phone—now I just kind of keep in touch with him, going from the fanboy phase into just being friends phase—and he said, "Hey, I actually have this other game, *Jericho*. If you'd be interested in scoring that, maybe we can finally make this thing happen." I said, "Of course," and was in negotiations with Codemasters about it, and something happened where they actually stopped taking my calls. And that was that. I was just not on *Jericho* at all. This was apparently unbeknownst to Clive. He thought I was working on it the whole time. And then about a month before the release of *Jericho*, I get a call from Codemasters saying, "Hey Chris, could you come in and rewrite all the music for *Jericho* in like three weeks?" It was almost two hours of music, and I was already working on two projects at the time. I thought this was finally my opportunity to work with Clive, and I knew I couldn't drop the other things because I'm not going to let my clients down. But I thought somehow I'll make this happen, so I said, "Sure, I'll do it." I called up Clive and asked him what happened. He said they hired somebody else and he didn't know about it. They had just had a big meeting at Clive's house, and he had apparently flipped out when he heard the music and asked if I had actually written the music.

So they hired me, and I worked very hard, and not only did we churn out two hours of music for the game, but in that time, we also went up to Skywalker Ranch and recorded a live choir for it.

ScoreNotes: Wow, what a topsy-turvy adventure that was!

Cris Velasco: Yeah, it was bananas.

ScoreNotes: In that one month when all this was happening, what was your average day like during that time period?

Cris Velasco: My schedule was a minimum 18-hour workday, and maximum was 20 to 22 hours. It was brutal.

ScoreNotes: It must have been tough remaining creative for such long hours at a time, no?

Cris Velasco: Well, you know, I couldn't say no to this dream project, and you have to do what you have to do.

ScoreNotes: Earlier in our conversation, you mentioned that you got a late start in the business. Did you find that you had to work harder to catch up, or did composing just seem to come naturally for you?

Cris Velasco: It just kind of clicked naturally. When I graduated from high school, I had just started playing guitar, which was the only music I knew at the time. I had a death metal band actually [laughs]. From there, I didn't know what I wanted to do with my life. I didn't go off to a university right away; I went to my local junior college just to figure my stuff out. I took a class in pretty much everything to figure out just what I was actually interested in to make it my life. Nothing was really clicking, and then I took a music appreciation course, which just seemed like an easy credit but seemed interesting, too. That course changed my life.

We were listening to the last movement of Mozart's 40th Symphony, and I had an epiphany in class that this is amazing and this is what I wanted to do with my life, which was kind of hilarious because I didn't even know how to read music. I'm not sure if I had even been to the symphony at that point, but just something about that Mozart piece really spoke to me so profoundly that it did change my life. From there, I kind of dropped everything and enrolled only in music classes. A year later, I transferred to UCLA in their composition department, studied really hard over there, and got my degree. And here I am today.

27 *Keeping Score* with Jesper Kyd

Used by permission.

Jesper Kyd.

J esper Kyd is entrenched in the heart of today's game music movement. Having worked on such notable titles as *Assassin's Creed* and the *Hitman* series, Jesper has a strong grasp on what a videogame needs from its score. In fact, I feel it's composers like him who are playing a key role in the rapid rise of game music as an accepted and popular option for soundtrack lovers.

In this interview, Jesper gives us a rather enlightening glimpse into his motivations as a composer in this field. He also discusses some of the inner workings that went into the creation of his scores and touches on the need for an increased availability of videogame soundtracks in the commercial market...

Jesper Kyd (2009)

ScoreNotes: What is it like to write scores for such an interactive medium as game music?

175

Jesper Kyd: I guess it depends on what you compare it to. It's definitely very challenging to think that videogame music is easy. It's definitely not the case. Videogame music had kind of a bad reputation there for a while, which has pretty much changed now, but the bad rep being that it's not as well composed as film scores. I just want to add that it is very difficult to create music for a videogame that stands out. For film, you have film music schools, you have teachers, you have educators, and everything to help you fit into what a good Hollywood film score should sound like. For games, I have had to, on a personal level, just kind of figure everything out on my own. So yeah, of course you can always come in and say I'll do my film style for the videogame and treat it like that, which is fine and it's being done, but it's not really a case where the videogame music shines the most or is being pushed as far as it can. It should be handled with a kind of attention to detail and attention to what makes a good score for a videogame, which is not the same as what makes a good score for a film.

ScoreNotes: So is it safe to say there is more of an institution in place around film scoring and that the nature of game music just might be too new?

Jesper Kyd: Yes, it is, but there is a flip side to that. There's definitely an institution. There are certain ways things are when it comes to film music. If you're interested in listening to game scores, or you play a game and you like the music and you want to find it, it's a little bit harder to find the music. It's not as readily available. I don't want to say it's an "underground" scene because there are so many fans and gamers, and they are so into the music when there is a good score out there, but it's definitely more in that [underground] area.

The thing about it is that there are at least as many fans of videogame music as there are, I feel, for film music. It's just that film music is much more visible; there's a promotional package behind it, and they do things the way they've done [them] for years regarding the way that they promote their scores. In games, sometimes a great score is never even promoted. The game sells eight million copies, and suddenly all the fans are like ripping the music from the game and going out there and finding the music anyway, even though it was never released. Things like that can't happen with a film. I mean sometimes you have a DVD that has its own soundtrack, but it's really rare that you'll find a movie [for which] you can play the soundtrack option without the sound effects. But in a videogame, the fans go inside the game, they rip out the music, and they spread it around on the Internet. There are tons of different bootleg versions of the *Assassin's Creed* score out there because it took us over a year to get the soundtrack out.

ScoreNotes: This is all probably to the detriment of the composers who are working very hard in creating these scores. Ideally, would you like to see a regular interval of soundtrack releases with these games?

Jesper Kyd: Yes, that would be great. I probably have more scores out than other composers working in the game industry (at least 10 on iTunes). Some of us are able to get it out, but there is no set way in which these things always get put out. That's something I would like to see improve.

ScoreNotes: What aspect do you enjoy the most about being a composer for games, and what would you say is the most difficult?

Jesper Kyd: Oh, that's easy: the creative freedom. It's also the hardest part. If you are able to convince the team to give you almost creative freedom, then you know you are in for a rewarding ride but also a tough ride because you have to come up with a lot of ideas. But it's very cool because you actually get to come up with ideas to help the team find the right music style. In movies, and personally with the films I've done, it's been more a collaboration between the director and the composer. Sometimes the director knows what he wants, and you kind of go in that direction, and obviously other times you get a bit more creative freedom there as well. But with game scores, the creative freedom is just vast because you don't always have the images—you don't have the picture. So you don't have to slave to the picture; you can pull back further. You don't have to be so up-close and look at every little scene that changes. You have to be aware of these things in videogames as well, but you have to be aware of the overall mood and atmosphere, so you have to pull back a little bit further.

ScoreNotes: One of the marquee projects of yours, *Assassin's Creed*, offered quite an interesting palette of music. Did you find any aspect of the game particularly challenging to score given the rather distinct differences of the game's locations?

Jesper Kyd: Yeah, the hardest part was probably scoring the escape sequences for the game, which, funnily enough, are the tracks that people seem to be responding to the most. But they were tricky to find because we didn't quite know what we wanted, but we knew we wanted something that was really "out there." And finding the fine line of sci-fi scoring—because there is a sci-fi element to *Assassin's Creed*—and not going too far with it because we had to make sure it fit the rest of the score, which is inspired more by the Middle Ages. Finding that line between those two [sci-fi and fantasy] was probably the hardest part about that score.

ScoreNotes: How motivating is it when you're brought on to score ambitious projects like an *Assassin's Creed*?

Jesper Kyd: When I was involved with it, it was probably a year and a half before it was released. So what I saw was not much. I was working more from concept art and these things. I knew it was an extremely ambitious title, but never really knew from the beginning if they were going to be able to do everything they said they were going to do; it was just so out there. They told me things [about the game] like its mysticism, the tragedy of the crusades, people getting killed in the name of religion. It was very interesting to put all these elements into a videogame score. It's not very often you get to have underlying tragic elements; it's more like the film realm where you're used to dealing with those things.

ScoreNotes: Is there a type of videogame you enjoy writing for more than other types? I'm not referring to genre—rather, specific to the gameplay (for example, first-person, arcade-style RPGs).

Jesper Kyd: Yeah, there is. I like to write for games that take the story seriously. I think all games have somewhat of a story, but some games take the story and put it much more into focus. Just as in writing for film, you get to do really dramatic stuff. So that's definitely my preference, to support a great story.

ScoreNotes: It seems more and more that game scores are indeed heading toward the seriousness and respectability of film. Just how bright a future does game music have, in your opinion?

Jesper Kyd: I think we've come a long way. There's been a lot of emphasis put on quality composition lately, and film composers coming into the game industry have certainly brought a sense of quality composition. I do think we have to remember that quality composition isn't everything. I think, right now, it's being looked at as one of the most important things. I could be wrong, but that's the sense I get, and I think we need to remember to focus on creating original music also. Just because a game sounds as good as a movie, that doesn't really impress me. If you hire a good film composer, your game will sound as good as a film. But is that really what it's about? I think it's more about creating something as original as the game. You have these highly original games coming out, and I think we need to match that with highly original music. Music that's highly creative and really out there. When you hire a film composer, you usually hire them to do their thing, and then you get that film sound for that game. But, again, a game is not a film, unless all you support are the cut scenes and the cinematics; then obviously there is basically no difference. But what about when you're running around and exploring, or you're sneaking around or engaged in combat? All these things are not the same as the kind of music you'd write for film.

ScoreNotes: Yes, and it could probably take a film composer off guard because I imagine some of the nuances in game playing require a certain, different type of approach be taken for the music to work correctly in the context of a game.

Jesper Kyd: Yeah, you do. I've scored eight feature films so far, so I'm getting pretty familiar with scoring film. It's very interesting. For example, you can have like an action scene, and you have 30 seconds of build up, and then you have one minute of really intense action maybe, and then you have dialogue where you have to go way down to make room, and you go into some suspense and tension... and this is all like in three minutes! But in a game, you're often asked, "Oh, we need a four-minute combat cue. And the intensity needs to be on 11 for all four minutes." You realize that's not the same as writing what I just described for film. It's about staying in the same mood for a long time. How do you do that and keep it interesting? It's a different mentality... it's almost like writing a song, a combat song.

ScoreNotes: As we wrap up here, I often wonder if game composers like to sit down and actually play the games they write music for. Do you consider yourself an avid gamer?

Jesper Kyd: I am a gamer. I don't have as much time to play as I want, but I definitely like to pick up the game pad and play some games.

28 *Keeping Score* with Jason Graves

Jason Graves.

Used by permission.

There is much to like about the music of **Jason Graves**. Here, we have a composer who has delivered one highly effective score after another in the videogame medium and has established a track record of reliability amongst fans and game developers while doing so. His work has earned him numerous accolades including the two prestigious BAFTA awards (British Academy of Film and Television Arts) for his superlative work on *Dead Space,* the immensely popular horror-action title released in 2008.

As that fine line of fan popularity between game music and film scores is blurred even further, it's the effective, memorable work from composers like Jason that is making the difference ...

Jason Graves (2009)

ScoreNotes: What are some of the creative directions in which you were able to guide the music of *Section 8*?

Jason Graves: The only real instruction that TimeGate provided was for the score to have a gung-ho "exploring the stars with really big guns" feel to it. Some of the tracks they picked as suggestions were very breakbeat-based, like "The Chemical Brothers" or "The Prodigy"—pretty much no orchestral music in there at all. However, they seemed less concerned with those tracks and more concerned with what I could bring to the game that would create a unique playing experience.

So I took the idea of the orchestral score I had in my head and tweaked it out a little bit—a breakbeat here, maybe a dance beat there, me playing some nasty guitar in this one, tweak and play my analog synths for that one. I was like a kid in a candy store! Sometimes specific genre games can be very limiting, but no one ever said things like "We don't want any trumpets or woodwinds" or "All the pieces have to be fast with breakbeats." I was given total freedom to brainstorm and try different things. There was one piece where I was asked to change a snare drum sound. That was pretty much the extent of the corrections involved once the main theme was established. Of course, if the score isn't well received in the game or as a soundtrack, I have only myself to blame! But I am personally happy with the final result, regardless.

ScoreNotes: Is the creative freedom on a score like *Section 8* one of the reasons that makes writing game music such a great place for composers?

Jason Graves: Absolutely! I don't know of any other medium that allows such creative freedom, and I've spent lots of time in film, television, commercials, and radio. I think it has a lot to do with the sheer amount of music that needs to be produced, combined with the nonlinear aspects of music for games. For TV and especially film, an AAA composer has a team of five to ten people who are there to help with anything from finishing up last night's cue, orchestrating, or making travel arrangements for the recording date. The same goes for the director you're working for. They have plenty of people helping and can devote time towards musical corrections, conversations about plot points, etc.

In games, we're a much smaller, though more voracious, group of artists. I don't have any assistants to compose music for me, fix my computer, or get me a cup of coffee. The audio director I'm working with is the sole person responsible for *all* the audio in the game—not just my music. We're always very focused and well-meaning towards each other, but there's a general unspoken understanding that everyone is working at max capacity and time is short, so let's do the best job we can as quickly as we can and get it all in the game before it ships. And there are two of us, not ten or twenty. That kind of "survival instinct" can bring out the best in people. You know, the whole "grace under fire" thing.

Speaking of creative freedom, I feel extremely lucky to have minimal corrections to my music once it's been submitted. There were a few pieces we tweaked a little for *Dead Space*, there was the snare drum fix for *Section 8*, [and] another recent game had two or three tweaks out of the 40-plus cues. Compare that to a commercial I did this week: The fifteen-second version had more than ten revisions! I would like to think that's a reflection on the music approval process in these different mediums and not directly related to my music.

Combine all of that with the idea of nonlinear storytelling in games and you have a whole new way to represent the story through music. No longer are you dependent on frame rate, minutes, and seconds to make the scene play perfectly. My general instructions for any game are pretty much things like: "We're going to need a few more of those three-minute combat cues. While you're at it, go ahead and do four more of the pre-combat cues as well; two minutes each would be fine, thanks." I get to score ideas and emotions, free of any markers, hit-points, or video edits.

Not to say that I don't enjoy composing to picture for film or game cinematics. It's actually one of my favorite things to do—like trying to figure out a musical puzzle. But it does have more restrictions and requirements than the open freedom of in-game music.

ScoreNotes: Can you talk about the combination of orchestral elements and electronic tools that you were able to bring together for the music?

Jason Graves: That was the main reason I decided to take the job when TimeGate called with the offer. I was their first choice, which is very flattering, but I wasn't interested in composing the same kind of score I had done in the past. I was afraid that was exactly the kind of score they were going to ask me to do. Fortunately, that was not the case. I saw *Section 8* as a great opportunity to take my three musical passions and blend them together into a soundtrack: orchestral music, guitars, and synthesizers. The best part about using such diverse instruments is I was able to perform all the guitars and synths myself, which was an absolute blast to do.

While the score is based firmly in the orchestral world, I was able to bring the other elements in and treat them as additional members of the ensemble. The end result is a score that uses guitars and synthesizers more as textural elements that blend and support the orchestra and sometimes take the lead when needed.

There are two main locations in the campaign mode of *Section 8*: temperate and desert. I used a more traditional orchestra, as well as more traditional music composition, for the temperate location. The desert has the hybrid rock/synth edge to it, along with more dissonant harmonies and [a] modern approach to the music. I also used the desert as a great excuse to pull out all my percussion instruments and record myself playing.

Used by permission.

ScoreNotes: I'd like to look back on another project of yours—the harrowing and intense game, *Dead Space*. Please tell us about the feedback you received for your work on this?

Jason Graves: There were two very distinct experiences I remember from *Dead Space*. The first was during the composition, wondering if such a brutal, non-melodic score would find any favor with critics or fans. The second experience was the feedback after the game was released. Truthfully, I was a bit overwhelmed at the response. I continue to get e-mails and messages from fans, both people who play games and [people who] make them. I think the entire audio team from *Dead Space* was pleasantly surprised, albeit happily satisfied, at the awards and press that the audio garnered.

ScoreNotes: Can you discuss the rather elaborate implementation of your music in *Dead Space*?

Jason Graves: The main direction I had from EA was to create a score that could seamlessly move from subtle and spooky to extreme tension in a moment's notice, depending on the gameplay. In order for a single piece of music to have this kind of flexibility, *Dead Space* needed an adaptive score, meaning music that actively changes with gameplay. EA had already determined we needed four individual levels of music to smoothly transition from the lowest to the highest intensity levels.

I approached the music one of two ways. I would compose a high intensity cue and then deconstruct it and break it down into those four levels. This technique worked well for large creature battles—pieces that were fairly loud from the first level and simply got more rhythmically intense as the levels increased. The second technique was to compose the cue from the ground up, first creating a very creepy, quiet "level one" and building the whole piece up from there. This was the way most pieces were composed because it allowed for the entire dynamic range of the music.

ScoreNotes: As someone who composes game music, how well versed do you have to be about the technologies that are being used for today's titles as it relates to the audio?

Jason Graves: An easy answer to that question would be the following: "Your knowledge of game audio technology need only be as deep and detailed as your desire to work in said field." Another easy answer would simply be "*Yes.*"

Seriously, the more informed you are about the technology that will be placing your music in the game and triggering your music at the (hopefully) proper time, the better off you are as both a composer and part of the team. Integration is *everything* when it comes to game scores. The worst-sounding score could get a world-class implementation in a game and come out winning awards. On the other hand, a brilliant score can get positively mangled by the implementation and not even get noticed or, even worse, turned off and replaced by an iPod.

The bottom line is the more you know about the way your music is being implemented, the better music you can compose for the game.

ScoreNotes: Can you share the details behind the BAFTA award you had won and what it meant for you personally?

Jason Graves: Wow, where do you start? I know it sounds like a cliché, but just to be nominated for something like that is a really amazing feeling. I simply assumed if I made plans to attend the awards in London that I would obviously not win anything, but if I didn't attend, I would win and would regret missing it. I finally decided it would be a wonderful experience just to be there, regardless of the outcome.

The audio in *Dead Space* was nominated for two awards—"Use of Audio," which included sound effects, dialog and music; and "Original Score." We won "Use of

Audio" first, which truthfully I expected to a certain extent and happily went onstage to accept on behalf of the whole team. When they announced my name for "Original Score," it was truly one of those out-of-body experiences you read about.

I put a lot of pressure on myself to always learn something new and compose better music with each project I score. So how do you top two British Academy awards? I've been lucky to not have to go down the same horror/survival road too much since then—my work since *Dead Space* and *Dead Space: Extraction* has been refreshingly horror free. Though some games, such as *Section 8*, do have a certain hint of that feeling in them. Now that I've had some time away from the horror genre, I finally feel like I have something meaningful to contribute once again.

ScoreNotes: As the popularity of game music continues to grow, do you feel that more composers will be recognized in the future for their work in the medium?

Jason Graves: I certainly hope so. It's interesting to see the popularity of music for games increase along with our capabilities as composers to get closer to hearing in games what we hear in our heads when we're working. Game music will continue to become more popular as the medium itself matures and comes into its own.

Unlike film and television, game composers are completely dependent on technology to relate their music to the people listening. It was only a few years ago when we were stuck in the "turn music on here, turn music off there" confines of PS2 and Xbox. Now we're finally getting into true dynamic music that follows gameplay and reacts accordingly. *That's* the kind of score that will turn ears and get a composer noticed.

ScoreNotes: As we close here, what do you think are some ways in which game soundtracks can be better publicized to score fans?

Jason Graves: Unfortunately, as a composer my hands are often tied. My publicist, Greg O'Connor-Read, gets the word out whenever there's a game score worth listening to. Music4Games is definitely the go-to site for people who want to keep up with the world of game soundtracks. However, game publishers need to make soundtracks more of a priority, especially when it comes to marketing their game. Of course, I'm really talking about just getting game soundtracks released in the first place. That's really the most challenging thing to do.

I think live concerts like Video Games Live and Play! are doing a lot to get the music out to the masses. I'm hoping that digital distribution systems such as iTunes will make the idea of releasing game soundtracks more appealing to publishers. Unless you're scoring a big game, it can be difficult to convince someone that spending money on pressing your CDs, doing the artwork, and working out the legal rights for a soundtrack are worth it. If you bypass the expense of physically pressed discs, the whole equation becomes a lot more appealing, from an income/expense point of view.

Also, I think game music will get more attention from fans, and probably more publicity as well, as it continues to come into its own. Technology is finally starting to allow composers to create really interesting, immersive scores that merit people's attention, whether listened to in-game or on their own. I know that beyond supporting the game, that's always my ultimate goal with every project I score.

Interviews with the Composers of the Future

The following interviews depict, in my opinion, the next generation of composers to look out for. Of those featured, some have worked on prominent, commercial films already while others are earning their stripes on various independent productions. I've also taken into account, in some cases, the modern approach that a composer of the future must harness, which includes speed, quality, and the use of cutting-edge technology for today's fast paced world of film and television scoring.

In all, there is a wealth of talent to discover in the following pages with great experiences to read about. Whether the following composers are new to you or you have already listened to their fine work, I hope you enjoy getting to know them through these chapters and that you have a chance to explore the soundtracks that are discussed. After all, if one were to judge by talent alone and not merely by a string of lengthy credentials, I think we might come to the conclusion that the future has already arrived.

29 *Keeping Score* with Kyle Eastwood

K yle Eastwood has shown promise as a composer of the future. His tactful approach to the films he has worked on exhibits a certain sense of craftsmanship that I feel will serve him well in the future. For example, I very much enjoyed the stirring theme from Kyle (and writing partner Michael Stevens) in *Letters from Iwo Jima*, an effort that solidified his spot in this book.

Kyle has had an ongoing collaboration with his father, Clint Eastwood, dating back to their work on *Flags of Our Fathers*. I spoke with Kyle during the time that *Gran Torino* was making its ascent in early 2009 and thought it would be interesting to find out more about the family dynamic involved in Clint and Kyle's working relationship...

Kyle Eastwood (2009)

ScoreNotes: Starting the discussion off with *Gran Torino*—how pleased are you with the positive manner in which the film was received?

Kyle Eastwood: I'm very pleased, actually. It's nice to see the reaction be so good for the film. It's always nice to be a part of a film that the public seems to accept widely.

ScoreNotes: Given that the film was a smaller-scaled, personal drama, was it challenging to determine which moments in the film required music?

Kyle Eastwood: There's not a lot of music in the film, really, so you have to kind of pick your spots where you want to go in, where you think it needs music. The main thing we concentrated on was the song at the end and the key moments in the film.

ScoreNotes: Can you tell us about your involvement with the film's Golden Globe nominated song?

Kyle Eastwood: My writing partner, Michael Stevens, and I had started to do some work on the film, and my father came up with a melody at the piano. Michael and I fleshed it out into a song, and we had done a little work with Jamie Cullum over the last few years and thought it would be a good idea to see if he would take a shot at writing some lyrics for it and possibly sing it. He read the script and wrote the lyrics and changed a couple of little things in the song, and we ended up recording him singing it.

ScoreNotes: It came out really well, as the award nomination can attest to. It was a great job done by one and all.

Kyle Eastwood: Thank you.

ScoreNotes: How important was subtlety in the score for *Gran Torino,* where there is such limited, focused music throughout?

Kyle Eastwood: We kind of incorporated the theme from the song in a few cues, and the rest were atmospheric and tension kind of things. We used a military snare drum for Walt's theme for the film. My father really is more about "less is more" with music in films anyway, so that's the direction we took.

ScoreNotes: Looking back a couple years ago at your work on *Letters from Iwo Jima,* can you tell us about what it was like to work on a project with such a unique perspective in storytelling?

Kyle Eastwood: Michael Stevens and I had done a lot of work on *Flags of Our Fathers,* so we were actually doing the score for *Flags* when [Clint Eastwood] decided to continue on and make a second film back-to-back. We were in the mode of that storytelling [on *Flags of Our Fathers*] when he asked us to continue on and keep going with the other film. I just read the script, and we actually started writing it before we even saw any of the film. We had an idea of what it was going to look like, and we knew what the story was. We started coming up with themes even before we started seeing any of the picture.

ScoreNotes: Your theme for the film impacted more on a human level than a country-specific tone. How important was it to represent the characters with music that would be relatable to a general audience?

Kyle Eastwood: We consciously decided not to go down the whole route of doing too much of the ethnic or Japanese kind of sounding things. There are a couple of themes we came up with on Japanese–sounding instruments, but [we] ended up transferring them over and playing them on the piano or trumpet—things like that. We decided to stay more away from that and just do something that sounded a little bit more military and kind of bookend the music from the other film.

ScoreNotes: What was the creative chemistry like with your father as you worked on each of these films? I'd have to imagine this is one director-composer relationship that really must work well!

Kyle Eastwood: We have a good working relationship. When you work with him, he has a pretty definitive idea about what he wants with certain things. But then a lot of times we'll pick a scene that needs music, and he'll let me go and just come up with something that I feel is necessary for that scene. So it's good like that. He'll listen to something and give you a little bit of direction to go in. But it's a good working relationship; you get quite a bit of freedom in a lot of respects.

ScoreNotes: I'm always curious about what it's like when you work within family dynamics on commercial projects. It sounds like it works out quite nicely for the two of you.

Kyle Eastwood: Yeah, it's good. I have a studio set up in his guest house, and that's where a lot of the scores are actually written. Quite a bit of them are actually recorded in there as well. So it's nice he can come over and just pop in and listen to things in progress. So it works out well that way.

ScoreNotes: What inspired you to take the steps toward being a film composer?

Kyle Eastwood: I've always loved film music and music in general, really. I was a part of some scores here and there when I was a musician years ago when I was living in Los Angeles. I used to play in film orchestras sometimes, so that was my initial experience with it. I started just writing bits and pieces and some songs for films over the years, and it's been the last, sort of, three or four years or so that I've been tackling entire scores.

ScoreNotes: Is this a direction you're looking to continue pursuing?

Kyle Eastwood: I'm thinking about doing it more and more. I split my time between doing [film composing] and my band and my own albums, which I'm doing as well. So right now it's been a pretty good balance of the two.

ScoreNotes: Could you tell us more about the music you've been producing apart from the world of film music?

Kyle Eastwood: They're predominately jazz albums. I live in France a good part of the time, and the usual working band I have is based in Europe, and we play quite a bit over there, and we get over here to the States to play now and then. I've been splitting my time between going out to Los Angeles, working on film projects, and going back and doing the jazz thing in Europe.

ScoreNotes: Kind of a global operation you have going on there [laughs]!

Kyle Eastwood: [Laughing] Kind of, yeah.

ScoreNotes: What's the pulse of the film-going audiences overseas that you've noticed?

Kyle Eastwood: I guess the European audiences are somewhat different. *Letters from Iwo Jima* seemed to do pretty well over there, but that was kind of a foreign film, I guess. I think they're interested more in the smaller, independent films over in Europe.

ScoreNotes: The character-driven, nonblockbuster types.

Kyle Eastwood: I mean there are certain ones that go over well in Europe as well, but I think the French are more interested in more of the smaller dramas and things like that.

ScoreNotes: Now growing up in the family that you did, I am sure there was a lot of creativity going on. Were you tempted to catch the acting bug at any point?

Kyle Eastwood: I did a little bit here and there years ago. I was actually really more interested in directing. I went to Film School at USC for a short period of time but then shifted over to doing more music and never really turned back after that. I'm still involved in film through music, which I enjoy quite a bit. The music's kind of taken over.

ScoreNotes: You have a varied talent going on over there for you. Do you think that will ever lead you to directing *and* composing similar to your father?

Kyle Eastwood: It's possible. I would never say never. Just between the band and doing music for films, it's been keeping me pretty busy over the last few years. It's possible that it could develop into that, but we'll see.

ScoreNotes: Thank you for taking time to chat with us; it was really nice being able to have this discussion.

Kyle Eastwood: Thank you very much.

30 Keeping Score with Richard Wells

Photo by Birgitte Truelsen.

Richard Wells.

If I were to tell you before 2009 came to be that the score for *Mutant Chronicles* would outshine *Wolverine*, *Star Trek, and Terminator Salvation*, what would you have thought? Well, you would have probably considered me to be a bit mad or eccentric. However, I kid you not! This rich, orchestral score by composer **Richard Wells** was one of 2009's best, and it immediately put him on my composer appreciation radar. A score simply isn't *this* good by accident.

In this interview, Richard goes into some of the detail behind his excellent score and also provides many other interesting tidbits about himself as well. I hope you enjoy the discussion and that you also set out to experience some of Richard's music, preferably starting with *Mutant Chronicles* (which is actually a decent B-movie–viewing experience as well!).

After being involved with film music for so long, I can get a good read on emerging talent, and Richard is definitely someone who has formidable contributions to offer...

Richard Wells (2009)

ScoreNotes: If we may, please tell us about your composing background and how you got your start in the business.

Richard Wells: Studying archaeology at university and then doing accountancy was an unhelpful distraction from what I always wanted to do, which was write music. My first professional job was playing keyboards and doing programming for a Dutch band called Xymox in the '90s. Soon after, I met a guy called Dave Punshon who was writing music for computer games. I worked with him and on my own on about 20 games, and that is when I was lucky enough to start composing and getting paid for it! During this time, I met director Jake West who was working on some live action scenes for two of the games, and he asked me to write the music for his debut feature, *Razor Blade Smile*. That got me into movies and subsequently into writing music for movie trailers, of which I've done over 50. Through Jake I met Simon Hunter, as they had both been to the same film college.

ScoreNotes: When you first met up with director Simon Hunter, what did you think about his early concept behind *Mutant Chronicles*?

Richard Wells: When Simon first came to me, it was for the music for the teaser he was making for Ed Pressman. The budget was nonexistent, and Simon was very honest and told me that if he got the money to make the feature there was absolutely no guarantee that I would be writing the music. So he certainly didn't promise anything he couldn't deliver! I enjoyed doing the teaser, and once it was finished, I just forgot about it. I was very surprised when Simon called me a year later to ask if I would do the feature. The concept had changed a lot, from a gritty and grimy horror film to a much more expansive and ambitious project involving world conflict. The original steam punk theme was retained, and I think it gives the movie a very distinctive and original look. I particularly liked the oversized guns! The other thing I thought was impressive was that it didn't look like anything else I had seen before.

ScoreNotes: Can you talk about the different approaches that were considered, musically, for the film?

Richard Wells: What was never in doubt was that the score would be mainly orchestral. We both thought it was important because the concept behind the film was quite daring and unreal, so we needed to ground the audience in something familiar, and particularly to deal with the human emotional side. However, I didn't want it to be purely orchestral, and we mixed in a lot of electronic music as well, although it is not always apparent. We also decided to use a few unusual instruments including giant panpipes played by the legendary Tony Hinnigan *(Mission, Titanic)*, theorbo, and lute for some of the religious music, and we also hauled an old grand piano I had in my garage into Air-Edel's studio and basically bashed it, scraped it, and finally dropped a large brass door stop on it! It was probably the most useful sampling session I've ever done, and a lot of the drum sounds in MC are in fact piano samples.

ScoreNotes: How pleased were you with the choice of proceeding forward in an orchestral direction?

Richard Wells: I was very happy with it, as long as I was allowed to add to the palette of sounds, which I was.

ScoreNotes: Your score achieves a great balance between military heroism, stirring drama, and visceral terror. Can you tell us about some of the themes that made up the construct of your score?

Richard Wells: The movie for me splits into two halves, pre and post the take-off sequence. This is where the mission really begins. I felt strongly that despite the apparent hopelessness of the mission that we needed to at least give the soldiers a good send off and generally say to the audience that amidst all the death and destruction, there is a heroic element to what this ragtag [band is] going to do. And, in particular, they are not doing it just for themselves, but to save the human race. So out of this came the heroic "Take Off" theme. I also wrote a choral theme, which was very simple and pure. Some of it got lost in the U.S. edit, but is available on the CD. It is meant to represent an old-fashioned religious purity and is used as a total contrast to the demonic atonal aggression of the mutants' music. Andy Reynolds played multitracked detuned erhus over a lot of the mutant music, which gave it a very unsettling feeling. We also used the piano samples as percussion and Tony's giant panpipes for punctuation. Finally, there is the theme of "Hope and Despair," which played during moments of extreme human drama, both positive and negative. It is a slow string theme, which also intertwines with the religious theme.

ScoreNotes: The audio quality of your music had a great depth to it. Can you tell us a little bit about the orchestra you used as well as the recording process?

Richard Wells: We were incredibly lucky with the orchestra. We recorded on January 3, and there were no other sessions in London that day, so as far as I know, we got everyone we approached. We had about 30 strings, a full brass section, and a very small woodwind section. They were expertly conducted by Ben Wallfisch, and we got through everything in one day, including recording the choir, which was in fact only four people, tracked once and backed up by symphonic choirs, singing rubbish Latin—proper words, but badly constructed sentences! All the orchestral stuff was recorded in the main hall at Air Lyndhurst, straight into Pro Tools by Jake Jackson, who has a lot of experience working at Air. Before we started the session, we discussed going for as big a sound as possible, and I think Jake certainly delivered.

ScoreNotes: In general, are you a fan of science-fiction fare?

Richard Wells: I'm no fanatic, but I am a fan of some sci-fi/action/horror (*Alien, Aliens,* the original *Planet of the Apes*). But I would have to say the story is the most important thing to me. I'm pretty good at suspending disbelief, so I don't really mind what the setting is, as long as there is not too much exposition.

ScoreNotes: What can you tell us about the music of your recent project, *Doghouse*?

Richard Wells: *Doghouse* is a very different score from *Mutant Chronicles*, because although it is a horror/splatter movie, it is at heart a comedy. I found it very challenging, as musical comedy does not come naturally to me. I'm much better at dark, moody, violent stuff. Don't ask me why, as I am very antiviolence in real life. Maybe I just like the big emotions, and comedy often needs a much lighter touch. But I did really enjoy working on *Doghouse* despite the tight schedule.

ScoreNotes: I understand that while working on *Doghouse,* you were also hard at work on the television series, *Being Human.* I suppose it's not often that one gets to write music for a vampire, a werewolf, and a ghost in one story arc?

Richard Wells: *Being Human* came very much out of the blue, and I was incredibly lucky to be offered it, as I had absolutely no track record of writing for TV. I think the one thing in my favor was that the look is very filmic. But, nonetheless, they took a big risk on me. *Being Human* is a very intriguing and engaging series, brilliantly written by Toby Whitehouse, and I honestly believe it's an original take on the whole genre. Although you might expect it to be a comedy, it is very much a drama, which, due to the situation, is often funny and sometimes horrific. The premise is that three young people who happen to be a werewolf, a vampire, and a ghost are sharing a flat in Bristol. They all have their individual hang-ups, but they are trying to get on leading normal lives as human beings. Of course, it doesn't work out like that, and all kinds of things both horrible and moving happen to them.

I would urge everyone I know to catch it when it is shown in the States. I can honestly say that even had I had nothing to do with it, I would still have said it was the best thing on TV while it was being shown. If you check the blogs, you will find out I was not the only one saying that. The other good news is that it has been recommissioned for a bigger second series at the end of this year, and I'm really looking forward to having another go at it.

ScoreNotes: Horror movies so often rely on proper timing with their music. Can you tell us about the precision that goes into making an effectively frightful score?

Richard Wells: A frightful score sounds good! That's a difficult question though. A lot relies on instinct and remembering one's initial reaction to a scene. You only get one chance to react like the audience, and after that it's never the same again. Particularly with a horror scene, it's a combination of knowing when to hold back, ramp up the tension, mislead the audience, and go for it flat out.

ScoreNotes: What films of the past do you think showcase some of the best examples of horror scores?

Richard Wells: Some favorite examples: *Alien, Aliens, Halloween, Scream, 28 Weeks Later, Planet Terror, Jaws, Psycho, The Omen, Terminator.*

ScoreNotes: Being based in the U.K., what is your overall perception of the current crop of scores from Hollywood? Also, do you plan on relocating to Los Angeles in the near future?

Richard Wells: There are always great scores coming out of Los Angeles and particularly from a technical point of view. Some of the orchestration is just phenomenal. Although I mixed *Doghouse* in L.A. with Mark Curry, I don't currently have any plans to move out there full time. Having said that, I certainly would not rule it out if the right offer came along, but we do have the issue of moving a whole family, which is a bit more complicated than just me. But I have to say I had a great time in L.A., and I certainly plan to come back for more meetings and hopefully to work with Mark again.

ScoreNotes: What excites you the most about the prospects of film composing?

Richard Wells: It is probably the journey of discovery. Starting with a blank canvas with no idea of what to do and then finding themes and the whole art of putting a giant jigsaw puzzle together. It's totally consuming and, combined with the deadline and general lack of time to think, pretty terrifying as well. The fear of failure drives one on relentlessly to the finish line!

ScoreNotes: If you had a chance at composing a "dream project," which orchestra would you ideally choose for the task?

Richard Wells: It would have to be the full LSO [London Symphony Orchestra], recorded at Air Lyndhurst.

31 *Keeping Score* with Abel Korzeniowski

bel Korzeniowski has already had an interesting adventure in getting to Hollywood. His path is literally a global trek that began in Poland where Abel was a big fan of movies and film music growing up. His schooling and eventual achievements led him to find a good deal of notoriety across Europe and eventually placed him on a trajectory to Hollywood.

I'm glad he made it.

After hearing his work, I found that he brings a fresh insight to the world of films with music that is commercially viable but also thought provoking. His first commercial project was for the animated sci-fi fable, *Battle for Terra*, which he spoke to me about during our conversation in early 2009...

Abel Korzeniowski (2009)

ScoreNotes: What is the general premise of *Battle for Terra,* and what kind of score did it require?

Abel Korzeniowski: *Battle for Terra* has a reverse alien invasion plot, so instead of aliens invading Earth, it is the humans who are the aggressors and attack a peaceful alien planet. The great thing about this plot is that it is not black and white. Both humans and aliens, who are called Terrians, are neither fully good nor all bad. There is a very intricate relation between these two worlds, which made scoring this movie even more interesting.

What was required from the very beginning was a score that would sound different, and which would set a unique mood for the whole movie and for the Terrians in particular. At the same time, it had to be as functional and dramatic as a regular Hollywood score.

ScoreNotes: This definitely does not sound like a routine science-fiction movie. Was this the first time, in fact, that you'd worked on an animated feature? If so, how did it differ from your work on live-action films?

Abel Korzeniowski: Usually, writing music for an animation means much more work. In a typical animated story, everything changes very quickly. You don't have the luxury of long scenes; a two-minute dialogue never happens. Even if you are given a scene that is a minute long, it will consist of six sections, and you will have to switch mood every ten seconds.

Now, with *Terra*, it was not a typical animated movie. It is more like *Wall-E*. When you think about Pixar before *Wall-E*, it used to be just comedy, nothing too serious. On the other hand, *Terra* is more like a live-action movie with real character development and drama. Its 2D version premiered in Toronto in 2007, and we were very happy that a year later, *Wall-E* opened up this new genre for wider audiences.

ScoreNotes: Sounds like a refreshing change of pace from the typical comedic, animated features we've been seeing. I also have high hopes for your score. Can you give us some background on your soundtrack?

Abel Korzeniowski: What I tried to achieve with the soundtrack was to contrast the two worlds. You will notice that the world of Terrians is full of strange looking items, mostly wooden. Technology seems to be on a very primitive level, but this is only the surface. It is all very warm, soft type of materials, and the music for Terrians also has a very characteristic orchestration that doesn't use any harsh sounds. In fact, it doesn't use any brass at all. Even in the action sequences, while you can hear the action drive, it is made with a different set of instruments than you would expect from a regular action score.

In contrast, cues related to the humans are different because they come from a position of power and are the aggressors. They have this military vibe. This was the place for brass instruments and much stronger and open sounds evoking power and determination. This was the basic concept behind the music.

ScoreNotes: Excellent! It seems like the director embraced your creative and accurate approach toward the content.

Abel Korzeniowski: Absolutely. This was a rare case, when a composer had been asked to produce a score that would sound different and that he was actually given a chance to do so. The work was really, really rewarding, and we didn't have a lot of fights [laughing] on how to approach the score.

I don't know if you know the story around it, but the movie started as a short, and this short got some festival awards. Then the director, Aristomenis Tsirbas, found the producers at Snoot, and they decided to make it a full feature-length project. I have seen some clips from this short film, and it is amazing how much the original concept has evolved and how complex the movie has become. The original short was really sad and depressing. The feature version, even though still carrying a lot of weight, is told in a more gracious way. There is space for both levity and graver moments. There is a lot to like about it.

ScoreNotes: What were the recording sessions like?

Abel Korzeniowski: We had really great, full-fledged recording sessions, which was a big achievement in itself considering that this was not a major studio production, but a small, independent company. [With an] 80+ piece orchestra, choirs, and various drum and solo instruments, there was an enormous amount of power in it. We were recording at Warner Bros., which has one of the greatest scoring stages in Los Angeles. We had some of the most incredible instruments like a seven-foot frame drum, which was used for the scenes with the terraformer—an apocalyptic weapon used in the movie by the Air Force. When you hear an instrument like this, it is really, really profound. By the way, this drum was used before *Terra* in *Transformers 1,* and I think was built specifically for that movie. We also had some very strange instruments like a glass harmonica, an instrument consisting of a set of glass bowls tuned to the chromatic scale. A little engine spins them around, and you press the rotating bowls with your fingers, which have to be wet. This produced a very unique, ethereal sound. Another interesting example was the lithophone, a kind of vibraphone, but made of stone. We really used a lot of unusual devices to make this score sound different.

ScoreNotes: Your path to Hollywood has been an interesting one and spans multiple countries. Can you tell us what this journey has been like for you thus far?

Abel Korzeniowski: I studied classical composition in Poland and then started writing music for live theater, which eventually brought me to film. My first feature was *Big Animal*, a stylish, black and white movie written by Krzysztof Kieslowski. For this music, I received the "Golden Lions" for best musical score—the most prestigious film award in Poland. After this, more projects followed. The next milestone in my career was the new score for Fritz Lang's *Metropolis,* which was a huge 147-minute live project with a 90-piece orchestra, two choirs, and two solo voices. After doing it, I started looking for an agent in Hollywood. Actually, I just sent e-mails to six agencies that I thought were matching my profile. Three of them responded, asking for my reel, and a couple weeks later, I received a phone call from Seth Kaplan of Evolution Music Partners, who is now my agent and a great friend. And this is when the real adventure began.

ScoreNotes: As we close, I would like to say it was really great getting to chat with you for the first time. I am definitely interested in hearing your material for this movie as well as your future work. I sincerely wish you all the best.

Abel Korzeniowski: Thank you. It was a pleasure to talk to you.

32 *Keeping Score* with Scott Glasgow

Scott Glasgow.

Another of the bright, emerging talents on the Hollywood composing scene is **Scott Glasgow**, a composer who brings a cross-blend of innovation and classical fundamentals to his craft. In this in-depth interview, Scott sheds some light on the struggles that up-and-coming composers face in today's industry, while also touching on a varied array of insider topics that I feel many of you will find of interest...

Scott Glasgow (2009)

ScoreNotes: What would you say are some of the biggest hurdles that an independent composer in today's Hollywood has to face?

Scott Glasgow: I'm not sure what the "biggest hurdle" is; in reality, there are many. I think starting from the top of the list, finding the job is very difficult and based almost entirely on friends hiring friends or contacts leading to other contacts through recommendation. I don't think I've sent out a single demo CD to get a job in a few years now; it's all through recommendations and contacts. The next challenge is getting the contract signed, when most of these independent films have more producers than needed, which leads to "decision by committee" that lasts weeks instead of hours, like I hear some of the big studio films do.

Then there is the crush of time to get it done fast, only to have the film flop around for a year or more trying to find distribution—"hurry up and wait" is a big part of this business. I usually aim for four to six weeks to score a full feature but end up with either much longer due to edits to the film or much shorter leaving a lot less sleep. Finally, there is [the] budget, which I guess would be the biggest hurdle, which I am guessing you are referring to. That's where you have to try to make something happen for a tenth of the budget a composer on a regular studio film would have, even though many of these films look as good as big-budget films seen in theaters. They have well-recognizable movie stars, [are] shot well, and [have] other qualities making it sometimes hard to not think of them as a studio feature.

Also, by the end of these low budget films, they are usually completely out of money when they get to the music. Orchestras are expensive, and that is why I end up recording in Europe mostly right now. I don't consider myself an "independent film composer," just a composer who happens to work on independent films right now, hoping some day soon to get to the next level. My ultimate goal is to do that big summer blockbuster that's in every theater, everywhere!

ScoreNotes: For those who are not directly associated with the inner workings of the business, can you provide an indication of just how competitive a field it is for composers today?

Scott Glasgow: Oh it's *very* competitive; however, as I've already mentioned, friends hire friends; it's finding the new friends or the film that is totally out of left field that is hard—*Gene Generation* I found on MySpace, but that is rare. Now it [has] changed from people getting the films to directors saying, "I heard this composer's demo the other day that sounded live when it wasn't. Can you make your demos more live-sounding like his?" Suddenly, I am researching what samples they used to make that score; however, the guy doesn't get hired.

Literally, there is a technology and music-programming race—who can make their demos sound as live without being live. I think the problem with that is it will never sound live with fake orchestra. My ears will always hear the difference. I'm not so sure for the film makers. Many out there, especially ones who have never sat in front of a live orchestra, can't hear the difference. Funny thing also is that these young composers spending weeks programming some cue don't realize that when you have to write 100 minutes of score, you don't have time for all that. It's not realistic in the fast-paced world of professional film scoring. These hyper-programming composers do more damage than they realize with the fake orchestra demos, which will probably lead to no independent films ever having live orchestra again and only the top 10 percent of Hollywood having the budget to really do it right. It'll become a world of mostly fake orchestra, sadly, and I think most of us can really hear the difference.

ScoreNotes: Can you talk about some of the differing, creative approaches you have to take when working on films of a smaller budget?

Scott Glasgow: A smaller budget can mean compromise in either finished sound quality or, worse, to creative ideas, but I try not to let it do that. I think it depends on what size of score they are trying for. A big-action sci-fi film needing a larger-than-life sound but having the budget for nothing live is basically an impossible scenario, unless you go *Blade Runner* Vangelis style, but that hardly works unless you are Vangelis! A comedy can be dealt with using a small chamber orchestra generally.

I think I just try to stay creative regardless of budget, such as my work in *Bone Dry*, which I knew was *not* going to have a live score; however, later I did convince the director to get one session with an orchestra. In that score, I used a plucked cactus and bunch of other organic sounds to fill out the sound with the fake orchestra, all leading to the cathartic end with the large live orchestra; it gave the film a sense of a journey, which is what I aimed for. It's difficult when a film is temped   that is, temporary music from another film score is dropped in to create pacing or tone for the editor—by large live orchestra film scores, then the film makers want something that sounds like that but don't have the budget for it! This happened to me on *Patriotville*—large, live orchestral temp music that I had to re-create without an orchestra; it was an impossible scenario, but I just did what I could with the resources I had. I sort of doubt I will ever release a CD of that score because of it. I am proud of the music in that film, but it just is a pale shadow of what it should have been in my ears. By the way, it is really a charming wonderful film worth seeing. Also, it allowed me to explore my "Goldsmith *Patton* and Morricone *The Good, The Bad, & The Ugly*" side.

ScoreNotes: What are some of your tools of the trade that you use in your studio?

Scott Glasgow: It's all computers for all us composers now. I have two eight-core Power Macs running tons of RAM filled with [orchestral] samples on one, and my main work system is the other where I do more creative-type sample manipulations in addition to tracking. This is much better than a few years ago when I was running six computers! What a mess that was, trying to get all those computers to work daily and work together. Wow, how technology has grown. I record live solo musicians in my studio all the time to enhance the scores, but mostly it is all me.

The one thing I do try to do differently than some of my other composer friends is to try and create custom sound sets for each project, even if the sounds are commercially available. I try to personalize it with effects, delays, edits...then save it in its own project bank. I try never to settle for the stock sounds out of the box. I do also occasionally record custom, live orchestra effects when I am working with an orchestra, too, so I have a nice palette to work with that sounds very live—because it is!

ScoreNotes: For you, personally, how much of an importance do you place on innovation with your music? Also, is there ever a concern about being too unique for the formula-driven world of commercial movies?

Scott Glasgow: I think being unique is a benefit in this business. Sounding like John Williams is the kiss of death for a new composer on the scene. Also, as you move up in the business, why would they hire you when they can get Williams himself? No, as a composer, you must develop sounds or chord progressions only you like to do. Too many guys just wanna sound like John Williams—why they don't pick Goldsmith is a surprise to me. Even I've done my version of John Williams style (i.e., *Robotech*), but it's all about how you do it or how close you get to someone else's style. There have certainly been quite a few composers working on big films getting too close to their models. I really try to do my own thing, but not forget what great scores have come before me. I think it's important to look forward but not forget or discount the past.

I'd say, for me, my own personal innovations were developed while I was studying in college. Music based on elements around me. As an example of that, one day seeing clouds shifting over me in the sky reminded me of two radically different chords slowly fading over each other (this can be heard at the opening music to *Bone Dry*).

ScoreNotes: What has been the most rewarding project you've worked on thus far in your career?

Scott Glasgow: You know that's hard to say since they all seem to have good moments for me, but I think *Chasing Ghosts*—my first real feature for director Kyle Jackson and released by Sony—seems to have been my best experience on so many levels. Creatively, I think many tracks in that score really came out nice—"Interrogation" and "Karis" are two shining moments for me. Also, the film has been the best received of all my films so far—well in France especially. Finally, it was really my first break as a film composer. I certainly had done a ton of work before then, even a feature when I lived in San Francisco, but it was my first "real" film, in my mind. Also Kyle is a good friend, so working with him was so easy, and [it] didn't seem as complicated as the other films have been.

ScoreNotes: You've recently made a foray into writing music for comedies. How much of a departure was that for you from what you've been used to working on, and is it a genre that appeals to you?

Scott Glasgow: I think I feel more at home musically in dramas, sci-fi, or thrillers, but it is a welcome change of pace. I also feel I'm still finding my comedy voice and realize there are some musical clichés that simply really work well in comedy scenes [such as] the pizzicato strings or silly bassoon lines. I keep hoping I will discover an utterly new way to score comedies—that is, if the film makers are open to that—most are not; they wanna sell their film, and most want their film to look and sound like other successful comedies. It's less about being unique, as in a sci-fi film, and more about being a function of selling a film.

There's also a surprising perception that somehow a comedy score is less important than say an action-fantasy score. It's hard to even get a CD release of a comedy score, even with a large live orchestra recording—probably due to lack of sales versus an action movie CD release. I've also noticed when a comedy movie gets reviewed, rarely is the score mentioned, whereas an action-adventure film with an interesting score will almost always gets some sort of mention. Comedy scores seem to get ignored, sadly, but serve just as important [a] role in films. I'm not sure I understand it, but I know I would never want to be pigeonholed creatively into comedy films only, as a few composers in Hollywood seem to have been. Then, again, working is better than not working!

ScoreNotes: Can you describe your relationship with the soundtrack labels, and, specifically, might you explain how involved they are in promoting your work?

Scott Glasgow: Well, as I've said already, relationships are everything in this business, from getting the film, to working with musicians, to working with the labels. I've had a few fellow composers ask how I am able to get my scores released when so many other composers struggle to, and I always say, "Because I've been lucky enough to meet the people at the labels." For instance, I met Doug Fake [Intrada] in Europe when I was recording *Hack!* and he was there to record *Spellbound*. Robert Townson [Varese Sarabande], I met years ago on a session for another composer, and we became friends, so I just started sending him my scores; luckily, one day he listened. Mikael Carlsson [MSM], I met online, and he approached me about releasing *Chasing Ghosts*, and we became friends—he even scored a scene for me in *Toxic* when I was too busy.

Another aspect is that I think you need to have film music that works well on CD. An all-ambient score probably will not get released. The labels are a business, and they don't want to put out CDs that are less likely of selling. The truth is soundtrack CDs don't sell very well anyway. They hardly make enough money to pay for the expense to manufacture them; there are quite a lot of costs—from mastering, to artwork, to manufacturing and distribution—that are well beyond the cost of the disc. As for promoting, I don't think they do much—labels like Varese Sarabande just have a following, where people just buy anything they release. They do have clout to get it into stores, and it gives the release a little more importance to have it released on a record label versus self-releasing a album.

I would say [that] almost all the interviews, CD signings, or other promotions I usually instigate myself, but without the CD release, I doubt these things would happen. The CD reviews on the various Web sites are totally up to the person who runs the site. There are some sites that simply do not have a single mention of any of my five CDs. There's nothing I can do with those.

ScoreNotes: With so many media options to choose from, what would you say is the best method for a film composer to promote his or her work?

Scott Glasgow: iTunes and other digital distributions are the future of music media— and movies for that matter, with sites like Hulu streaming movies at DVD quality for free. At this point, I think record labels making physical products to sit in a warehouse waiting for people to buy them is not a good business plan. With successful bands like NIN [Nine Inch Nails] giving away their new CD online for free, it would seem the future is here. Ironically, my first CD [*Chasing Ghosts*], which was a digital download only, is my least-known work and sold the least. Soundtrack collectors seem to not like digital downloads of CDs. I guess that is the "collector" mentality—like collecting comics, digital is just not the same. However, personally, I prefer digital versions of albums and listening on iPod.

As for other film composers and how they should promote their work, I'd say use whatever means to get the scores out there—CD Baby is as good as a digital download by a record label, except it loses the exposure that comes with that label; self-promotion just doesn't have the weight of a record label. More importantly, composers need to focus on getting the work; the CDs will happen automatically if they just find a way into a good film and write good music.

ScoreNotes: Who are some of the composers working today that you most admire and why?

Scott Glasgow: I am always inspired by the composers who keep themselves fresh or reinvent themselves. John Williams, even after all those scores, always surprises me. The chords he uses are wonderfully unique and fresh. I'm tired of hearing the same chords, mostly entirely diatonic, and they go right where I expect them to go in. The aggressive sound of Elliot Goldenthal still inspires as does the quirkiness of Danny Elfman. Then there are Alan Silvestri and James Horner, who are always doing great work. Jerry Goldsmith is a *huge* influence on me—possibly the composer who inspired me to go into music years ago. These are at the top of their game because they are all doing fresh, interesting work with great musicians and great production values.

Some of the younger but not newer guys that get my attention are guys like Marco Beltrami, Thomas Newman, Chris Young, and Brian Tyler. Then there are quite a few new composers of my generation working today that catch my ear—Ryan Shore, Bear McCreary, Christopher Lennertz, Atli Orvarsson, Jeff Grace, Ceiri Torjussen, Gordy Habb are all doing really interesting work.

Finally, I have to mention the composers who do not work in film but do "classical music" that inspire me—Peteris Vasks, Michael Torke, Christopher Rouse, Arvo Part, Michael Daugherty, and James MacMillian change the way I think of my work. I'd say I listen to more modern classical composers than I do film scores.

ScoreNotes: If you were looking to introduce new listeners to your music, which two soundtracks would you recommend that they start off with?

Scott Glasgow: You know I really hope everyone gets a chance to hear *Chasing Ghosts* since it is some of my best work, but unfortunately the digital-only release makes it not really a contender for this question [Note: the contract has been signed to release *Chasing Ghosts* as a physical CD someday]. To answer your question, *The Gene Generation* is a very unique score and the newest release, so I'd have to say that one is my first suggestion to listeners. As for my second suggestion, *Bone Dry*, since it also is a unique score with the cactus and the [symphonic attributes]. In many of my scores, the final couple tracks are really worth listening to—it seems my CDs have a balance of opening and ending on a strong note. Some of my best tracks are at the ends of these CDs.

33 *Keeping Score* with Simon J. Hunter

Simon Hunter.

S imon J. Hunter is a highly talented and versatile composer who has a clear understanding about what the needs of today's fast-paced mediums require. Having composed music featured on television and in theaters, Simon's unique and flexible approach has helped him gain the type of expertise that more and more producers are turning to for their projects.

Here, we talk about his contributions for shows like *CSI*, the music he's created for commercial film trailers, and other topics of interest...

Simon J. Hunter (2009)
ScoreNotes: Please tell us about yourself and how it was that you landed in the music business.

Simon Hunter: I grew up in Melbourne, Australia. I played in bands from a young age around Melbourne. After high school, I was awarded a scholarship to study at Berklee College of Music in Boston. After being there for a couple of years, I moved out to Los Angeles and got the first job I could find at a recording studio, to learn how to record music. After working there for a while, I started making recordings and collaborating with artists and eventually started getting asked to produce bands, write music for film/TV, and eventually score TV shows, films, and now video games.

ScoreNotes: What has it been like to contribute your music to such a successful, ongoing television series like *CSI*?

Simon Hunter: I'm very happy with the fact that all three of the *CSI*s have found my music to be useful to their shows. I really enjoy my music being part of such a high-quality and highly visible drama. As contemporary music has evolved, so has the sound of the show, so it's never static. I like to stay ahead of the curve generally, so I have been lucky enough to have created what they need in many cases!

ScoreNotes: Your music has been noted as defining some of the key moments on the show. Can you tell us about the type of research and planning that goes into writing music for pivotal scenes?

Simon Hunter: Generally, I watch a lot of TV and see a lot of films and listen to heaps of music. This really informs my work and keeps it current. For a show like *CSI*, currency and emotional content seem to be very important.

ScoreNotes: Why do you think American audiences are so captivated by crime dramas like *CSI*?

Simon Hunter: I couldn't say for sure! But I can say that the *CSI* shows have some of the best production value of any of the shows on TV at the moment. They're constantly upping the ante on what they're doing on TV. People tend to like the scientific, procedural type shows, and when they include strong story and characters, that makes them even more compelling. Add to that the awesome music soundtrack by the composer and the use of source music, and it's a really compelling show.

ScoreNotes: Outside of the television venue, can you tell us about some of the musical artists you have worked with thus far in your career?

Simon Hunter: I can't name names, but one major rock diva I worked with ended up completely trashing the recording studio I was working at while on a rampage, with furniture smashed, drug paraphernalia scattered throughout the studio, and band members pretty much running for their lives. Other artists were really professional, and they are the ones I gravitated towards. One of my favorite projects was with the producer Hugh Padgham, who was incredibly down to earth and fun to work with, for such a prolific guy.

ScoreNotes: What are some of your favorite instruments or tools that you like to employ?

Simon Hunter: I love my Yamaha upright piano. It has this really dark, emotional sound that I just can't get enough of. When I got it, I tried a bunch of other pianos out, and it was the darkest, moodiest, most sentimental, and expressive instrument I found. When I add it in a track, it really breathes the life into it way more than synths or samples.

ScoreNotes: Generally speaking, where do you think the future of television and film music scoring is headed? Do you foresee a landscape of continued innovation on the horizon?

Simon Hunter: Productions left and right seem to be cutting costs. So the big, high-priced gigs seem to be reducing, which is a struggle for some composers. I feel like the people who will really shine moving forward are the quick, adaptable composers that can come up with new ways of making the process more efficient, while still keeping the quality of music at the maximum.

ScoreNotes: To follow up on that point, can you relate to us the level of preparation a composer must have in order to be quick, efficient, and adaptable?

Simon Hunter: Definitely the more real instruments you can play and the more experienced you are with different styles of music on a deeper level will set you apart from the rest, as a composer. I think if you are asked to do something "impossible" in no time, it becomes more possible if you can just quickly play it yourself instead of trying to program something to sound real.

ScoreNotes: What would you say is the most exciting thing about working in television for you?

Simon Hunter: For me, the most exciting things about working in TV are the fast deadlines and intensity and speed. When I'm working on a show under an impossible deadline, I come alive. There's nothing like creating 30 to 40 minutes of music to picture in a couple of days and sending it out as fast as possible. I love the challenge.

ScoreNotes: What do you feel is the key principle to writing effective and impactful music for film trailers?

Simon Hunter: In movie trailers, it seems like there is a set structure of the piece that must fit pretty well with the overall structure of the trailer. Most of them start out small or wide and empty and, of course, end up huge and epic. If the track can build up consistently throughout the piece and still end on a very strong point, without ever feeling like it's going backwards or down in intensity, then it will be a winner.

ScoreNotes: The popularity of trailer music as a stand-alone listening experience is growing more and more with listeners these days. Can you comment on that developing trend?

Simon Hunter: I absolutely love the drama of the best movie trailers. Some of the better trailer music is so epic and huge, and I think that is really entertaining to most people. Also, it's a very popular and commercial form of the film score genre, so theoretically most people can sit down for a two-minute piece and get into it without investing as much time as they would [diving] into a full-length movie score. It's more accessible, and oftentimes the drama is more obvious. I think that's a great aspect of the genre.

34 *Keeping Score* with Assaf Rinde

Assaf Rinde.

Photo by Adam Meir.

To be considered as a Composer of the Future, I believe the individual should have a masterful grasp on the classic, symphonic attributes of film scoring as well as a keen handle on the modern tools currently available today. **Assaf Rinde** certainly meets these criteria and then some.

Assaf's style combines the best of both worlds: the influences of classic-era film music and the modern inspirations of today's sound. When brought together, as he did for a score like *Kill Zone*, it's easy to see why this talented composer is someone you're sure to hear more from in the not too distant future...

Assaf Rinde (2009)

ScoreNotes: Please tell us about the type of music you were exposed to during your childhood and what impression it made on you.

Assaf Rinde: I grew up in Israel and was exposed to almost every kind of music possible. Israel is one of those places, a bit like LA, where there are so many different cultures and backgrounds meeting together and creating a wonderful mix.

I was exposed to everything from Jewish and Arabic traditional music to jazz, pop, rock, Hollywood soundtracks, European classic, modern music, and many other types. Growing up in such an environment made me feel like I could use whatever style of music blended with any element possible from different genres without feeling like I'm out of focus. As a child, I always added groove elements to Bach's music and other elements, and I believe that kind of stylistic freedom attracted me and subsequently drove me to film music.

ScoreNotes: At what point in your life did you feel that being a composer was a path you wanted to be on?

Assaf Rinde: My first real composition was written when I was 11 years old, and I had already been playing the piano since the age of three, so it was very clear to me that music was what I really wanted to do with my life. I think it was around the age of 15 or 16 when I noticed for the first time the real power of film music, and that, together with my continued love for music of all genres and music composition, locked and solidified my life's ambitions.

ScoreNotes: Your versatility and knowledge enable you to work on a variety of projects in different capacities, such as composing music for blockbuster movie trailers, writing original scores for independent films, helping to develop game soundtracks, and more! Can you tell us a little bit about the valuable experience you have gained thus far in the entertainment industry?

Assaf Rinde: One of the things that I was so attracted to in this field was the fact you "can," or more suitably stated, "have to" do more than one thing while working on a project. You have to serve much more than just the composer function.

On a typical movie project, the composer should also produce, perform, orchestrate, conduct, mix, and edit the entire score. On bigger movie projects, most composers will have a big team working with them to support all these countless occupations. I was involved in almost every aspect of these various roles before, as well as working as part of the team for other composers as a producer, orchestrator, mixer, and conductor.

As a composer, I was involved with writing music for movies like *Nailed, Kill Zone, Mandingo in a Box*, as well as a few documentaries and animation projects among many other film projects. I've been writing a lot lately for movie trailers such as *Race to Witch Mountain, Starship Troopers 3, Tinkerbell & Her Friends Saving Energy, The Orphan*, and many others. In the videogame world, I've collaborated with such composers as Inon Zur, David Kates, Mark Morgan and have written for a few videogame projects as well.

Although I started to compose many years ago, I have actually started working as an orchestrator for several high-profile projects in Europe as well as composing the music for short movies along with a few concert pieces.

ScoreNotes: Your work on the independent film *Kill Zone* made for quite an intelligent, highly stylized soundtrack. What were some of the cross-genre themes you looked to get across in the music for this score?

Assaf Rinde: *Kill Zone* was lots of fun to work on. One of the first things we locked in on this project was the fact that it is a western created as a tribute to Sergio Leone's westerns, but with a much more modern feel to it. The director, Vitor Santos, wanted the Ennio Morricone feel with the music, and when I started getting deeper into the writing process, I felt that it was a really great instinctive decision on his part. On the other hand, I knew it would have to be much more modern musically because of the contemporary feel and look of the movie. Once we had established the musical direction for the score, we started to concentrate on the more hidden elements in the story, so what we ended up with is more of a modern baroque western drama movie/soundtrack, and I think it works for this particular movie.

ScoreNotes: Can you shed some light on your time commitment and the sacrifices you made while bringing *Kill Zone* to completion?

Assaf Rinde: *Kill Zone* didn't have much of a budget to begin with, but the movie itself was so interesting to me as a composer that I just had to take it on. Being such a low-budget project made me go for some different solutions musically that I wouldn't have thought of without being cornered with budget decisions. Most of the score was performed electronically, but there are some key moments in the score that I just couldn't let go of without the live touch. I brought in my friend Sean Hennessy to perform the trumpet lines; another colleague of mine, Israel Klich, who played guitar; and my wife, Iris Malkin, who performed all the vocal lines. The live component was used to take the emotional impact to the next level, since there is only so much that samplers can actually do. I must say I was very lucky with having such amazing friends/musicians around me, and they helped me tremendously in giving this score a real signature sound.

The schedule on *Kill Zone* was a bit hectic. We started spotting and scoring the movie, and after about two reels in, we stopped for almost six months. The main reason was that it got into post-production with almost no money at all, so every step forward took much longer than it should have. But that also gave us the time to really evaluate every single detail, which you usually don't have the time for with a normal scoring schedule. So after this long break, we got back into scoring, which, on and off, took over a year to complete.

ScoreNotes: Who are some of the composers you have worked with in the business, and what are some of the valuable lessons you've learned from them?

Assaf Rinde: Along the way, I've been working with so many different composers in Israel, Europe, and the U.S. I've worked a lot with Christopher Young, Andrea Morricone, Inon Zur, Rafi Kadishson, Uri Hodorov, and many others. I've learned a lot from each one of them.

My work with Christopher Young gave me the opportunity to work on some of the biggest movies ever made, like *Spiderman 3*, *Ghost Rider*, *The Uninvited*, *Drag Me to Hell*, *Untraceable*, and more. Working on these really big movies showed me how tight some of the schedules are, how many people are actually involved in the decision-making, what goes on screen and what's not, as well as the power of a real team effort. With Inon Zur, I had the opportunity to be involved with the music production of some of the biggest videogame titles, and that has shown me a different perspective and approach to telling a story, musically.

But at the end of the day, you really have the opportunity to explore what methods work for you and what approaches are not working, and you can learn from other people's experience as to what to do or not on a project.

Photo by Tomer Stolz.

As a Composer of the Future, Assaf Rinde is well suited to conduct orchestras for use in any medium.

ScoreNotes: What would you say are some of your most valuable composing tools that you use, and how much do you relish exploring new technologies for use in your craft?

Assaf Rinde: I have two writing environments that I use, based on the project's needs. The piano is one of my favorites because this is a great place for me to experiment and improvise, and this is where I develop most of my themes and elements, melodically. My other composing environment is the computer and all the studio gear around it, and this is where I finalize my compositions. The piano hasn't changed much since Bach's days, (except for a few Yamaha revolutionary models), but the technology on the electronic side of the studio is constantly changing. I'm really into all the tech gadgets, and I do consider myself a "gearhead," but at the same time, I'm trying to remind myself that the gear isn't the important component of my studio. It is the musical idea that makes the difference at the end of the day. Every day I learn some new programs and new approaches in music making and producing. I keep up with the technologies, since I feel that once you've stopped for even less than a year, you are already far behind, and it might be very hard to catch up with everything you've missed. I'm constantly exploring new technologies and new composing techniques and environments every day. I must say I feel really comfortable in both worlds, classic and tech, and the constant battle between the two keeps me focused and creative.

ScoreNotes: What is your opinion on the state of videogame music today, and how encouraged are you about the opportunities that the medium has to offer?

Assaf Rinde: Videogames are one of the best places today for composers to make a living composing music. At the same time, it is one of the only avenues in music where you can compose music that is very close in its concept to concert music, since most videogame scoring is not done to picture but to a storyline or state of emotion of the game's characters. Another thing that is really nice about videogames is the simple fact that you can be based almost anywhere and still be constantly working in this field because much of the communication between composers and the developers happens over the Internet and phone. When you work on a movie, usually you need to be at the same place where the post-production takes place, which usually limits the possibilities to LA, London, or New York.

I was already involved in so many ways in the music production side of some of the biggest videogames out there, and I'm open to any idea of composing music for a good storyline whether it is onscreen, on stage, or in a videogame. I actually prefer to keep switching media since it keeps me really fresh creatively.

This is also why I'm so deep into films and videogames. The fact you can compose a big action score this month and a real drama score following that, or sometimes at the very same time, makes it all much more attractive to me. I need this constant change in order to keep myself as inventive as possible.

ScoreNotes: On a bit of a side note, I often notice that videogame projects cannot be discussed or promoted until, essentially, the time of their release. Why is there such secrecy associated with the videogame titles?

Assaf Rinde: The videogame world is always running against time in terms of developing new technologies. The videogame companies are not only developing the content of the game, but also developing graphic engines, audio engines, and interactive engines and tools, [such as the] Wii remote or the guitars for Guitar Hero, so they want to be far ahead of everybody in terms of releasing their new trend to the market. The guys from Nintendo who created Wii, for example, enjoyed the power of being first in doing something that revolutionary, and of course having this power translates easily into money and opportunities for their company. So working on a new revolutionary graphic engine that will show everything onscreen faster and without using up your entire computer's CPU power is something very delicate that you don't want anyone to know of before the right time. The same happens with the game's storyline, the character design, and the animation, and other aspects of the game's content.

ScoreNotes: Have you been involved with any projects where extra measures were taken to safeguard the secrecy of the film?

Assaf Rinde: On almost every film I've ever worked on, I had to sign a nondisclosure agreement that basically forbids me from talking about certain aspects of the production with anyone besides my team. All the film content, [both the] audio and visuals, is being developed between so many people, and since there are so many people involved, it is really hard to keep all of it to secrecy, so the production companies have lots of different agreements to protect themselves from information-leaking, but they have to additionally use some other techniques in protecting their investment. Some production companies will give the entire film content a different "working title" from the final movie's name, just to protect their property in case someone gets access to these tapes/scripts/hard drives; the same often applies with videogames. There are so many movies that are using new technologies and effects that change the landscape of the industry, and everybody in these productions is doing everything possible to not give up any of this revolutionary and valuable information before the official release date. Think about *The Matrix* and about all the movie productions that tried to follow this technology in movies that came thereafter. Can you imagine what could have happened if this revolutionary technology was being used before the official release? That could have taken all the magic out of the original *Matrix* release.

ScoreNotes: Be it in film, games, or television, where do you hope you can make the biggest impact as a composer?

Assaf Rinde: As a composer, my real goal is to touch people with my music. I love writing music for different media. With my music, I'm trying to let you feel and experience something that you can't describe with words, but you can just feel it without processing/thinking about it too much. I'm always trying to communicate and connect with people's hearts rather through people's minds, because I believe this is where everybody's truth really exists. Writing for the concert stage, film, TV, or videogames is all about telling a story musically and emotionally. Although the environments and techniques being used are different, you're still telling a story, so my goal is not really to choose which medium is the right one for me, but to find the way to touch as many people as I can through my music.

35 *Keeping Score* with Boris Elkis

Boris Elkis.

Photo by Ree Kadivar.

I like where this is going. **Boris Elkis's** first solo scoring assignment was for David Twohy's thriller, *A Perfect Getaway*, and it was a debut that he capitalized on. In his work, I felt that he lent a sense of freshness to an overworked genre, a style of music that foreshadows a great career in the making.

Having worked with veteran composer Graeme Revell, a collaboration we discuss in the interview, Boris took hold of the opportunity that *A Perfect Getaway* presented and placed himself, formidably, on the film scoring map.

An interesting back story, a relevant talent, and another composer to keep an eye (or ear) on . . .

Boris Elkis (2009)

ScoreNotes: When did you first meet director David Twohy, and what were some of the steps that led you to the scoring assignment for *A Perfect Getaway*?

Boris Elkis: Graeme Revell introduced me to David. He scored the last three David Twohy pictures and originally was approached by David as a composer for *A Perfect Getaway* but could not do it due to scheduling conflicts, so he passed the torch to me. Graeme arranged a meeting between the three of us and worked as a music producer on the film.

ScoreNotes: Please tell us about the type of emotions your score conveys for *A Perfect Getaway*. I found that the contrast between the warm tones of the early tracks and the suspense of the darker cues made for an engaging listen.

Boris Elkis: I was fortunate to be able to write a score that transforms and takes an emotional journey. With a film score being a by-product of the story, a composer is not always afforded the opportunity to cover a lot of musical ground. From a dramatic perspective, it is always good to be able to start and finish at the extreme opposites. The film starts out on a positive note, then things progressively turn for the worse, and the music reflects that transition as it goes from happy to menacing to terrifying. At its core, the film is a romantic thriller, as it centers around the main couple (Steve Zahn and Milla Jovovich), who are on their honeymoon, so there is a strong romantic element to the score. The romantic chemistry of the main characters and the breathtaking beauty of the Napali coast inspired the music and gave it the warmth and the scale.

ScoreNotes: How important was it to engage the audience with themes that were bold and subtle?

Boris Elkis: The film plays upon the genre expectations of the audience. The film is cleverly written and follows its own internal rhythm, as it takes turns when the audience least expects it. This is not a typical formulaic thriller, as there is quite a bit of character development. The film's tension comes from subtle things, like double entendres between the main couples. The task and the challenge were to guide the audience without giving too much away. I concentrated on three main themes, so the score is basically based on them. There is a romantic theme, killers theme, and the island—which later in the film becomes a battleground for survival—has its own leitmotif. I'm a strong believer in the use of melodies in film scores, and I think of this as the best all-around tool in a composer's toolbox.

ScoreNotes: I honestly felt that you brought forward an original and fresh take on the horror/suspense genre. Given that Hollywood productions often guide their scores toward that of temp music, how important is it for you to maintain a personal signature on the music you write?

Boris Elkis: With film scoring being a collaborative process, a lot of factors come into play that determine a score's final outcome. I was lucky to work with David Twohy; he is a truly creative individual who instinctively knows how to value and nourish creativity in others. David allowed me be creative, and he was incredibly supportive of me throughout the process. And that is not always the case, as at times a composer ends up having to please several people involved, and the results often end up being different from the composer's original creative vision.

As for the temp track, the use of temp music is not going to go away. I think it is a valuable tool, as it provides insights into the director's dramatic intentions. Part of a composer's skill is to be able to interpret the temp at the dramatic level, without copying it musically. It is a cerebral process, and it requires analytical skills and acute dramatic sense.

As far as the personal signature is concerned, that is for the listeners to say. I honestly do not know where the creative process comes from. The process is subliminal, it's intuitive, and it is divine. Some composers seem to have that unique quality more prevalent in their works. I don't think they know how to write any other way.

ScoreNotes: As one of your first major solo scores, did you find anything about your work on the production side of *A Perfect Getaway* to be particularly challenging or surprising?

Boris Elkis: I've been a big fan of David Twohy. *Arrival* and *Pitch Black* are some of my favorite movies, so at first it was a little intimidating to be in his company. I was pleasantly surprised by the creative leeway David afforded to me. Also, Graeme Revell, whom I consider a close personal friend, vouched for me. That upped the stakes for me emotionally. I did not want to let him down.

ScoreNotes: Can you tell us how productive it was working with Graeme Revell, and when it was that he first noticed you?

Boris Elkis: Graeme was a featured speaker at a Film Music Network event. After the event, a long line of aspiring composers had formed—myself included—with everyone trying to pass their demo CDs on to Graeme.

A couple of years later, I got a call from Graeme, saying he liked my demo and needed some help, and eventually it led to bigger things. Working with Graeme has been a wonderful experience, as he's been a great mentor and a big influence on me. Having scored almost a hundred films, Graeme has developed very keen dramatic sensibilities. His creative and intellectual capacity never ceases to amaze me.

ScoreNotes: Preceding even that, can you tell us what it was like to grow up in Moscow while having aspirations of being a film composer?

Boris Elkis: Growing up, I was one of those painfully shy kids. Going to the movies was a form of escape for me. Back then in Russia, we did not have the latest movies playing in theaters, so I remember watching *Some Like It Hot*—I must have seen that movie a dozen times. Every time I watched it, I was overcome by a feeling of joy. As I got older, I remember going to see political thrillers like *Three Days of the Condor*. Watching them made me question the political system we had in Russia at the time. I think films have an incredible power. One good film can alter society's consciousness. Russian government knew that; that's why they had an iron-grip censorship on films from the West. I always thought, what a privilege it would be to be involved in a medium that has the power to change lives.

ScoreNotes: What composers, be it classical or in the arena of film music, have inspired you the most?

Boris Elkis: Russia is a country rich in culture and musical history, with many great composers. My favorites were Igor Stravinsky, Dmitri Shostakovich, Sergey Prokofiev, and, above all, Alfred Schnittke. If you are not familiar with Alfred Schnittke, I recommend that you give him a listen. He was particularly influential on me because he mixed styles from different time periods, which is essentially what film music has evolved to. From the concert music arena, Arvo Part, Michael Nyman, George Crumb, and Steve Reich have also been influential on me. Growing up, I quite enjoyed the progressive rock movement, and I was an avid King Crimson fan. In film music, Bernard Hermann takes the crown for me. He was actually an influence on me for this score. There are a lot of talented composers working today. In all fairness to the film composers that are still living, this subject merits a separate discussion.

ScoreNotes: Please tell us about the soundtrack release for *A Perfect Getaway* and what listeners can expect from the album presentation.

Boris Elkis: I would say to expect the unexpected. This score is a mixture of different styles, as I wanted to keep the music evolving to make things less predictable. Main themes are the backbone of the score, so they keep it cohesive. The orchestra is used as another color in a rich palette of sounds, so sometimes it disappears and other elements take over. There is a strong island element to the score, so I used native flutes and percussion. Basically, it is a modern score with a strong melodic underpinning.

ScoreNotes: As we look ahead to the rest of the year and beyond, what are some future opportunities you plan on exploring?

Boris Elkis: With *A Perfect Getaway* being my first major score, my future opportunities are somewhat contingent upon the reception of the film and the score. As of now, I'm up for several projects, but nothing has been penned down as of yet. Ask me again in a few months.

36 *Keeping Score* with Clinton Shorter

Clinton Shorter.

O ne of the more popular movies from 2009 is Neill Blomkamp's modern-day science fiction tale, *District 9*. Produced by Peter Jackson, the film took hold of the top spot at the box office in its opening week and was greeted with positive feedback from the majority of viewers and critics who experienced the saga.

Equal parts documentary, sci-fi, and drama, *District 9* was a challenging project to score given the film's wildly diverse themes and structure. However, it was an assignment that gifted composer **Clinton Shorter** was duly ready for . . .

Clinton Shorter (2009)

ScoreNotes: *District 9* appears to be an original and most welcome type of science fiction movie. What kind of score did this film require?

Clinton Shorter: It ended up being a very dark, percussive score. It was quite a hybrid of acoustic and electric instruments. We spent about three weeks experimenting with different types of sounds and trying to get our palette together. After that, we nailed it, and it was full steam ahead.

ScoreNotes: Were you going for more of a raw, visceral experience?

Clinton Shorter: Yeah, Neill [Blomkamp] pretty much had two key words: raw and dark. That was basically all he was looking for most times. He really wanted to keep this as African as possible, but generally the music and instruments of the southern part of the continent are quite positive and happy. We really had issues, specifically with the drums—there just weren't any that were big and dark enough for him. So we had to take a lot of liberties and just go with some larger taiko drums, artificial drums, and that kind of thing, just to give it what he was looking for. The other issue was with the lead instrument; we tried so many different things, and in the end, it just came down to vocals as the only thing that carried it for us. So the only key elements that were African left in there were some smaller percussion and the vocals.

ScoreNotes: It's really a matter of just finding out what fits musically for a movie like this.

Clinton Shorter: Absolutely. And really it's set in Africa, and there's an underlying apartheid theme, but it's an action/sci-fi film. We decided not to try and treat this like it was some sort of musical study on African music because it just wasn't going to work. But we sorted it out over those three weeks, and I think the sound of it works pretty well with the picture.

ScoreNotes: What are some of the unique directions that the film's storyline will take audiences in, do you think?

Clinton Shorter: The first act is primarily a documentary, which is really interesting and posed some interesting challenges for me. For the first little while, I kept scoring a lot of it, and we were having lots of problems. In the end, I finally figured out what he was looking for, and it was that he just didn't want anything "scored." Nothing was needed to be accented; he didn't want me framing any dialogue or anything; he wanted it to be treated just like a documentary where you would literally just move the fader up and down. So I basically just did some blanket score and rhythm tracks over the first act, and as the film became more cinematic and dramatic, we introduced more of the orchestra for the more heroic moments and actually scored scenes.

ScoreNotes: Nice to hear about a movie actually building up toward something these days!

Clinton Shorter: [Laughing] True. Fair enough.

ScoreNotes: Was this the first time you had worked with the director Neill Blomkamp?

Clinton Shorter: No, I've known Neill for a good seven or eight years. I was first introduced to him when he was probably twenty-one or twenty-two. I had a buddy that was working at a CG facility, and Neill was there, and everybody said he was going to be a superstar. I was introduced to him and saw a bunch of his reels, and they were phenomenal. I ended up doing a couple of commercials for him, and I ended up doing the short, *Alive in Joburg*, and that was the thing that Peter Jackson saw. So that's how the relationship started, and it's been going strong ever since.

ScoreNotes: And speaking of Mr. Jackson, how advantageous is it for *District 9* to have Peter Jackson's credentials attached to it?

Clinton Shorter: Well, obviously it's incredibly advantageous. The following he has and the talent that goes along with it can do nothing but really help a film. But the one thing that people may not realize was just how much leeway he gave Neill; he really let Neill make his own film here. I mean if you think about it, we've got a first time feature director—Neill had done lots of commercials and shorts, but this was the first feature he had done. A first-time screenplay writer in Terri Tatchell. We had a director of photography, Trent Opaloch, who had done only commercials to that point and was Neill's guy. We had a first-time actor. So it was quite funny because myself and the editor, Julian Clarke, were really almost like the elder statesmen on the show. It was quite funny, even though neither of us had done a show of this magnitude either. But it's just a real testament to Peter Jackson and his belief that there are talented people out there that can get the job done that are outside the system. So, yeah, it was really refreshing, and we were really lucky.

ScoreNotes: Do you think the industry could use more of that independent spirit in an era where sequel-mania and comic book movies are running rampant?

Clinton Shorter: Sure, I think so. And I think you're going to see more of it with costs coming down and less money being available to make the bigger shows. It's going to force people to actually find shows that can be made for less. Like it or loathe it, it's just the way it is. But you know, there are tons of talented people out there who don't get a shot, so I absolutely hope there's more of it.

ScoreNotes: Getting back to the music, can you tell us about the planned soundtrack release of *District 9*?

Clinton Shorter: Yes, Sony closed a deal to release the soundtrack on iTunes and Amazon.com. It's very exciting to have it released; I hope people enjoy it.

ScoreNotes: Can you tell us about your background in TV as it led up to your work in movies?

Clinton Shorter: I spent quite a few years assisting a local composer in Canada by the name of Terry Frewer. I think we worked on about three hundred episodes of TV. He was primarily a television composer, and he did some features and some movies of the week. That's where I learned everything that had to do with how to get in and out gracefully with music and when and where to have it. I learned a ton from Terry.

ScoreNotes: What are some of the goals that you've set for yourself as a composer in this entertainment business? What are you setting your sights on next?

Clinton Shorter: As always, I just try to work on shows that challenge me and that people are going to want to watch. It's really just about being on projects that I enjoy working on and especially with people that I enjoy working with, people that care. I've done shows where people didn't really care about the product so much. You know, you get paid, but there's not a whole lot else that goes with it. That's not why I got into this business in the first place. It's a lot of fun when you're actually doing it. So, yeah, I just look for gigs that are fun, well-written, and with good people.

ScoreNotes: At the time of this interview, *District 9* is about to debut nationally. How do you think sci-fi fans will receive this picture?

Clinton Shorter: Well, I'm a big sci-fi fan, and even if I wasn't working on this show, I would have been lining up to see it. When I saw the first cut back in January, the first thing I said to Neill, Julian, and Terri was, "I'm telling you right now, this is the type of movie my buddies and I would kill to go see." It's a blast, a ton of fun. It's not exactly what you would expect.

ScoreNotes: I also think they staged the trailers cleverly without giving away too much. It doesn't reveal everything like so many trailers do these days.

Clinton Shorter: Absolutely. Neill had talked about the same thing. They had to recut and recut because he felt they were giving away too much. There's enough eye candy in there to get people interested, and combine that with the brilliant ad campaign they've got going—you'll get people in the seats without giving away the story.

ScoreNotes: It's definitely a score and movie combo that I am looking forward to as well. Thank you for sitting down with us today to talk about it.

Clinton Shorter: Thank you. It was a lot of fun.

Finale

Now that you've reached the Finale of *Keeping Score,* what is it that I hope you've taken away from this experience?

First off, it's my sincere wish that you've enjoyed learning more about the composers featured in this book and that you get a chance to discover or revisit the tremendously entertaining scores they've produced. A wealth of inspiration and entertainment awaits you, and the experience will open up your imagination to all-new wonders.

Second, I hope you now find that engaging in soundtracks offers you a new, exciting manner in which to follow movies. As I've indicated earlier, the composers are often the unheard voice, ironically, when it comes to movies and their discussion points. It's my goal that a book like this opens up the communication channels a bit more. After all, composers offer a completely unique viewpoint on the films they work on and have opinions that may provoke you to think about a movie's storyline in ways that you might not have thought of before. I certainly get more out of hearing a composer speak than I do listening to an actor on a routine press tour.

Third, I feel that an often untouched subject in this industry is the lack of opportunities for some of the veteran composers who are still interested in scoring films. In fact, common speculation may lead you to believe some composers have retired when they actually have not! As you have noticed in the bonus interviews, there is a bit of a gap between today's industry and yesterday's composers. I hope that gap closes.

Lastly, this book was written to show my appreciation for the magic of film, television, and videogame music. May your next steps now lead you to the music of these great composers you just read about so that you can discover that magical spark as well.

Index

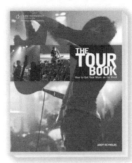

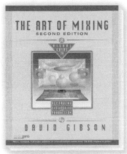

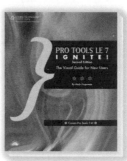